The Proper Study
of Mankind . . .

BOOKS BY STUART CHASE

The Proper Study of Mankind . . .

by *Stuart Chase*

in consultation with Edmund deS. Brunner

REVISED EDITION

> Know then thyself, presume not God to scan;
> The proper study of mankind is man.
> Alexander Pope's *Essay on Man*

 HARPER & BROTHERS PUBLISHERS NEW YORK

Library of Congress catalog card number: 55-11278

Actually there is a continuous chain from physics and chemistry to biology and anthropology, and thence to the social and intellectual sciences, a chain which cannot be broken at any point.

MAX PLANCK

*

It is easier, someone has said, to smash an atom than a prejudice.

GORDON ALLPORT

*

We are discovering the right things in the wrong order, which is another way of saying that we are learning how to control nature before we have learned how to control ourselves.

RAYMOND FOSDICK

*

Contents

Foreword

When this book was first undertaken, shortly after the second world war, it seemed a rather daring project, and I hesitated a long time before starting it. It still seems daring, and in many ways it has been my hardest assignment.

My lifelong interest in social science had prepared me to some extent, but my specialty had been economics rather than the behavior sciences. As a professional accountant—my first occupation after leaving college—I had to learn to survey a new situation thoroughly in a short time, and be responsible for the results. Journalists and accountants have that in common.

A group of social scientists approached me with tales of a mine of fresh material accumulated during the war, and asked me to investigate it. Fresh material was much needed just then, for the postwar problems, especially atomic problems, were on everyone's mind. The warnings and appeals of the atomic physicists had put these problems squarely up to social scientists. But were the scientists capable of meeting them? There was plenty of intellectual virtuosity in physics, but where was its equivalent in the study of human relations?

I dropped everything else and began the exploration. I had some expert guides, especially Donald Young of the Social Science Research Council, and Charles Dollard of the Carnegie Corporation, and through them the help of many scholars. They gave me every assistance (though the dealings with the publisher were my responsibility) and I leaned heavily on them for advice and contacts.

I visited research projects, laboratories, government agencies, universities, interviewing many leaders and students. I read endless monographs, made endless notes, and, with the help of Young and Dollard, sent a questionnaire to a representative group of social scientists all over the country. One question, "If you were given ten million dollars for research how would you spend it?" brought in some significant information on what should be done next.

My first task was to round up work which had been carried on during the war—aptitude testing for flyers, "area studies" in the Pacific, group analyses, opinion research with soldiers and rationed consumers, price control techniques, and so on. After Pearl Harbor social scientists had left their ivory towers in the universities and gone to work for their country. Funds larger than they had ever known were suddenly at their disposal for research and engineering. One sociologist whom I visited at the Pentagon had the whole Army, eleven million men, as subjects for opinion research. New ground had been broken, and some spectacular results achieved, as will be described later.

Beyond these crisis-encouraged operations, where was social science going? What had scientists to build on, as outstanding accomplishments of the past? What were some of the barriers to progress, and some of the unanswered questions? Was the scientific method, as it is known, say, in physics, genuinely employed? Was social science really science, or just disciplined talk about social problems?

The months went by and I became increasingly encouraged. I began to feel that a real foundation was being laid, that some answers to my queries were apparent, and more would come. As a member of the philosophy department at Antioch said to me, there isn't any other way to go. Only science can learn to control what science has created. Good will, intuition, common sense, can help, but they are not enough.

My book was published in the fall of 1948 and on the whole well received. Many specialists were surprised and encouraged, like myself, to hear of work outside their own fields. It seemed useful to place these fields in some sort of perspective, however incomplete the view. Though no one human being could see them all at once, it seemed useful to offer concrete illustrations of what had been done in various departments, and suggest gaps that needed to be filled. Specialized critics rightly pointed out certain technical omissions and deficiencies in the book, but not too severely. Most readers seemed to understand that it was a sample, not an encyclopedia.

The present revision is still a sample. I have tried to take advantage of various suggestions and criticisms raised earlier, and also to bring the subject matter up to date. As the book now stands, about a third of it is new, mostly accounts of research findings that have come in since the first edition. Another third is material from the original, extensively edited, and the remainder stands substantially as first written. A bibliography has been added, and the index extended to selected subjects as well as proper names. Though the accent on work during World War II is somewhat modified, the trend, so exciting in 1948, is perhaps even more exciting today, as social scientists turn to the arts of peace.

As before, I have selected only the cases which I felt competent to discuss and which specially interested me. Many fine examples have been neglected. As in natural science and invention, new researches grow out of old ones, and increase like compound interest. The figure of the ladder, which is applied in an early chapter to natural science in atomic discoveries, and to social science in population studies, could be extended to practically every subject in this book. Even in drawing up these sample ladders, I have had to leave out many rungs, each perhaps the life work of a brilliant man. I am well aware of the devoted scholars whose work has been inadequately appraised here or by-passed completely. Perhaps in some later study I may catch up with them.

In this edition I have had as consultant a uniquely qualified scientist of wide experience. Edmund deS. Brunner, officially Professor of Rural Sociology on the staff of Columbia and Teachers' College, has sent out many teams of scientists, and planned many surveys through the Bureau of Applied Social Research. He spent the year 1953-1954 visiting universities in South Africa and advising their social science staffs. He has called my attention to a great deal of valuable work, and drafted accounts of some of it for me, as well as reading the entire manuscript and making criticisms and suggestions. He is not responsible for errors, of course, or for general conclusions.

My wife has spent untold hours in research, copy-reading, proof-reading. She offered many helpful ideas, and is largely responsible for the bibliography. I was also fortunate in having two neighbors who helped me with secretarial work—Lola Donnell and Christine Loring.

My thanks go also to the many distinguished scientists who have patiently dealt with my ignorance and cleared up difficulties for me, both when *The Proper Study of Mankind* was first undertaken and in its revision.

STUART CHASE

Redding, Conecticut
October, 1955

The Proper Study
of Mankind . . .

1

Is Social Science Science?

In 1733 Alexander Pope said in a famous poem that "the proper study of mankind is man." Not many could have agreed with him then and some people still disagree. More than two centuries later, in 1954, a committee of the American Congress severely criticized the big foundations for financing research in the social sciences. Nature can be studied scientifically, but not human nature, the committee said.

This book takes the side of Alexander Pope. In it we will try to show that while human behavior may be more difficult to study, the scientific method is applicable to both man and his world. Already we know a good deal more about human relations in industry, in communities, families, face-to-face groups, about people under stress, than doctors knew about the human body, say, in 1800.

Indeed, the story begins at least 300 years ago, long before Pope wrote his *Essay on Man*. A group of famous scholars and scientists used to gather for a weekly discussion in the rooms of Sir William Petty at Oxford. Petty had been by turns a cabin boy, surveyor, physician, professor of music, member of Parliament, statistician, and political economist—in brief, a sturdy descendant of the versatile Elizabethans. The men around his table included Robert Boyle, Christopher Wren, Bishop Wilkins, Ward the astronomer, and later Hooke the physicist. When the club began holding occasional meetings in London, the King asked to become a member. One Isaac Newton also joined the company.

They called themselves the "Invisible College" and took issue with the dry scholasticism of Oxford and Cambridge. Following

Galileo and Francis Bacon, they wanted fewer abstractions, less logic chopping, more observation and experiment in discovering the secrets of nature. Sometimes a member would perform an experiment before the group and they would sit late over their wine, discussing its implications. Yet they were only 50 years from the time when a chemist in the Sorbonne at Paris had to conform to the teaching of Aristotle on pain of death. Soon after the King became a member the Invisible College was re-christened the Royal Society. To this day it has fought for experiment and first-hand observation against purely logical demonstrations and unconfirmed speculations.

Presently Sir William Petty published a study on population theory, and then his unique work, *Political Arithmetick*. John Graunt, another charter member, made a careful analysis of mortality rates in the London plague. Halley, the astronomer for whom the comet was named, constructed the first life expectancy table and became the father of actuarial science and the principles of insurance. The Royal Society published his table in 1693.

Thus these great pioneers of the scientific method, while they were chiefly concerned with astronomy, gravitation, chemistry, navigation, did not neglect to inquire into social statistics as well. They set in motion the modern sciences dealing with man and his behavior, as well as those dealing with energy, space, and matter.

It is important to recall this, for since their day the natural sciences have forged rapidly ahead, with the dismemberment of the atom as a stunning climax to their advance. Now that man has found the secret of ultimate energy in nature, can he find also the knowledge to control it? This is the task before the social scientist today. The success of the Manhattan Project in producing an atomic explosion is forcing social scientists to come of age.

From another point of view, atomic energy is but the capstone on a series of problems with which natural science has presented mankind. Ever since the first power-driven loom began to throw cottage weavers out of their livelihood, technology has been breaking up customs worn smooth by the centuries. Many of our troubles today, from the threat of guided missiles to strikes and the divorce rate, can be regarded as by-products of the successful solution of technical problems. Once these successful inventions came out of the laboratory into the workaday world, they created a whole category of acute social problems. Henry Ford, for instance, gave us the Model T, and presently the robot on the assembly line.

It is the task of applied social science to repair some of the dislocations of technology and so keep society on an even keel. We *could* invent ourselves right off the map, and a number of imaginative books have already anticipated this outcome—such as *First and Last Men* by Olaf Stapledon.

Six Methods for Solving Problems

Before we go on talking about social scientists, we need a clear picture of what the term "science," rigorously interpreted, refers to. Fundamentally, it is a method for obtaining knowledge and solving problems. Down the ages mankind has evolved a variety of approaches to meet the questions and uncertainties which have continually confronted him. It is possible to identify at least six methods:

1. Appeal to the supernatural.
2. Appeal to worldly authority—the older the better.
3. Intuition.
4. Common sense.
5. Pure logic.
6. The scientific method.

These approaches, of course, are not mutually exclusive but often overlap. Any of them may be temporarily helpful; some may be disastrous. Only the last furnishes a cumulative storehouse of dependable and consistent knowledge.

Common sense and logic have their place in the laboratory, and so has intuition, which is a loose term for a half-conscious blend of many minute observations. A good outfielder starting to run for the fence at the crack of the bat is an example of trained intuition. The supernatural is the only method which has been entirely banished by our technical experts; yet to primitive men magic may have been a crude attempt at science, as Sir James Fraser suggested in *The Golden Bough*.

Thus the analogy between the magical and the scientific conceptions of the world is close. In both of them the succession of events is assumed to be perfectly regular and certain, being determined by immutable laws, the operation of which can be foreseen and calculated precisely; the elements of caprice, of chance, and of accident are banished from the course of nature. . . . The fatal flaw of magic lies not in its general assumption of a sequence of events determined by law, but in its total misconception of the nature of the particular laws which govern that sequence.

Eddington, in a famous passage in *Space, Time and Gravitation*, has shown the limitations of common sense. What nonsense, he says, to think that the table on which one writes is a collection of electrons moving with prodigious speed in spaces relatively as empty as the spaces between the planets in the solar system! What nonsense to believe that this thin air presses on every square inch of one's body with a 14-pound weight. What nonsense to think that the light one sees in the eyepiece of this telescope left a star 50,000 years ago.

Common sense tells us that the world is flat, that the sun goes around the earth, that heavy bodies always fall faster than light bodies, that boats made of iron will sink. The practical man, that paragon of common sense, was once defined by Disraeli as "one who repeats the errors of his forefathers." Yet a technician without common sense is a laboratory liability.

The Greeks and Egyptians caught a glimpse of the scientific method, but even the great Pythagoras, who established the nature of proof, went wandering off into the mists of number magic, and the great Aristotle, father of logic, perpetuated many errors that might have been cleared up by a few simple observations—such as the number of teeth in a horse's mouth.

WHAT IS "SCIENCE"?

The scientific method tells us not how things *ought* to behave, but how they do in fact behave. Today it is universally applied to problems connected with matter and energy, and occasionally applied to many other sorts of problems, as we shall see. It is the only method yet discovered which produces knowledge that stays put, at least until a closer fit to reality is found. One can think of scientific achievement as a storehouse with many well-filled shelves, their contents neatly classified and ready for use by any qualified student. An engineer could not build a bridge without going to the storehouse for the equations of stress and strain. A doctor could not write a prescription without referring to carefully tested knowledge on the shelves. Engineers in a dozen countries are now drawing on recent deposits of knowledge to build their first atomic power plants.

Some people, as we have noted, say that social science isn't science. Some say that astrology is a science, and so is dowsing. Some speak of the science of boxing; while if you call a person a "scientist" in certain of our sunnier states, he may think you mean a Christian Scientist.

"Science" is a roomy term, covering a wide range of subject matter and behavior. There is no one proper meaning. For instance, *Webster's New World Dictionary*, 1953, gives six different meanings:

1. Knowledge as opposed to intuition.
2. Systematized knowledge derived from observation and experiment.
3. A branch of knowledge—as the science of music.
4. A branch of natural science—as physics or chemistry.
5. Skill, based on training—as the science of boxing.
6. Christian Science.

The two-volume *Oxford Dictionary* explains how "science" formerly applied to philosophy, and was often synonymous with the "seven liberal arts" of grammar, logic, rhetoric, arithmetic, music, geometry, and astronomy. About 100 years ago the concept of the "exact sciences" came in, referring to astronomy, physics, and the natural sciences; but the other meanings still have plenty of life in them.

If we select "exact science," and add the idea of the "scientific method" or the "scientific attitude" in approaching a given problem, we shall come close to what is meant by "science" in this book.[1]

Morris R. Cohen, in his *Logic and Scientific Method*, examines the various techniques for discovering truth, and finds none but the scientific method free from human caprice and wishful thinking. None of the others, he says, is flexible enough to admit an error. "What is called the scientific method differs radically from these, by encouraging and developing the *utmost possible doubt*, so that what is left after such doubt is always supported by the best available evidence." As new evidence comes in, new doubts may arise and must be taken into account. "It is the essence of the scientific method to make them an integral part of the knowledge so far attained."

Science as thus defined—corresponding to Webster's second definition—is dynamic, open at the top, and thus able to come ever closer to the truth. It has abandoned absolutes in favor of relationships and probabilities. Nothing in modern science can be dogmatically taken as 100 percent true, though quite a few things may be 99.999. . . . For a long time physicists regarded Newton's laws of gravitation as 100 percent so—Absolute Space, Absolute Time, Absolute Motion. Einstein's principles of relativity shattered these absolutes. Newton was not wrong in terrestrial areas, but his laws did not always apply in astronomical areas. Einstein found a closer fit to the space-time world. Presently some genius may discover a still closer fit.

Einstein's work gives us a clear idea of three cardinal steps in exact science:

[1] *The American College Dictionary* defines social science as: "The group of studies seeking to establish a science of the social life of human groups." Increasingly one hears the term "the behavioral sciences."

First, he was worried and curious about the relation between matter and energy, and got together the knowledge already available.

Second, he assembled his thoughts in the language of mathematics and came out with a startling hypothesis governing the conversion of matter into energy.

Third, he proposed various experiments to verify the hypothesis, such as the bending of light rays as they passed the sun in an eclipse.

The experiments were performed and in due course relativity was put in the storehouse of knowledge, later to be abundantly verified by the Manhattan Project. If the experimental results had been persistently negative, the theory would have gone into the wastebasket, together with thousands of other brilliant theories which have not survived the test of verification.

Human emotions are excluded as far as possible from scientific discipline. Alone among man's activities, science can resolve problems independently of our desires and wills. Scientific method, as Morris Cohen said, is systematic doubt. To fudge an experiment, to slant a conclusion, to report anything but the whole truth as one knows it alone in the night, brings ignominy and oblivion. There can be no secret processes, no patent medicines, no private understandings or payoffs on the side. The calculations must be laid on the table, face up, for all the world to see. In this sense, science is perhaps the most *moral* of all man's disciplines. It will be corrupted and debased if ever its direction falls permanently into the hands of national governments and ideologists. It is as international as the north wind.

One comforting thing about adopting the scientific attitude is that you no longer need try to save face when you find that you are wrong. You expect to be wrong a good part of the time. Ehrlich was wrong 605 times before he found the famous specific "606" for venereal disease.

A rough test of science is the amount of argument a conclusion generates. Men used to argue violently about the composition of water, and about the nature of heat. Today they know the answers and arguments are stilled. An argument may answer a debater or a politician, but it will never answer an experiment. An experiment can be answered only by a more careful experiment.

FINDING A PATTERN

Another broad definition of science is *finding a pattern in a set of phenomena*. Once the pattern is determined, prediction becomes possible. Failing prediction, we are still in the pre-scientific stage. One of the earliest scientific patterns was the movement of the stars across the heavens. For millennia men had watched them in wonder and perplexity; but some 5,000 years ago a few of the more curious among the watchers began to name them, trace their courses, and predict when they would return.

Mendeleev's Periodic Table is another revealing example of finding a pattern, this one in the atomic weights of the various elements, and with it predicting new elements which no one had ever found on earth. Presently they were found, each in its proper place. Another pattern is the Reproductive Index whereby future population curves can be predicted.

Observation, whether in astronomy or sociology, identifies the pattern and checks it. Prediction then becomes possible. The magnetic compass, for instance, can be relied on to tell us which way is north. Next we invariably inquire: *Why?* Finding an answer is the next long step in science. The planets move so and so, we can plot them to the second. *Why* do they move that way? This is a much harder question. Nobody even suspected why planets moved the way they did until Newton worked out the laws of gravitation. Nobody yet knows much about the magnetic field governing the compass.

PATTERNS OF HUMAN BEHAVIOR

A good deal of natural science, and more social science, is still in the prediction stage. If this occurs, then that will follow. The *understanding* stage, finding the why, is far advanced in physics, just beginning in sociology. But the difference is in degree, not in kind. Scientists can find patterns in the behavior of people as well as in the behavior of electrons. On this level of discussion, there is no difference between social science and natural science. On this level we define social science as *the use of the scientific method to answer questions about human behavior*. Science goes with the method, not with the subject matter.

If the whys are carried far enough, they take us into the realm of unanswerable questions, where no operations can be performed to obtain an answer. Some questions, formerly supposed unanswerable, have yielded to new techniques of investigation, which themselves have uncovered still newer and more baffling problems. Many are likely to remain forever closed to human understanding. We shall have more to say about this later.

"The social realm," said the great sociologist Emile Durkheim, "is a natural realm which differs from the others only by a greater complexity. Now it is impossible that nature should differ radically from itself in one case and the other in regard to which is most essential. The fundamental relations that exist between things . . . cannot be essentially dissimilar in the different realms."

The informal picture I carry around in my mind of a social scientist is that of a man with a notebook watching people behave. He may be watching a town meeting in New England, a religious riot in India, a nursery school in Pasadena, a Japanese internment camp. Perhaps my most vivid picture is of the man with the notebook at the Hawthorne plant of the Western Electric Company, finding out in a world-famous experiment what makes workers work.

The scientific investigator puts down what he sees, not what he wants to see. He puts it down in such a way that other observers can verify his findings. Without a situation where the findings of one observer can be checked by other competent observers and agreement reached, we must surrender the idea of the scientific method.

Scientists study nature, and man is a part of nature. If certain of his characteristics may be beyond analysis, others are not. "Look, here is how a lever works, a bee steers home, a star explodes, a group comes to a decision." In some respects, a social scientist can push an inquiry deeper than a natural scientist. By a cautious use of introspection he can obtain a rough check on outside observations—something which cannot be done with a bar of steel or an exploding star.

Neal E. Miller of Yale, who has worked in both natural and social science, has this to say (in the *Journal of Personality*, September, 1951):

Large portions of human behavior are highly predictable. For example, a driver on the highway may bet his life 100 times within an hour on the predictability of human behavior—that none of 100 drivers coming the opposite way at a closing speed of eighty miles per hour will suddenly decide to swerve in front of his car. . . .

The author has been held up by a considerable number of mechanical failures, hotboxes, broken driving rods, washouts, etc., in the course of extensive experience riding on railroads; he has never been delayed because the engineer decided to get out and pick daisies. The mechanical behavior of the physical structure of the railroad was less predictable than the human behavior of the engineer . . .

2

Scientific Ladders

A scientist and his friend were driving through Wyoming and saw a flock of sheep up on a mesa.

"They've just been sheared," said the friend.

"They seem to be, on this side," replied the scientist.

You do not take anything for granted when you enter the monastery of science. You take the vow of skepticism until the evidence comes in. This is contrary to normal human thinking, which abhors explanatory vacuums. So it is not surprising that congressmen sometimes think scientists queer, and that the Army called the men on the Manhattan Project "long-hairs." There is a curious paradox here—the men who know most assert they know nothing at all except under rigorously limited conditions. "We have come to have a great caution," says Dr. Robert Oppenheimer, "in all assertions of totality, or finality or absoluteness. . . ."

Let us emphasize again the great change which Einstein wrought. Before he demonstrated relativity, assertions of totality and absoluteness were standard. The mechanistic view culminated in Laplace's concept of a completely determined world in which, from the present state and velocity of every material body in the universe, the entire future could be theoretically predicted. "Twentieth century physics has not demolished this view in the sense of proving it definitely wrong. But it has, in effect, pulled the rug out from under it. From the time Heisenberg demonstrated the impossibility of determining simultaneously both the position and the velocity of individual electrons, physicists have had to speak in terms of probabilities instead of exact determinations. . . ."[1]

Probabilities fit human behavior much better than exact determinations, and a little appreciated result of the Einstein revolution has been to give social science a far more secure standing. With this in mind, suppose we prepare two ladders of development, one in the natural sciences, one in the social, and note their similarities and differences.

ATOMIC LADDER

The popular idea about the atomic bomb, according to the late Selig Hecht in *Explaining the Atom,* was that a long-hair named Einstein had a kind of midnight vision about it. He took the vision to President Roosevelt and said it would cost two billion dollars. The President, being a sporting man, accepted the gamble and appointed an Army general to direct the production, as long-hairs are notoriously impractical. There lingers among us, says Hecht, the fancy that a scientist is a man who has crazy ideas which occasionally work out. Ideas are supposed to come by spontaneous combustion, with little or no relation to the past. The scientist is thus the modern magician.

Scientists are not like that at all. Nowadays they stand, like teams of acrobats, on one another's shoulders in a pyramid which spreads upward. Atomic fission, far from being a sudden apparition in Einstein's brain, was the culmination of the lifework of hundreds of scientists, extending back for at least 150 years— not to mention Democritus, who in 400 B.C. first suggested that matter might be discontinuous and made up of indivisible particles called atoms.

With the assistance of Dr. Hecht we will sketch a ladder reaching back to the beginning of serious work on the atom. It will give us a picture of science as a continuing process, one discovery leading to the next, instead of a series of unrelated

[1] One of the conclusions reached at a scientific-philosophic conference at Washington University, St. Louis, in 1954, as reported by Huston Smith in the *Saturday Review,* April 2, 1955.

brainstorms. If one of these rungs had been missing, there would have been no chain reaction in 1945. Note also how war and politics affected the ladder. Had Hitler not challenged the world in 1939, the development might have taken longer, and culminated in entirely peaceful uses.

Dalton in 1808 formulates early atomic theory. All atoms of a given element, like iron, are alike and combine with atoms of other elements to form molecules. The concept was that of a tiny billiard ball.

Mendeléev in 1869 sets up his famous Periodic Table.

Becquerel in 1896 discovers that uranium is radioactive.

J. J. Thomson in 1897 discovers the existence of charges which he calls electrons.

The *Curies*, Marie and Pierre, find radium and receive the Nobel prize in 1903.

Rutherford wins it in 1908 by breaking into the atom. The billiard ball model is replaced by the solar system model—a nucleus surrounded by revolving electrons. (No one, of course, has ever seen an atom or probably ever will.)

Bohr works out the electron circuits of various atoms.

Soddy in 1910 evolves the idea of isotopes, essential to understanding the atom's insides, and *Aston* in 1919 finds that nearly all elements do indeed have isotopes. The *Curies* of the next generation, Joliot and Irène, produce them artificially in 1933.

Urey gets the 1934 Nobel prize for heavy water containing the hydrogen isotope. We are coming closer.

Chadwick locates the neutron in the atom's nucleus, for which he receives the Nobel prize in 1935.

Einstein's equation, $E = MC^2$, first evolved in 1905, is now in the 1930's brought in to explain the loss of mass when protons and neutrons combine to form helium. Matter has been transformed into energy, as Einstein predicted. *Cockcroft* and *Walton* confirm by experiments.

Hahn and *Strassmann* in 1939 bombard uranium with slow neutrons and get barium, considerably to their astonishment.

Lise Meitner, contemplating the above, evolves a revolutionary hypothesis. Suppose, she asks, this bombardment can be made to continue releasing neutrons and energy in a chain reaction?

Frisch, Fermi, Szilard, and others in March, 1939, confirm Meitner's hypothesis. Terrific excitement in the scientific world! More than one hundred papers on atomic fission are published within a few months.

Chadwick is now certain that anyone can make an atomic bomb with the published knowledge available, provided he wants to spend the time and money. The storehouse is stocked.

Einstein, fearing that Hitler will get there first, writes a letter to President Roosevelt in August, 1939, and the Manhattan Project is born.

Fermi puts an atomic pile in operation under the stadium at the University of Chicago in December, 1942, and the Atomic Age begins . . .

This long ladder, rung by rung, has at last led to the secret of atomic energy and unlocked it. There are many more rungs, of course, than have been included here. We are not trying to explain the atom but to give a brief indication of how one discovery leads to the next. "The real secret," says Hecht, "is that there is no basic secret." In 1936, before the work of Hahn and Strassmann on uranium, no one could have made a bomb, not with all the money in the world.

True, the Manhattan Project was a miracle of teamwork and developed some astonishing methods for taking knowledge about nuclear fission, which was now in every university, and making a practical explosive with release mechanisms and other intricate devices. But the next group of scientists and engineers to make a bomb might do it more simply or cheaply. In 1940 five separate processes were known for accumulating fissionable material. Yet one American congressman was so ignorant of the atomic ladder that he introduced a bill providing the death penalty for anyone who gave away the *scientific* secrets of atomic energy!

Ignorance like this is hardly an ideal approach to the atomic age. Western civilization, if not the whole world, is now committed to applied science. Without it perhaps half the population would rapidly die off. It is a very serious matter when statesmen, generals, and industrialists lack a clear idea of this man-made activity which both sustains and threatens the race. Not only our leaders but the man in the street should have at least a rough notion of what science is up to. So far, the toothpaste ads sum up the popular conception—a chap in a white coat and a Van Dyke beard peering down a microscope . . . an "egghead," a "long-hair."

A Ladder in Social Science

In the field of human relations, long scientific ladders are harder to find. But there is one at least which goes back to the early days of the Royal Society. It concerns population theory, and runs like this:

1654. Pascal and Fermat formulate the theory of probability as a result of their interest in gambling odds.

1693. The Royal Society publishes Halley's life expectancy tables, the basis of actuarial science and a branch of probability.

1749. The Academy of Science in Sweden conducts the first national census of population.

1790. First United States census is taken as provided by the new Constitution. Recognized to be the best national count so far.

1798. Thomas Malthus, aged 32, publishes his immortal essay attempting to prove that the "exponential curve" of man is steeper than that of his food supply.

1801. First British census. It bears out certain statistical predictions by Sir Frederick Eden.

1812. Laplace carries probability theory another long step forward. (A more useful contribution than his mechanistic concept.)

1836. Quetelet in Brussels publishes some observations on statistical regularities as disclosed in population figures. His *Social Physics* is bitterly attacked as exhibiting the philosophy of determinism.

1883. Galton, a cousin of Darwin, publishes *Inquiries into Human Faculty*, developing the principle of frequency distribution curves.

1890. Hollerith introduces punch cards in the United States census—a landmark in social statistics!

1899. Karl Pearson publishes the *Grammar of Science*, which still dominates statistical theory.

1932. R. R. Kuczynski develops the "reproductive index," to predict population growth, based on potential mothers.

1933. Lorimer and Osborn publish *Dynamics of Population*.

1936. Dublin and Lotka publish *Length of Life*.

1941. United States census comes out according to prediction, with error less than 2/100 of one percent!

Observe that this ladder is full of "regularities," and that it supports not only population theory and social statistics, but also probability mathematics, which is now vital to the development of biology, physics, and natural science generally.

Social Science Is Science

The population ladder may be less rigorous than the atomic ladder, but both show the same kind of mind at work. The difference is in subject matter, not in the technique for tackling a problem. Social science, in its exact meaning, has fewer geniuses on its roster to date, a smaller research staff, less money at its disposal—despite the growing interest of the big foundations— less public understanding of its goals and achievements, and a long time lag to make up. Its predictive power is usually still below the range found in most natural science—about on a par, one might guess, with the Weather Bureau. We swear at the weather man from time to time, but nobody seriously proposes to abandon his services.

Social science in many departments, as we shall see in detail throughout this book, has forged ahead of intuition and common sense. Paul Lazarsfeld of Columbia, for instance, has prepared a list of ideas firmly held by most of us about United

States soldiers, which social scientists in World War II found to be quite wrong. Among them:

It was not true that better educated G.I.'s showed more mental instability in combat.

It was not true that recruits from the farms bore hardship better than recruits from the cities.

It was not true that troops from the South stood the climate of South Sea Islands better than troops from the North.

It was not true that Negro privates were less eager to become officers and noncoms. (The standard stereotype that Negroes lack ambition.)

FEEDBACK[2] ON SCIENTIFIC METHOD

Let us recapitulate the chief elements of the scientific method, as described so far. There are ten of them:

1. A problem to be solved which bothers somebody, maybe cosmic rays, maybe juvenile delinquency.
2. Gathering the available facts about it, searching the literature.
3. A theory to explain the problem, a pattern sketched.
4. Rigorous verification of the theory by other scientists. Emotion and bias ruled out.
5. A stubborn atmosphere of doubt. The cheerful ability to say, "I was wrong."
6. Prediction in terms of probabilities, not absolutes.
7. Thinking more in terms of process than of linear cause and effect.
8. Thinking in terms of *structure*. How things are related to one another; the order in which they come—the structure of a sky-scraper, a corporation, a community, a conference, an argument, an agenda.
9. No closed solutions; room always allowed for new data which may give a closer fit.
10. No secrets, no monopolies, no payoffs. The storehouse open to all men everywhere.

[2] *Feedback:* a useful term from cybernetics, rapidly becoming popular. It means: "let's see where we've got to before going on."

Dr. Oppenheimer, testifying on the National Science Foundation bill in Congress in 1946, provided a kind of theme song for this study of ours:

I am aware of the difficulty of establishing in these fields [the social disciplines] rigorous criteria of competence and qualification. Nevertheless at a time when the whole world realizes that many of its most vital problems depend on an understanding of human behavior . . . and of the regularities which underlie the operations of our varied society, we should recognize the great benefits which may come from attracting men and women of prominence to the study of these questions.

Oppenheimer is calling for the scientific method to be applied to the "regularities," the patterns, which underlie human societies. It is easier, someone has said, to smash an atom than a prejudice. The path is difficult and stony; but this has not stopped social scientists in the past, and will not stop them in the future.

3

Varieties of Social Science

What are social scientists up to today?

A television camera could show a number of professors lecturing to more or less eager students in more or less stuffy classrooms; experiments being performed in psychological laboratories; two-way communication systems between men and management being installed in large corporations; teams of investigators taking notes in communities like Middletown; social workers making case reports on their rounds; a battery of electronic computers clicking away while they sort cards for opinion polls; interviewers taking a sample of the unemployment situation in Illinois; sunburned persons in pith helmets asking questions of puzzled natives in New Guinea. Finally, the camera would focus on shelf after shelf of books. Many of the volumes are famous; many of them contain prose as good as the advice is bad—for instance, Plato's recipe for the communal rearing of children.

Here in America, 165 million people, scattered over three million square miles of plain, valley, and hillside, form and re-form into numberless groups and organizations, with loyalties and sentiments woven around each. (In Newburyport, Massachusetts, a recent study showed more than 800 clubs and organizations among 17,000 people.) The camera might go on to indicate the many curious methods by which Americans earn their living, or try to offset the boredom of earning a living under machine-age conditions. In New York City a great glass-walled cube shelters delegates from some 70 nations, of all human skin colors and languages and belief systems, trying to find roads to agreement.

This is the field of the social scientist: watching these people behave, and searching out the laws which govern that behavior. Kurt Lewin, the originator of group dynamics, believed that the laboratory of the social scientist is living society, that observations must have a date put on them, for society is always changing, and that a small *controlled* change can be made to provide a scale for measurement and comparison.

THE MAJOR DISCIPLINES

Schools and colleges offer courses in history, philosophy, mathematics, chemistry, psychology, and so on. Teachers, after long years of training, teach these subjects; students pass them or flunk them. Some are classified as "natural science," some as "social science," some as "the humanities."

Actually, of course, neither the physical world nor human behavior is cut up into any such neat classifications. Reality out there beyond our heads is all of a piece, one area flowing into the next by "insensible gradations." A cat or an eagle treats it as all of a piece, but because of language, which permits us to classify, we humans can cut up the all-thing verbally and consider the various areas under appropriate labels.

Increasingly, however, we are finding that the pieces when reassembled do not fit together. So we are taking down the verbal partitions from time to time, to permit a broader and truer view of what is going on. A big research project these days may include most of the disciplines. The natural sciences flow into the social sciences via medicine and public health; anthropology flows into sociology, and both into economics. During World War II partitions were falling right and left; we will return to this important subject in the next chapter.

The separate college courses remain, and necessarily will remain for a long time—to be supplemented, one hopes, by more orientation courses. Which of them fall under the head of social sciences? In preparing this book I asked a number of social scientists around the country to name and rank their disciplines. Some subjects were always clearly inside the "social science" classification, but others were cloudy, bordering on natural science or the humanities. Obviously no hard-and-fast distinction had been made—or probably ever can be made for the borderline subjects. The following five had the most votes as authentic social sciences in my questionnaire:

> Cultural anthropology
> Social psychology
> Sociology
> Economics
> Political science

The order corresponds inversely with their age, for anthropology and psychology are the youngest of the disciplines, while political science is the oldest. Aristotle, as the author of *Politics*, might be nominated as the father of political science.

Economics, which once was called "political economy," became a formal discipline with the work of Adam Smith in the late eighteenth century. Sociology was launched in the nineteenth century with such sponsors as Durkheim, Le Play, Giddings, Small, Cooley, and Lester Ward. A little later social psychology gathered impetus from William James. Cultural anthropology seems to have started with Morgan's work on the family systems of Seneca Indians, and began to be prominent after the turn of the century; a landmark was the publication of Sumner's *Folkways* in 1906. "Physical" anthropology as a science was much older, but it dealt more with the measurement of skulls than with human behavior.

In addition to the above Big Five, various other disciplines were named by my respondents. *History* received almost as many votes as political science, but usually with a reservation. Because they deal with events which have gone into limbo, historians cannot use the full scientific method. To predict the future from the history of the past is risky business, especially when science and technology are forcing rapid social changes. History, as some one has said, is an irreversible process, and perhaps the discipline should stand by itself, like mathematics, as an aid to all the others.

Demography, or population study, received a number of votes; so did *human geography, linguistics, public administration, legal science, educational science*. Today we find some of the older categories dividing into such specialties as public opinion research, group dynamics, communication studies, labor relations analysis.

A double movement can be noted: in one direction social science is specializing and thus putting up more partitions; and in the other it is tearing them down—integrating the social studies into one university department, or into a given large research project, for instance an "area study."

I received no questionnaires from abroad, although similar movements are known to be under way in Canada, Britain, and Western Europe. Europe set the pattern for the social sciences, but in recent years the United States has forged ahead in developing both theory and research techniques. UNESCO is now exerting its international influence to make social science more widely known.

Philosophy, ethics, comparative religion, were classed by most of my respondents with the humanities, along with literature and the arts.

Assisting the social scientist are four tools: mathematics, statistics, logic, and semantics. Each of these tools is a formidable discipline in its own right; each is useful if not mandatory where problems are to be solved. The scientific method would be practically unrecognizable without mathematics. Without logic it could not draw inferences, or formulate hypotheses and theories. We are beginning to realize that people often do not know what they are talking about without some functional understanding of language and its pitfalls in meaning—which is the domain of the young discipline of semantics.

Between social science and natural science is a zone where various disciplines and studies cut across both fields. Is fingerprinting social science or biology? Obviously it is both. What about Sherlock Holmes and all his professional descendants? How about Dr. Yerkes's revealing studies of the habits of chimpanzees? A strong case can be made for *psychiatry* as a bridge between the two major fields. Not only has it contributed enormously to social science, but it draws on it as well. "Psychiatry," says Dr. William C. Menninger of the famous clinic in Topeka, "is a medical science but it is also a social science. The psychiatrist, more than the physician in any other medical discipline, must concern himself with the social situation of his patients." Race prejudice and involuntary unemployment, for instance, can cause mental breakdowns.

Every doctor knows how much psychology is involved in medical practice. In one sense, a good general practitioner in a country town is as expert in human relations as in the pharmacopoeia. Would Mrs. Jones be really sick if she were not sick of Mr. Jones?

Some Outstanding Accomplishments

With the help of my questionnaires, personal interviews, visits to universities, and the reading of many monographs and books, I have accumulated a long list of outstanding accomplishments in the social sciences. Some are brilliant individual research findings, some cover whole groups of studies.

The culture concept developed by anthropologists and sociologists is frequently named as the most important accomplishment of all. It covers a body of principles derived from field studies, all revolving around the basic idea that an individual cannot be understood apart from the culture which contains him; or, to put it in a more familiar way, that man is a social animal. It is a broad and general concept, on the scale of Darwin's theory of evolution, and perhaps equally important. The anthropologists, by studying living cultures around the world and checking with the records of past cultures, have worked out some of the laws which govern all human societies everywhere.

Other accomplishments which received high ratings include:

Studies in race relations by Boas, Benedict, Myrdal, Young, Klineberg, and others. There is as yet no proof of racial inequality that will meet the test of science. The real problem today is how to apply these scientific conclusions in practical problems—such as desegregation in the public schools.

William F. Ogburn's extensive work on social change.

The Cross-Cultural Index at Yale—a kind of Rosetta Stone of anthropology.

Dr. Alexander Leighton's work with interned Japanese-Americans during the war. He discovered some fundamental principles of the governing of men.

Sampling theory and its application to census figures, population, insurance; the remarkable techniques of the Social Security Board.

The polls of public opinion—also founded on sampling theory. They are at present enjoying a great vogue, and when properly conducted add to our understanding of human behavior.

Elton Mayo's scientific approach to labor-management relations, combining anthropology, psychology, sociology, and economics.

The various "Middletown" surveys, beginning with Quaker Hill.

Measurements of IQ, and other testing and scaling techniques developed by Binet, Terman, Seashore, Rorschach.

"Area studies" by social scientists during the war, especially the preparation for the Okinawa landing.

Manpower analysis for recruiting soldiers and war workers—an outstanding statistical achievement.

Development of Gross National Product and other economic indices during the war.

Linguistic research, including the metalinguistics of Benjamin Lee Whorf.

Communication research and semantics.

And so on, and so forth. A number of the above accomplishments will be described in detail later. The sample list is presented here to give the reader an idea of the depth and richness of the field.

LABORATORY AT HARVARD

Social scientists have adopted the word "laboratory" from natural science, but their version usually lacks the noble stinks and sinks and Bunsen burners of the traditional lab. It is a fixed place where experiments in behavior are conducted, or the results of other experiments gathered and codified. Sometimes it looks and smells like a biological laboratory, if experiments on rats are in progress; sometimes it looks like a photographer's studio, as in the perception experiments of Ames and Cantril at Princeton; more often it looks like a college class room, with chairs arranged for a seminar and a tape recorder humming—as in the group dynamics laboratory at Bethel, Maine.

Here is the Laboratory of Social Relations at Harvard, under the direction of Samuel A. Stouffer. It is primarily interested in two tasks: verifying hypotheses in social science, and improving research techniques. The application of theory to practical situations is of less interest to the Laboratory, but of great interest to Harvard's allied Department of Social Relations. Perhaps the most interesting piece of equipment in the Laboratory is the one-way window, where experimenters can see and hear a group in action—say a family conference or a labor-management negotiation—but the group cannot see the observers.

The staff includes social anthropologists, sociologists, social and clinical psychologists. "However, there is no interest in pigeon-holing research as especially belonging to one or another of these disciplines. Rather, the concern has been with a problem, with the hope of attacking it freshly from more than one point of view." Periodic staff discussions bring many points of view to bear, and prevent specialists from burrowing their way too far underground.

A recent report lists 95 projects under attack, with more than 100 papers published. Here is a group of studies in the way children form habits in various cultures. Do different child-training practices lead to different sets of values when the child grows up? Here are experiments on dogs—following the great Pavlov—with findings which are "central to any thinking about so-called compulsive or phobic behavior, and may have applications—in the Armed Forces, for example—to training people to handle anxiety better." Here is a mathematical model constructed to reconcile two theories of behavior; and another model to support von Neumann's theory of games and its important implications for economic behavior.

The Laboratory is studying how we perceive things and people, how we form prejudices. Here is a detailed psychiatric study of 98 patients with ulcerative colitis, all of whom had lost someone dear to them. Evidence "tends to strengthen the conclusion that the bereavement crisis is of great pathogenic significance for such an illness." More evidence for psychosomatic medicine.

Finally, we note a long series of experiments aimed at improving the techniques of experiments—scaling and computing procedures, new mathematical and statistical methods, psychological measurements of emotion, sentence completion tests, Murray's Thematic Apperception Test, a hard look at the Rorschach (ink blot) test, and so on.

How does the Laboratory select its projects? Says Stouffer: "The Laboratory believes that it is now more important than ever to choose carefully among problems of basic inquiry those which seem to have the greatest potentiality of generating results ultimately useful to mankind." Such a choice illustrates how ethical judgments may get into scientific research, through the selection of the problem.

APPLIED SOCIAL SCIENCE

The oldest of the university research organizations is Columbia's Bureau of Applied Social Research. More than Harvard, it concentrates on applying theory to practical problems, and it is also seriously concerned with techniques and methods.

The Bureau has made studies of the impact of mass media on the attitudes and values of those exposed to them—and who today is not?—studies of how voters make up their minds; studies in the role of religion in contemporary life; in professional aptitudes—what it takes to become a doctor or a lawyer; studies in world population trends.

Its researchers have gone to the Middle East to find out what people there think of the United States, the stereotypes they hold. In Europe they have evaluated the Voice of America on the spot. They have gone to a small Midwestern city to study the power structure—who runs the town; to a village in the South to analyze the support of voluntary health organizations; into a labor union to study democracy or the lack of it. (Here the Bureau concluded that democracy in the union depended more on the nature of the job and the local environment than on the goodness or badness of union leaders.)

The Columbia Bureau is supported partly by funds from the foundations, and partly by its own earnings. Specific projects are undertaken for the Armed Services and other government agencies, for business firms, labor unions, social welfare agencies. Since its inauguration the Bureau has conducted more than 300 research studies, and published 200 reports, of which 40 are full-length books. It accepts commissions to conduct applied research only where such research can satisfy basic scientific concerns along with solving a sponsor's practical problem. This policy has paid off handsomely as measured by the quality of the Bureau's work. In turn, the Bureau has had an important influence on some aspects of government policy, on labor-management relations, on public health programs, on the content of certain mass media programs.

There are now some fifteen university research organizations like those at Columbia and Harvard. The two so briefly sketched give an indication of what social scientists are up to today, and how far they have departed from an exclusive preoccupation with the books and the ideas of the past.

THEORY AND PRACTICE

The above samples of social science research make it evident that theory runs into application, and application often demands new theory. It is not easy to draw a line between the theorist in his laboratory and the practitioner in clinic, survey team, or village.

Natural scientists, however, have a similar problem. Lancelot Hogben points out how the practice of deep-shaft mining in the sixteenth century opened up acute questions of air pressure, ventilation, and explosives. Mining could not go deeper until they were answered, and this forced chemists and physicists to develop new theory in a hurry. Without this practical urge, says Hogben, chemical theory might have stayed where the Greeks left it.

Theory may suddenly emerge as a by-product of observation. When Malinowski was studying the natives of the Trobriand Islands, he noted that if they fished in the protected lagoon they used the reliable method of poisoning. There were few dangers, and the catch was assured. Also he noted that in the lagoon the natives had no recourse to magic. When, however, they ventured beyond the lagoon into the open sea, winds and currents produced serious and unpredictable hazards; there was no sure control of the catch and magic rituals were called in to help. So Malinowski evolved the theory that magical belief arises to bridge the uncertainties in man's practical pursuits, a supplementary technique for reaching practical objectives.

Two centuries ago, medicine in the West was largely magic. Doctors did not know much about disease or how to control it. Today, the magical element has declined to the patent medicine ads. Malinowski's theory has wide application: *the less we know, the more magic we invent to explain the mystery*. Social science theorists and social science practitioners work hand in glove, and both are essential. The practitioner takes the theory off the shelf and puts it to work; in doing so he may discover new theory.

There is, to be sure, no lack of theory in social science, but much of it has never been adequately verified. This is what the Harvard Laboratory is especially concerned with, the verification of theories now at large. There are other difficulties and growing pains, too, and in the next chapter we will look at some of them.

4

Growing Pains

A favorite phrase of social scientists is "cultural lag." It means old and useless customs and beliefs which still survive despite new conditions—like whipsockets on early automobiles. Social science itself is handicapped by a good deal of cultural lag. Hippocrates was a great physician, but no modern doctor in a critical diagnosis would dream of consulting the writings of the father of medicine. The modern doctor respects Hippocrates, and recites his famous oath, but disregards most of his therapy. Not so in large areas of social science, where the great figures of the past are still regarded as the final authority on human behavior. If no better theory has come up, perhaps they are, but often the sheer weight of their names is taken for ultimate wisdom.

Social science got its title before the "exact science" meaning was in wide use, when the "seven liberal arts" were "sciences," together with the "science" of boxing. Natural science has now gone wholly over to the "exact" meaning as defined in our first chapter, but social science is split between the two, giving it a somewhat schizophrenic character, a symptom of its growing pains.

Although no Newton has yet arisen in social science, a number of figures stand out, together with some who thought they were Newtons—Ricardo, for instance, and Herbert Spencer. The great names include Plato, Machiavelli, Locke, Comte, Malthus, John Stuart Mill, Jeremy Bentham, Adam Smith, Thomas Paine, and many more.

These men were as distinguished as any natural scientist and far better known to the general public. They were not, however, scientists as defined, at least not for most of the time. Rather they were political or social philosophers—and there is quite a difference. Philosophical systems and speculations do not require an expedition by the Royal Society to verify a hypothesis, say by viewing an eclipse from a Pacific island. Sometimes, to be sure, the speculations are full of wisdom; but the mental approach is less humble, the pervasive aroma of doubt is missing, it is harder to admit one may be wrong. Where the scientist accepts the facts, the social philosopher often succeeds in ignoring them. Let us examine Karl Marx as an example.

WAS MARX A SCIENTIST?

The founder of "scientific" socialism is regarded by millions as a Newton in the field of economics. He is supposed to have discovered the laws which govern human societies as the law of gravitation governs the movements of the planets. Marx's adherents talk about economic determinism, and grow very impatient with people who doubt if matters are quite so inevitable.

Marx and his collaborator, Friedrich Engels, were not so much filled with curiosity about human society as they were filled with anger against capitalists. This was an unfortunate beginning, for it contradicted the first principle of the scientific method by letting in an emotional bias. Forty years of so-called utopian socialism had convinced Marx and Engels of the futility of preparing rational blueprints for the good society and then trying to argue them into acceptance. They were looking for stronger medicine.

Casting about the social structure, they presently discovered a number of facts, such as the uprising of discontented workers in Lyons in 1831, and the Chartist agitation in England, which seemed to be strung on a single theme, *the class struggle*. They evolved a hypothesis about the class struggle—a step which was quite legitimate scientifically—and went to the history books to find out about class struggles in the past.

"Then it was seen," said Engels, "that all past history, with the exception of its primitive stages, was the history of class struggles." Great excitement prevailed as this "law" emerged from the shelves of the British Museum. Not content with locating a dynamic group—the proletariat—who would automatically bring socialism, Marx went on to elaborate the conclusion by sweeping generalizations which covered all history, and which were difficult, if not impossible, to verify. We must also remember that the history books in the British Museum a hundred years ago left something to be desired.

In due time the anthropologists came along, with their patient observations of how men actually behaved in a given society. They found little to support the "law" of the class struggle. Says Ralph Linton, for instance, in *The Study of Man*:

> The class struggle is a special phenomenon which developed in only a few societies, and then as a result of a complex series of factors, the most important of which has been rapid cultural change. Most of the world's societies have not even been class-organized, and in those which were so prior to the sudden rise of machine industry, the classes . . . reached a condition of satisfactory adjustment.

Here is a flat contradiction of evidence. As between Marx and the anthropologists, any competent scientist will choose the latter. Linton has no ax to grind; he is not indulging in personal opinions or grievances, but summarizing accredited knowledge in this field. Anthropologists have agreed that the typical human society, except in periods of very rapid change, comes to rest with nearly every individual in it enjoying a definite status. The normal individual, moreover, takes pride in his status, and does not dream of revolting against it.

SOCIAL SCIENCE₁ AND SOCIAL SCIENCE₂

If Marx was not a social scientist in the exact sense, what was he? He certainly was an economic theorist, and by common acclaim one of the greatest. We may clarify the question by introducing a little gadget from mathematics—the index number, usually appearing as $a_1, a_2, a_3, \ldots a_n$.

Social scientist$_1$ follows the scientific method as rigorously as in biology, and demands verification before accepting theories. The exact sense.

Social scientist$_2$ is seriously concerned with human problems. His theories may be true, but adequate verification is missing. Fortunately, scientists like Stouffer are working to supply it.

Social scientist$_3$ is occupied with observation and speculation which has never reached the stage of clear-cut theory. William F. Ogburn observes somewhat ruefully that a large proportion of social science is in this class.

From here on our science grows mistier and mistier. Social scientist$_4$ might refer to persons who proclaim themselves as scientists, but are neither well trained nor really curious about human behavior. They have more mundane motivations. Professional psychology, for instance, has been so plagued by gentlemen convinced that the world owes them a living, that the American Psychological Association has had to draft a code of ethics to protect the public against them.

Much of the material classified as "social science" in universities and libraries has not been arrived at by the scientific method. Its exponents have not cut loose from the older methods of intuition, authority, and pure logic. The material may be interesting, stimulating, and educational in the scholastic sense, but it is not conclusive.

Did Plato mean this in the *Republic* or did he mean that? Did Machiavelli foreshadow Hitler? Did Spengler originate a fresh philosophy or was it the same old stuff? Is the capitalist system "mature"? Listening to this constant buzz soaring up the ventilators of many a classroom, one realizes that there has been good reason for asking whether social science were indeed science. Much of it is social science$_2$, if not social science$_3$.

DELINQUENCY AS A TEST CASE

Let us take another case to set beside that of Marx. Suppose juvenile delinquency is a serious problem in your community. You are put on a committee to look into the causes. First, let us say, you try speculative methods. This means calling a lot of meetings, thinking hard, and arguing. It means looking up what the good books say about bad boys. Some of the books say to reason with them, some say to punish them, some of the more recent say to give them playgrounds, or get them out of the slums. Doubtless in all this welter of advice you will find some stimulating ideas.

Another approach, however, would be for your committee to consult experts who deal in social science₁. Here, for instance, is what a team actually did some years ago. Delinquent boys and girls were paired with nondelinquents from the same families —143 pairs in 143 families, from three different cities. All were given a most searching examination, physical and mental, with IQ tests and psychiatric interviews. Their records were exhaustively studied.

No proof was found of inheritance as a prime cause of delinquency; nor was illiteracy, slum upbringing, or most of the other alleged causes responsible for delinquency. Nineteen of the cases came from well-to-do homes. *But in every case* an emotional maladjustment was found. Often it had its roots in the way the parents felt about that particular child. If they loved him and made him feel secure, the chances for delinquency were small, no matter how poor the family. If parents did not provide that emotional security essential to every human youngster, he might be robbing candy stands by the time he was eight.

Leonard Doob, the Yale psychologist, commented that Healy and Bronner's study rendered obsolete four fifths of all previous literature on delinquency. It put something definitive into the storehouse. It provides a useful point of departure for your committee, and for every serious attempt to do something about juvenile delinquency. It is not the whole story, a closer fit is sure to be found, but it will give you something solid to build on.

Unverified Hypotheses

It is of great importance, it seems to me, to grasp the distinction between these two wings of social science. Far out on one side are the speculations of great men like Aristotle, Hobbes, Mill—and others not so great. Nobody knows whether what they say is true or not. Far out on the other side are the plodding note-takers in clinic, Congo village, and laboratory, putting down what they observe, accumulating a store of relevant facts. In the middle is a zone where men with imagination may be using the scientific method part of the time, and letting their imaginations roam the rest of the time. William James and Benjamin Lee Whorf, the linguist, were such men.

There is no call to become severely critical because a good deal of social science is not rigorously scientific. We simply recognize that the speculative wing, social science₂, has not gone beyond the hypothesis stage, adequate proof has not come in, debate and argument are still wide open. Criticism can be legitimately leveled only when solid validity is claimed for what are only interesting speculations. The alert reader is now in possession of a rough test for validity. Has argument among the experts died down, indicating acceptance of the hypothesis, or is debate still hot and inconclusive?

Another test is suggested by Dr. Oppenheimer. Above all, he says, science gives us the means to detect error; it is continually self-correcting.

In fact one of the features which must arouse our suspicion of the dogmas some of Freud's followers have built up on the initial brilliant work of Freud, is the tendency toward a *self-sealing system* . . . which has a way of almost automatically discounting evidence which might bear adversely on the doctrine. The whole point of science is just the opposite.

Dr. Oppenheimer has presented us with a valuable term— "self-sealing system"—which, incidentally, he also applies to Marx. Social science, broadly defined as it must still be, has its share of self-sealers, guarding the "true doctrine" from any further objective investigation. When we find students so engaged, and more than a little emotional about it as well, we may be sure that we are in the presence of something less than social science$_1$.

The late Morris R. Cohen has given another example. Because different peoples have different histories it is dangerous, he says, to compare the institutions of one with another. To get around this difficulty, men like Comte and Herbert Spencer resorted to the arbitrary hypothesis that all peoples must go through the *same stages* in their history, and declared it legitimate to compare different peoples at the same stage. There is no support in anthropology for this. The Peruvians, for instance, cannot have passed through the sequence of nomad, pastoral, and agricultural stages because they never had enough cattle to be a pastoral people. The savants invented tribal customs to fit their theories. (They would hardly dare do it now, with the Cross-Cultural Index to check them.)

As late as 1870 Herbert Spencer could affirm that the starvation of the idle, the exploitation of the weak by the strong, "are the decrees of a larger, far-seeing benevolence. . . . Under the natural order of things, society is constantly excreting its unhealthy, imbecile, slow, vacillating, faithless members. . . ." Nobody could contradict this ferocious doctrine because neither anthropology nor social psychology had then advanced far enough to prove that it was wrong.

What it seems to come down to is this: All of us have a right to speculate about human relations and write books if we care to. But we should not publish such books without making it clear that we are offering *an unverified hypothesis*.[1] Looking back over the years, I fear that a book or two of mine should have carried that warning more explicitly.

IVORY TOWERS

Colin Clark, in the introduction to his classic study *The Conditions of Economic Progress*, bids farewell to his academic colleagues in London. He likes them all personally, he says, but is dismayed at their continual preference for the speculative

[1] See Chapter 19 for sad examples in economics.

rather than the scientific approach to economic problems. Not one in a hundred really understands the scientific approach, least of all those who most anxiously proclaim the scientific nature of economics. He observes many authors trying to solve exceptionally complex economic problems by logic and argument, often with hardly a reference to the facts. Others will base a book on theoretical arguments and then select a few hand-picked data to illustrate conclusions already reached. This neatly puts the theoretical cart before the factual horse, and reminds us of the attorney who, in summing up his case to the jury, cried: "These, gentlemen, are the conclusions upon which I base my facts!"

University schedules unfortunately are not easily adjusted to permit first-hand observation by social science students. They rarely take their notebooks to Congress during a heated session, to a dock strike in New York, to a revolution in Paraguay. Such a program would be expensive, but perhaps a greater difficulty is the enormous amount of trouble it would entail.

The social disciplines until recently have tended to be highly intellectual, bookish, and abstract. The best students have been those who could deal brilliantly with formal logic, cite chapter and verse, and correctly manipulate the verbal symbols. Professors have tended to sit in chairs writing books about each other's books. Students have sat in harder chairs, writing monographs about the theories of men long dead. As the science of man advances, the really good students may be found not among the chair-bound scholars, but among boys and girls who like people, enjoy talking to them and interviewing them, and are curious about human relationships. They will study living society more than they study the classics.

Elton Mayo, after a quarter of a century of university work, notes sadly how social science students are trained to argue and to cite authority, but not to handle concrete situations involving human relations. They are like the man who took a correspondence course in aviation; he knew all about flying but he couldn't fly. Mayo demonstrated in his experiments at

Hawthorne that scientific conclusions can be drawn by means of clinical as well as laboratory methods. He advises the universities to teach skills which can be used to answer specific questions. Many of Mayo's students are now using his techniques to solve labor-management problems in business firms all over the country.

GOBBLEDYGOOK AS SCIENCE

Without disclosing the source, for that would be unkind, let us quote a paragraph by a distinguished social scientist, written not a hundred years ago:

In conformity with the preceding point, if all the interacting parties (in marriage, in minority-majority groups, in different occupational, religious, political, economic, racial, ethnic and other interacting groups and persons) view the given overtly similar (or dissimilar) traits: A, B, C, D, N (physical, biological, mental, sociocultural) as negligible values or as no values at all, as comprising even no similarity (or dissimilarity), such overt similarities-dissimilarities are innocuous in the generation of either solidarity or antagonism.

Some professors seem to feel that if they can only get a terminology which is dense enough, they have somehow achieved the scientific method. All they have done is shatter the communication line.

Too often social scientists have blindly copied the techniques and language of the natural scientists, possibly hoping thereby to lessen their own feelings of insecurity—practicing prestige-by-association. Some of the transplanted mathematics, especially in economics, is fearful and wonderful.[2] This might be excused in a young department struggling for recognition, but the social sciences are grown up now. They should stand on their own feet, working out techniques which are not borrowed from physics and chemistry, but appropriate to different sorts of problems.

[2] See Bassett Jones, *Horses and Apples*.

Too Many Partitions

A brilliant graduate student in economics at a leading university once spoke bitterly to me about the partitions which hemmed him in. Faculty members are classified, he said, as "economic theorists," "economic historians," "economic statisticians," "monetary theorists," "labor economists," and so on. Each regards his field as a vested interest, on which no sociologist or psychologist may trespass in pursuit of a problem. At the same time he is cut off from their company. "We are like soldiers lying in isolated foxholes without means of communication . . . yet the social sciences are concerned with different aspects of the same critter—man—and the notion that we can abstract the economic or the psychological aspect of his behavior without regard to the rest, is nonsense."[3]

This is a blunt statement of a major difficulty in social science as we noted earlier. In the classroom it perhaps does not make so much difference, but once concrete problems are tackled in a factory, in a hospital, in the armed services, the partitions must come down.

When Alexander Leighton was charged with finding out what was going on in Leyte or Okinawa, preparatory to a landing by American troops in the war, he used not only anthropologists, psychologists, historians, economists, sociologists, but geographers, botanists, meteorologists, medical men. He threw nearly all the scientific disciplines into a massive combined operation, which undoubtedly resulted in saving thousands of lives! He was not teaching in a classroom, but facing an urgent problem in military intelligence. Later he went back to Cornell, his professional skills expanded and strengthened. All who took part in this area study were stronger for the experience.

Here, let us say, is a project in rural sociology. Almost immediately the director finds himself coping with the *geography* of the region, the *economics* of the region, its *political* structure, and its *history*. Similarly a geographer with a problem usually

[3] The young man was Dr. Jackson Toby, now on the faculty at Rutgers.

needs an economic and sociological analysis to get results. All large problems in group behavior, meanwhile, whether rural or urban, demand a vivid appreciation of the culture concept.

Chemists alone, says Professor George T. Renner of Columbia,[4] could not have made the atomic bomb—but the bomb could not have been made without chemists. "There is the same organic unity among social scientists as among the physical scientists when it comes to problem solving." But each social discipline, he observes, has been trying to produce a bomb by itself.

There are exceptions. Harvard, as we have seen, has set up a Department of Social Relations where teamwork is the order of the day. The Yale Law School welcomed economists and psychologists to the faculty many years ago. Columbia has had an integrated department for a generation. Michigan, Chicago, California, M.I.T., Case, and many other colleges are experimenting with integrating the social sciences.

At Palo Alto, the Ford Foundation is financing a Center for Advanced Study in the Behavioral Sciences, where outstanding social scientists are invited to pursue their special subjects in close contact with Fellows from all the disciplines. It is something like the Princeton Center in the natural sciences, now headed by Dr. Oppenheimer. The Social Science Research Council has long been a clearing house for research, theory, and practice among all the disciples. Man, as my graduate student observed, is one critter.

Taboo

The last major difficulty which we shall note is that certain aspects of human behavior cannot be freely investigated. Our Western culture permits almost unlimited investigation in the natural sciences, but not in the social sciences. Researchers must use caution in setting up projects dealing with sex, race relations, property relations, the function of government, international relations.

In 1954, cadets at West Point were forbidden to discuss the

[4] In a personal letter.

recognition of Red China. The Kinsey reports on sexual behavior have been bitterly attacked, while a congressional committee, as we have seen, has denied the possibility, let alone the utility, of any social science₁ at all. It used to be a kind of heresy to examine the gold standard objectively, but that day is passing.

The scientific method cannot operate in a climate of taboos and restrictions. One reason the natural sciences can be more liberal is the likelihood that foolish hypotheses will soon be eliminated by the shock of facts. Presently somebody will come along to say, "Very interesting; let's take a look at the experiments." In social science, foolish theories sometimes continue unchallenged for a long time. The situation is not yet so serious as it was in Victorian days, when bigots tried to silence Thomas Huxley for describing evolution, but neither is it as good as it was in Athens 2,500 years ago.

5

Nineteen Questions

Despite the taboos, lags, and difficulties set forth in the last chapter, the scientific study of man cannot be halted; it is too late. The hoary argument which says man is so unpredictable that he cannot be examined empirically has collapsed, and only the ignorant now raise it.

New knowledge has been discovered, tested, and stored on the shelves; much of it won during World War II. Already it can answer certain problems of society better than any dictator, better than a convocation of elders, better than intuition or common sense. Thousands of able, well-trained men and women are devoting their lives to increasing this store.

We must not expect to learn *all* about man and his behavior. No worker in the natural sciences yet knows what life is, or precisely what electricity is. But enough is known to stamp out yellow fever and light a thousand cities. Ralph Linton points to the still grander vision now before the social scientist: "The pioneer can only press on, sustained by the belief that somewhere in this vast territory there lies hidden the knowledge which will arm man for his greatest victory, the conquest of himself."

Suppose we turn the idea of social science the other way around. Suppose we try thinking about *problems* to be solved, rather than *disciplines* to be taught, and look at some major barriers to progress in the years ahead. In this chapter we will list 19 questions to be answered as the atomic age moves in on us. All of them must somehow be met, and in all we shall need expert help. Intuition, pure logic, common sense, appeals to ancient authority, even magic, will doubtless be used, but it is

hardly likely that they will be good enough. Most of the problems are a by-product of applied science loose in human affairs,
and it is a fair assumption that a further application of the
scientific method must be used to deal with them.

We will divide the questions into three classes—political,
economic, and sociological—and illustrate incidentally the tentative nature of classifications and partitions. Political scientists
alone cannot handle the first class of questions, economists the
second, or sociologists the third. Specialists may lead the team,
but they will need a great deal of help from the other disciplines,
and often from natural scientists as well.

PROBLEMS PRIMARILY POLITICAL

1. *Modus vivendi.* First and foremost today is the towering
question of finding what President Eisenhower has called a
modus vivendi between East and West. If the world is entering
a kind of "thermonuclear truce," time may be granted, or borrowed, to work out firm understandings and guarantees to make
the truce permanent, and so avoid the unthinkable disaster of
World War III. The statesmen building such machinery will
need social scientists to aid them, and need the utmost resources
of the storehouse. In chapter 27 we shall explore this cardinal
question in some detail, with suggestions for a more effective
use of social scientists. They were used to win a war, and now
they are doubly needed to win a peace.

2. *Civilian defense.* War or peace, we dare not evade a comprehensive program for civilian defense. Yesterday I listened
to part of a day-long program beamed from Bridgeport, my
nearest industrial city, spelling out what 200,000 people in that
area should do when the alarm sounded. Practically, it meant
wholesale evacuation. No city in the world ever faced such a
threat before, not even London in the blitz of 1941. What are
the psychological as well as the physical elements to be reckoned
with? Studies in handling disasters have been made by social
scientists at Michigan, Columbia, Chicago. Research teams have

flown to actual disaster areas—floods, tornadoes, great fires— to observe how people behave in panic. Their studies give us something to build on.

3. *A more effective United Nations.* The UN, as most responsible people agree, has more than justified its existence. But its structure is clumsy, its lines of communication scrambled, its grasp of the culture concept weak. Social scientists have been working to improve it, but a great deal more needs to be done, especially in improving communication. UNESCO had a group of outstanding social scientists working on international conferences,[1] but the project was handicapped because of insufficient funds.

As colonialism and old-style imperialism decline, rampant nationalism is rising, not only in states, like India and Indonesia and Egypt, which have shaken off their European masters, but in the Western nations themselves. How shall we keep national pride, yet avoid the clash of nations in atomic war? The UN is the only agency in sight to resolve the paradox. If it were abolished, another international agency would have to be created in the interests of survival.

4. *Foreign aid programs.* This question applies to the so-called Have nations, in coöperation with the Have-nots. It could be run exclusively through the United Nations and perhaps should be. In the United States it has been called Point Four, technical assistance, "handout to foreigners," and other names, while Congress blows hot and cold. Along with his technical equipment, a foreign aid officer needs to take with him the culture concept. Otherwise, as we shall see in case after case throughout this book, he will not know how to get on with the local people, and may be defeated before he starts.

5. *The clash of races.* Organized nationalism is a comparatively recent institution, but prejudice is based on an ancient, if not a universal response. The new nations in Asia are not without prejudice against the white man, while the white man in South Africa seems to be moving to some terrible climax with the

[1] Reported in my *Roads to Agreement.*

remorselessness of Greek tragedy. The clash of races in America has been steadily lessening but some critical tests lie ahead. There are social scientists, like Gordon Allport, who have specialized in prejudice and the means to reduce it. The world bitterly needs their knowledge today.

6. *Governmental machinery*. Few citizens in the democracies of the West wish to go back to kings or dictators. But the political machinery grinds and groans and often comes close to breakdown. The French Assembly offers one sad example, and the persistent war between White House and Congress another. How can political structures be improved so that "a government can govern," to use a favorite phrase of Walter Lippmann? Here is an outstanding challenge to social scientists. If the machine should really strip its gears, a dictator might be the only alternative to chaos. The British machine works pretty well; so does the Swedish. Why?

PROBLEMS PRIMARILY ECONOMIC

7. *Population pressure on the food supply*. This is the old question raised by Malthus, and may be the most serious long-term problem confronted by mankind. Though America does not face this problem at home—so long as we can hold our soils—we face its consequences in Asia, where it is transcendent. It is implicitly recognized in most projects of technical assistance. All the social sciences will have to help in solving it, and most of the natural sciences too, especially biology and chemistry.

8. *Revival of world trade*. States plagued with nationalism struggle for economic self-sufficiency—what the Germans used to call "autarky." World War I blocked trade routes. The depression, World War II, and the cold war, further distorted them. (Consider the huge synthetic rubber plants built by the United States government when Japan cut off the supply of natural rubber in 1942.) This question is tied to question Number one, modus vivendi, but here economists must take the lead,

with help on many cultural and psychological points, to expedite a reasonable flow of goods around the planet.

9. *Boom and bust.* How are we to prevent both mass unemployment, as in the 1930's, and the runaway inflation which afflicted many nations after both World Wars? Economists have devised some compensatory techniques against deflation and inflation, but the profound psychological problem remains of getting citizens and governments to use them. More research, too, is needed to refine the methods.

10. *Labor-management conflict.* This critical question seems to be on the way to solution in the United States and Canada, aided by social scientists as we shall see in detail later. In the rest of the world it is still virulent. Industrial psychologists, pollsters, economists, sociologists, are all helping management and unions in America.

11. *Automation.* Scientists who are engineering the displacement of men by the new electronic machines, in both office and factory, predict an industrial revolution greater than that wrought by steam power. If it should come with a rush, unplanned, it could result in wholesale technological unemployment. Social scientists are needed to advise both management and unions how automation can be eased into the economy without disaster.

12. *Ideological warfare in industry.* Some conflict between economic groups is inevitable and healthy. But conflict has been aggravated ever since Watt's first steam engine by a purely verbal demonology of "labor" against "capital," "business" against "government," "free enterprise" against "regimentation," "Wall Street" against the field. To banish these verbal spooks is a task for experts on communication as well as economists. We shall look at some progress along this line in Puerto Rico.

PROBLEMS PRIMARILY SOCIOLOGICAL

13. *Decentralization.* Something must be done about cities, industries, organizations, bureaucracies, grown so monstrous that

people can no longer cope with them. Our biological equipment is geared to smaller units. One way to appreciate this, I find, is to walk slowly through the canyons of lower New York. Even the suburbs are growing congested, while the urban parking problem has become astronomical. Civilian defense programs serve to point up the whole question and, to solve it, social scientists will be in acute demand, along with bulldozers, dynamite, and engineers.

Megalopolis has engulfed the small face-to-face community of a simpler age (there are still a few in Vermont), and the automobile has kept citizens on the move, hunting jobs and homes and sometimes sheer excitement. People on the move put down few roots; cliff dwellers in their city apartments have few neighbors in the old village sense. Ralph Linton believes that the disintegration of the small community, the timeless human band, is perhaps the gravest of all modern problems. The band has been the most constant of all social phenomena down the ages. It is tragic to lose its self-discipline and emotional satisfactions, with no substitutes beyond synthetic, publicity-created clubs and organizations.

14. *Mental illness.* A high-energy society, chiefly because of increased tensions, now reserves about half its hospital beds for the mentally ill. A good many wards are filled with sufferers from the allied disease of alcoholism. The psychiatrists are making some progress, but a mass attack by various disciplines is urgent.

15. *Juvenile delinquency.* As we have seen earlier, scientists know something about its causes, but much work must be done to apply the knowledge in a given community. Comparative studies are also in order: Why does the American rate go up, while the British rate goes down? Why do some societies have no juvenile delinquency at all?

16. *Crime.* How can prisons and criminals be handled more intelligently? This problem is intensified by recent prison revolts in the United States. Two hundred years ago convicted persons were hanged, drawn and quartered, broken on the wheel. In

England as late as 1820 one could go to the gallows for stealing a pewter pot. This ferocity had no appreciable effect on the crime rate. When a luckless pickpocket was given a big public hanging on Tyburn Hill, luckier pickpockets were busy among the crowd. We have reduced the ferocity but not the idea of punishment. An eye for an eye does not seem to work, and publicity seems to work in reverse. Here is Eddie Murphy of Detroit, proudly exhibiting the gold medal he received for being the first criminal in America to be convicted 100 times![2] Frank Evans is right behind him with 76 convictions. A criminal, like a soldier in combat, does not expect his number to come up. Effective prevention of crime apparently requires something different from punishment, not something in addition. What is it?

17. *Old folks.* There will be twice as many of us over sixty-five in the United States by 1980 as in 1955. This is what medical science has done to the life span. Now science must turn around and help citizens adjust to a longer journey. Ranch style bungalows, to say nothing of city apartments, have few chimney corners for grandpa to retire into, and both grandpa and grandma without work or hobbies will go nuts, and drive all the family nuts. Social scientists recognize this aspect of the problem, but it is only the beginning.

18. *Sex and marriage.* People need to think more sanely about marriage, divorce, and sex, in a changing culture where old certainties have been undermined, old penalties and safeguards removed by invention. This tough and urgent question is as far beyond traditional moralists as the question of crime and prisons. Dr. Kinsey has gathered important facts, as have other research workers. Constructive programs, however, are hard to find; yet society must have them.

19. *Education.* This question is last but by no means least; some might rank it first. Modern education is a complex of teachers, curriculum, school buildings, degrees, specialization—all providing headaches. One big headache is how to cut down

[2] John Barker Waite, "Revenge Costs Too Much," *Harper's*, May, 1946.

wasted years in school—wasted through the boredom or apathy of the students. Another is how to prepare them for an unknown future, as the world changes faster than teachers can be trained to keep up with it.

Innumerable research and foundation projects and expert studies are now going on in educational methods, many of them excellent. But there is a long lag in applying new methods, and many improvements already worked out may not be introduced for decades. Meanwhile several generations of students may go on daydreaming through school and college—as I did for a good part of the 17 years I spent there.

Among the projects to watch are those which show teachers how to use the spontaneous group energy of a class to help members learn, and various semantic techniques to encourage independent thinking and the power to adjust to a changing world.

Every one of these 19 questions calls for a vigorous use of the scientific method. Without it the problems are insoluble. For many of them we have a modicum of available knowledge which has not been put to work. For most we need more research, more experimentation, more verified theory. James Reston, the political writer, observed sadly in *The New York Times*:[3] "Everywhere is evidence of little men fumbling with big questions." True, but one reason the men seem little is that they are trying to answer big questions with inadequate knowledge and outdated tools.

Our list, it seems to me, not only highlights the role of social scientists in the years ahead, but it should challenge the mind and feelings of everyone who cares about the future of his children and of the race. The late Louis Wirth, professor of sociology at the University of Chicago, in answering my questionnaire, added some words which came deep from his heart, and I would like to close this chapter with them:

The great unanswered questions of the social sciences are the great unanswered questions of mankind. How can we get peace,

[3] May 8, 1955.

freedom, order, prosperity, and progress under different conditions of existence? How can we establish the conditions of human well-being that have been attained in some parts of the world, or by certain groups, so that they will apply to other groups, and to other parts of the world? How can we achieve consensus in a mass democracy? How can we get the advantages of a rapidly developing technology without destroying the other values which we cherish?

I know these are general and cosmic questions, but until social scientists make a usable answer to the ways and means of achieving such ends, they will be playing a game which may be interesting enough to themselves, but one which they have no right to expect society to support.

6

Finding Fliers

A good airplane pilot, like a good violinist, must doubtless be born with special combinations of genes. We can't all fly stratocruisers, and we can't all rival Heifetz. Both types of experts need training before their virtuosity can be expressed. In the case of the pilot, however, it takes a considerable amount of first-hand experimentation, some of it dangerous and all of it expensive, before the man with the good flying genes can be discovered.

Social scientists have now found a way to locate him before he ever shows up on the training field. The technique was worked out under pressure during World War II by a combination of theory, practice, and controlled experiments. It gives us a clean, neat demonstration of social science$_1$ in action. It also provides a good starting point for our exploration of accomplishments today.

In World War I most airplane pilots for the Allies were selected on the basis of courage. After many terrible accidents the generals began to wonder if all courageous men were equally endowed with ability to stay up in the air. A crude screening process was established toward the close of the conflict. As World War II approached, not much progress had been made beyond a few educational tests.

In 1941, President Roosevelt called for 60,000 planes. Despite skepticism in high quarters, he got 300,000 planes before the shooting was over. Who was going to fly them? With the threat of war on two fronts, a fantastic demand arose for pilots, navigators, bombardiers, ground crews. There were not enough college undergraduates in the whole country to meet the need, even if every one of them had been a potential ace. A screening process was necessary at once to handle not hundreds, but hundreds of thousands of young men. As the planes came off the assembly lines in Detroit and Seattle, pilots must come off assembly lines at the training fields.

Scientists were put to work designing planes, and social scientists were put to work designing pilots. In 1941 the Aviation Psychology Program of the Army Air Forces was organized, with the dual purpose of finding out the characteristics which make a young man a good flier, and constructing a series of tests to recognize such young men as they applied. Here was a challenge in aptitude testing beyond anything attempted before.

John C. Flanagan, psychologist for the testing service of the American Council of Education, was put in charge of the program. From the first he had excellent coöperation from the generals in the AAF. He began at once to recruit assistants, from the universities and from personnel departments of large corporations. By V-E Day he had more than a thousand persons on his staff.

It was soon discovered that the various IQ tests developed over the past 30 years were not much help in picking pilots. They measured scholastic aptitudes rather than ability to come out of a nose dive. It was found that the ten standard qualifying traits for a job were too limited. Some 20 traits were required to select a man who could pilot a plane in combat. It was found that a bad pilot might make a good navigator, and that a man who did well at one type of gun might do badly at another type.

The ability to reason, a wide and fluent vocabulary, skill in handling mathematical concepts, are fine for success in academic work but practically useless for pilots or bombardiers. Such abilities, however, help navigators. Probably the most significant advance made during the whole program was the development of tests which measured ability to fly rather than ability in a classroom.

THE FIRST SCREENING

Here we are, then, with thousands of youngsters clamoring to battle the Luftwaffe in the skies and a team of scientists trying to determine which of them are competent to do so. First of all, the experts set up a paper and pencil test, based on all that could be gathered from past experience in this field. Simultaneously, they set up a procedure to test the test, making it self-corrective, so that the initial screening constantly improved.

Altogether, more than a million young men took this pencil and paper test, and 650,000 passed it. How good was it? A controlled experiment was devised to get an answer. One thousand men were allowed to take the preliminary course for pilot training whether they had passed or not. Those who had passed did considerably better in the air than those who had failed. Thus it was proved that the preliminary screening of a million men had eliminated a lot of square pegs.

But not enough were identified by this method, and many still slipped through. To devise a really formidable barrier, one group of Flanagan's men concentrated on theory, research, and instrument-making. Eventually, they produced a test "battery" composed of two distinct parts.

THE BATTERY

A young man facing this battery first sits down with scores of his fellows to answer a far more searching pencil and paper test. This finished, he goes into a room full of strange mechanisms. The candidates sit in rows, each facing an instrument panel where he manipulates complicated controls. At the end of the row is a trained technician in charge of the experiment. He, too, manipulates instruments, some of them ingenious recording devices to score the candidates.

The battery measures such characteristics as speed of perception, mechanical comprehension, ability to read dials, mathematical reasoning, and so on. After some pretty complicated statistical operations upon the record made by each man, pilot candidates are separated from navigators and both from bombardiers. Each occupational group is then graded into nine "stanines," or classes, based on predicted ability in the air.

CHECKING THE PREDICTIONS

How good were the predictions? More controlled experiments were arranged. Take pilots, for instance. When a thousand men from all nine "stanine" classes were given primary field training only 4 percent from the top stanine failed, compared with 77 percent in the lowest stanine. Similar clean-cut results showed up for navigators and bombardiers. This seemed to indicate that the predictions were very good indeed.

Presently no candidate was allowed to train on the field for these positions unless he had made one of the three highest stanines. Those below Stanine 7 for all the aircrew officer positions were put into training for ground officers, gunners, mechanics, radio operators. Exceptions, of course, were the guinea-pig groups which were constantly being filtered through as controls.

The test battery was continually improved as aptitudes were more sharply defined. Battery scores were compared repeatedly with actual training records in the air; the good techniques retained, the poor ones discarded. One controlled group of 1,000 pilot candidates came up with these results:

	Eliminated in field training
No screen at all	75 percent
Prewar Army screening	61
Battery, 1944 model (3 upper stanines)	36

Consider the enormous saving in men, equipment, and money reflected in these figures! Think of the terrible crackups avoided, the combat defeats turned into victories. It was found that pilots placed high by the test battery had the best combat records.

Successful pilots were found to be quick in reactions, well coördinated, with high discrimination between visual objects and high visualization of mechanical movements; they were well educated and keen about flying. The best pilots were in the 18-20 age group. Pilots in the lowest stanine, it was found, had *more than twice the accident rate* of those in the highest. Education was clearly a factor, but only one of many.

How Psychologists Build Aptitude Tests

Neal Miller of Yale once summarized for me the steps psychologists take in building a testing battery like this one for pilots. Four distinct stages are involved.

First, analyzing the job. In doing this the psychologists pay particular attention to the critical requirements, the causes of accidents and failures, and the human qualities which make for exceptional success. Their methods of studying the job range all the way from analyzing records and interviewing candidates, instructors, and supervisors, to taking instruction and learning the task themselves.

Second, constructing the tests. The next step is to select or construct tests which seem likely to measure the aptitudes necessary to meet those job requirements. The psychologists start by drawing from the storehouse a large number of standard tests. Usually it is also necessary to devise some new ones. Certain tests look like those all of us once faced in school. Others may be very different, aimed at finding out, for instance, how quickly the candidate can notice the details of a map, or how accurately he can learn to manipulate a new and complicated mechanism.

Third, trial administration. After a number of promising tests have been selected or invented, the third step is to administer them to a representative sample of candidates. The resulting scores are *not* used to select who shall go into training, but are filed away until the candidates have had a chance *to make good or fail at the job.*

Fourth, validation. After some measure of the success or failure becomes available, the final step is to compare the test scores with training scores to see if candidates who earned higher marks on the tests also succeeded in practice. Tests which prove their ability to predict are kept, and those which do not are discarded. In the Air Forces program several hundred tests were tried out and only the best 20 or so were used in the final battery.

If a test is composed of a number of parts, each part is tested separately, and the poorer ones are dropped. In addition to determining how well each test predicts success or failure, there is a way of showing how far each test overlaps others. The best ones measure something related to success and failure, and something not already measured by the other tests. The statistical techniques for measuring and combining these factors, in order to compare tests, include the "correlation coefficient," and the "multiple-regression equation."

Many other technical devices are involved but the main idea is simple: study the job, make up experimental tests, try them out, and keep those which can predict with high probability the success or failure of the candidate.

GROUP DYNAMICS

Flanagan's staff did not confine themselves to the laboratory and the training field. Some of them followed the fliers right into combat zones to check their predictions and investigate tensions. One team made a special study during the winter of 1943-44 of the 8th, 9th, 12th, and 15th Air Forces in the European theater. Losses were high over Hitler's "Fortress Europa," almost 5 percent per bombing mission. After 25 missions, only 277 men out of 1,000 were left. A flier had one chance in four, yet morale was good. Why? The psychologists found that good leadership was certainly one reason, but another was even more important: the sense of being *a member of a group in which flying and fighting were the only accepted ways of behaving.*

Fliers lived together, played together, fought the enemy together in four-squadron units, and had little contact with outsiders. The individual came to identify himself very closely with his group, as a kind of extension of his ego. He took great pride in his outfit and was ready to beat the ears off anybody who criticized it. He also wanted to be constantly reminded that it was doing an important job, and doing it better than other out-fits. Group commanders had to assure their men that this was so.

To help fliers endure the intense strain of their missions and to maintain morale, they were encouraged to *talk it out* after a harrowing experience over Berlin. Leaders were advised by the psychologists to get every detail out in the open, not to let the boys bottle it up inside.

The relationship with the group was fundamental in the combat zone. Indeed, a kind of hierarchy of group loyalty was identified. First, the flier valued the *crew* of his own bomber—they were closest and best; then the *squadron* with which one's plane fought; then the *group of four squadrons*, under a full colonel; then the *wing* under a brigadier general; then the *Air Force*—the 9th or the 15th, or whatever. All these outfits pro-duced strong comradely feelings. The feeling for the United States Army was less strong, for the Allied armies still less so. Loyalty to the peoples of the allied nations was barely measurable.

If a boy identified himself with his immediate face-to-face group—crew, squadron, wing—the record showed he was a much better fighter than if his loyalty was ideological, expressed in such slogans as "fighting for freedom," or fighting "a war for democracy." People meant much more to the fliers than ideas.

Thus the scientists' work on aptitude testing presently branched out into the analysis of groups in combat, group loyalties, group morale. This type of research is now going like a prairie fire in the fields of labor relations, executive meetings, adult education, college classes, the training of army officers, and elsewhere. We shall encounter "group dynamics"—to use Kurt Lewin's term—repeatedly in the pages to come.

Three kinds of fear were identified by Flanagan's men: fear of injury to oneself, fear of injury to one's crewmates, fear of failing in one's duty. If the results obtained by one's squadron were believed to be poor (whether they actually were or not), fear *increased*. The individual must be encouraged to think that his death, if it came, would not be in vain.

Morale, meanwhile, was helped by a definite goal: so many missions completed and then home! It was helped by confidence in equipment—"the B-17 is the best damned ship ever built!" Morale was hurt by stories of slackers back home or strikers in war plants. It was hurt by lack of trust in commanding officers, by stories about returned fliers with combat experience who were not used to train recruits on United States fields. Questionnaires showed that 85 percent of the fliers were afraid on their first mission, 40 percent were afraid on all missions; only 1 percent said they were never afraid. We begin to see why courage alone was an inadequate standard for selecting pilots in World War I.

How many casualties were saved by this project? Your guess is as good as mine—the Army Air Forces make no guesses. I suspect the figures must run into tens of thousands. It is hard to name a more urgent and more useful piece of scientific work. Nineteen volumes in the report of the Aviation Psychology Program have gone into the storehouse of knowledge.

LESSONS FOR PEACETIME

Working with young men in large statistical groups, the Air Forces' psychologists found out many things about the learning process. One of the most serious difficulties in training pilots and airmen was "having individuals learn the wrong things," and thus waste their time—to say nothing of the taxpayers' money.

One trouble with regular school education, Flanagan believes, is that the individual is trained for the next course rather than for life and is often trained against his aptitudes. The program has thus an important lesson to contribute to educational guidance. Youngsters who today cannot pass the Seashore tests, however, do not attempt a musical career, for they may be tone deaf or in other ways handicapped. They lack what it takes to be successful in music.

Flanagan is now trying to extend this idea to the major professions. Working through a research organization connected with the University of Pittsburgh, he has prepared a battery of 14 aptitude tests covering such skills as coding ability, reading scales, arithmetic, communication ability, etc.[1]

This battery does not include all major aptitudes, but it does help pick good candidates for various professions, and helps the individual discover where he fits. Some 30 occupations—from "accountant" to "writer"—have been matched against the tests, with good preliminary results.

Flanagan's Institute has also been using the Air Forces program since the war to test pilots for commercial lines, including American Airlines, National Airlines, and others. Up to 1954, some 2,000 pilots had been selected. More than half of the lowest scoring applicants would have failed to meet training standards if a company had allowed them to enter. This has meant a large saving in dollars, and a more important saving through safety and efficiency. The Institute, furthermore, does not test green applicants, but only young men who have already met the airline's careful screening. This selected group was found to contain plenty of poor risks, candidates who looked initially very good but lacked the right natural aptitudes.

But Is It Science?

Let us pause for a moment and compare Flanagan's Air Force program with a large-scale undertaking in natural science, such as the Manhattan Project for the atomic bomb. Both were operating about the same time, 1941-45. We find three important differences:

First, there was less knowledge in the storehouse for the social scientists to draw on. Psychology has no unbroken ladder going back to Galileo. These scientists began by rounding up data from World War I, most of which turned out to be useless—though one good instrument test was resurrected. They continued with an investigation of Army tests from the twenties and thirties, which were also largely useless. They then gathered

---

[1] I have taken some of them, doing pretty well in arithmetic and communication, not so well in mechanical ability.

what was known about IQ tests, only to find they did not fit requirements. Data on aptitude testing before 1941 were helpful but in severely qualified ways. Some laws and conclusions in social psychology and anthropology were available and helpful. Reading the record, however, one cannot fail to notice how limited was the background, and how the group had to create new theory, forge new tools and techniques, as they went along. But observe: *the next scientist concerned with aptitudes can stand on their shoulders.*

Second, we note that successful prediction was not so high as in the investigation of the atom. If 1,000 boys passed the battery in the highest class it did not follow that 100 percent made good fliers. A small percentage of those in the lowest class meanwhile *did* become good fliers. This qualification has nothing to do with the scientific method. It only shows a larger margin of error in the social field.

Third, in Flanagan's group we miss the names of outstanding authorities and Nobel prize winners. The natural sciences still have more prestige.

Waiting for a Newton

Should a wider margin of error in the social field discourage scientists? I think not. Two centuries ago, medicine was emerging from the stage of alchemy and the laying on of hands. Not until useful *instruments* were invented to measure symptoms—clinical thermometers, stethoscopes, microscopes—not until doctors observed their patients more and argued less, did medical science move forward. Medicine even now cannot predict as accurately as physics and astronomy. We have all heard people boast: "Doctors gave me six months to live five years ago, and look at me now!" Medicine, too, deals with man and his variables, yet it is universally included with the natural sciences.

Mark May of the Institute of Human Relations at Yale draws an interesting parallel. Referring to astronomy, he says[2] that in social science we have a great deal of first-rate observation like

[2] In conversation with the author.

that of Kepler's forerunner, Tycho Brahe, who recorded the movements of the planets. We have some good deductions from the observations, such as distinguished Kepler. But we have no Newton yet to mold the deductions into great summary laws, let alone an Einstein to refine the summaries.

Perhaps, however, there is a Newton at this very moment in one of the graduate schools—in Cambridge, Michigan, Tokyo. And an Einstein somewhere in a nursery school, say in Topeka, Kansas, one of those alarming infants with an IQ near the boiling point, whom only the Menninger Clinic can cope with. We are going to need them.

7

The Culture Concept

The culture concept of anthropologists and sociologists is the cornerstone of the study of behavior. "The work of the social scientist," says Ralph Linton, "must begin with the investigation of cultures, the ways of life which are characteristic of particular societies." In this sense "culture" means far more than the arts and graces. Knowledge about it has been accumulating for more than a century in painstaking studies of hundreds of communities, both primitive and civilized. Here and in the next few chapters we shall examine this concept from various points of view.

An understanding of human culture enlarges one's perspective. The effect is something like that amazing photograph, taken from 80 miles straight up in a V-2, which showed the whole Colorado River region, the Gulf of California, and the great curve of the earth bending the Pacific Ocean far to the west. The concept deflates many a fixed idea and cherished notion about ourselves and our society. It takes us clean out of Western civilization and its values, and shows us what a Congo man, a Moscow man, and a Detroit man have in common—how all have similar needs, but meet those needs by habits, customs, and beliefs which vary spectacularly.

It shows how every human being is shaped by his culture in ways far below the level of consciousness. His language, his habits of thinking, his tool-using muscles, are developed in special patterns. To use them at all he must use them as he learned to do in childhood and in youth.

Without the presence of culture, conserving past gains and shaping each succeeding generation . . . *homo sapiens* would be nothing more than a terrestrial anthropoid ape, slightly divergent in structure and slightly superior in intelligence, but a brother to the chimpanzee. . . .

So says Ralph Linton in *The Study of Man,* a brilliant inventory of the major findings in cultural anthropology. We have already referred to it and we shall do so often in the pages to come. Walter Bagehot, writing long before Linton, had invented the phrase, "the cake of custom." Presently Sumner published his epoch-making *Folkways,* a classic which has, I suppose, influenced every social scientist working today. I read it just after leaving college, and it made a shambles of much that I had learned there. The first effect was to accent the differences in human customs around the world. It was pleasantly shocking to learn that this tribe consider it immodest to wear anything above the waist, while that tribe customarily killed, with due ceremony, the ailing aged.

The initial shock, however, soon gives way to something more fundamental. To the adult mind, the great lesson is not human differences, but *similarities.* Common needs persist in human behavior everywhere. They are the universals which govern Homo sapiens, from green tropical jungles to the jungles of Manhattan. To solve our current problems, such as those listed in Chapter 5, generalizations and theories will have to be grounded on the principles which affect all societies, the common denominators of human living.

Although no scientist can study his own species with the objectivity he applies to a colony of ants, he can study villages in Borneo more impersonally than villages on Cape Cod. He must learn not to be surprised at anything, not even when wives in a harem belligerently defend the institution of polygamy (or polygyny, if you want to be technical). Some groups, says Linton, not only tolerate epileptics, they honor them as agents of the higher powers. Many an inmate of our mental hospitals might be not only free but a respected oracle in some other society.

The investigator develops that tolerant sophistication which is characteristic of anthropologists: "Well, some do and some don't." Instead of applying his own moral values to a given custom, he concentrates on trying to understand its local meaning in that particular culture. Such an attitude may be depressing to missionary zeal, but it is a great help in acquiring dependable knowledge about human behavior. Any culture can develop antisocial customs—and most do—but no culture can continue them in a big way without running the risk of extinction. There is a tribe in New Guinea described by Margaret Mead which has been pushing head-hunting to dangerous extremes. Ultimate survival is the sanction hanging over every behavior pattern—including the use of atomic bombs.

Alexander Leighton[1] describes what he calls the "parachute technique" developed by a training school in the American Southwest. After a student has been instructed for some weeks in the culture concept, using local Indian and Spanish materials, he is sent to a remote Indian village to make his way, beginning with sign language. He must find his own lodging and food. Trainees are invariably astonished at their success in adjusting to a totally different situation. They discover basic questions which must be answered in approaching any culture, and how to find the answers.

It would be a fine idea to put technical assistance (Point Four) administrators through the "parachute technique" before they set out to improve local conditions in Burma or the Sudan.

When enough investigators have collected data from enough places, and comparative studies are made, the universal patterns begin to appear: the needs and functions which *all* tribes share, civilized as well as primitive. These common denominators, when adequately checked by competent observers, give vital information about human behavior, information which statesmen neglect at their peril. How, for instance, is it possible even to think intelligently about ending war, or about strengthening the United Nations, without an understanding of such universals?

[1] In a talk at the Washington Seminar, May 14, 1952.

Defining Culture

Along with eating and sleeping, one universal habit of our species is forming ourselves into bands, tribes, societies. We then evolve various ways and means for holding the group together and giving it structure.

A *society* refers to a group of people who have learned to work and live together.

A *culture* refers to the way of life which the group follows.

Culture is the cement which binds the group together. Without it, a group is not a society but a mob, an aggregate, a milling mass. Social scientists divide a culture into three chief parts:

1. *Habits*, customs, ways of behaving, which a child begins to learn almost as soon as he is born. How to keep clean, how to eat his food properly, how to dress, how to comport himself in church and school. The most important habit of all is how to communicate, including the unique gift of speech. He is born with large speech centers in his brain, but language must always be learned.

2. *Belief* systems, to give him his ideas of right and wrong. Religion, magic, patriotism, property standards, all the accepted symbols and credos of his society.

3. *Artifacts*, the tools, utensils, constructions, machines, which the society has developed or borrowed from other societies. The catalogue of a large mail order house gives us some idea of the artifacts loose in the American culture today. In 1800, it is safe to say, such a catalogue would not have been a tenth the size.

Customs and belief systems vary inside a culture, depending on the status of subgroups. In Europe, until recently at least, royalty had a different set of rules from those of the middle classes, and both differed from the rules for peasants and laborers. In the United States and Canada, while classes are very fluid, rich people do not observe quite the same pattern as journeymen plumbers—even though President Eisenhower's original cabinet in 1953 was composed of "a plumber and eight millionaires."

Journalists and fiction writers speak of the "unwritten law," by which they must mean the culture of the tribe. Culture comes ages before formal law. Nature peoples like the Eskimo have no formal law at all; there are no courts or statutes or jails, but the living law or culture may enjoin the death penalty just the same. Unless the formal law is in line with the living law, it cannot be enforced. The Prohibition law in the United States banning alcoholic beverages was an instructive example. One difficulty in setting up a formal international law today is that there is as yet no international *living* law, no planetary culture.

Dwelling together in groups is as characteristic of man as the shape of his teeth or his inclination to laugh. "A social organism," said William James, "is what it is because each member proceeds to his own duty with a trust that the other members will simultaneously do theirs. A government, an army, a commercial system, a ship, a college, an athletic team, all exist on this condition without which not only is nothing achieved, but nothing is even attempted."

It is difficult to overemphasize the importance of this observation—yet not many of us understand it. If most people were dishonest, if they failed to do what they promised to do, if they did not take care of the children, help others in crisis, society would fall apart. Most people are "good," just as the charge account statistics prove; they pay their bills, they can be trusted. The culture concept makes it plain why this must be so. If any considerable fraction—say more than 5 percent—could *not* be trusted to do what was expected of them, there would be no dependable culture, no living, growing society—just a prisoner-of-war camp, with a polyglot mixture of prisoners. A functioning society must be self-disciplining. When we talk about "dictators," "democracy," "the state," "freedom," we often forget this underlying condition.

In Homo sapiens, society rather than the individual has become the primary unit in the struggle for existence. For centuries in the West, philosophers, theologians, educators, business-men, have concentrated on the individual. They have affirmed that he alone was responsible for his sins, his sufferings, his tri-umphs, and his defeats. Social scientists find that the individual is not that kind of organism, and cannot be understood in such a conceptual frame. He is a product of his culture; he is a living part of his group, and can be understood only in relation to it. To judge him outside this matrix is like trying to understand a fish without reference to water.

A comprehension of the *double role* of the individual, ob-serves Linton, as a separate person and as a unit in society, pro-vides a key to many problems of human behavior. "Until the psychologist knows what the norms of behavior imposed by a particular society are, and can discount them as indicators of personality, he will be unable to penetrate behind the façade of social conformity and cultural uniformity to reach the authentic individual." Dr. William C. Menninger made the same point about mental health, as quoted earlier.

Social scientists are a long way from working out *all* the re-lationships between the individual and his culture, but they have led the study of man out of a blind alley. They have begun to ask the right questions, and have demonstrated that man is a social animal to a degree hitherto unappreciated. Apparently he has always been one since he came down from trees. Some-times his group comprises only a few families, living under the most primitive conditions. Sometimes it fills a continent; but it is always there.

On this broad base, the science of man begins. A baby snake can fend for itself about as soon as it can squirm. A human baby, without a group behind it, either starves immediately, or if natural food is by some miracle available, comes to resemble a gibbering idiot. Civilized man can do more things than the savage because he has the opportunity to learn more things; his culture is richer; it accumulates like compound interest. The innate ability of the savage, however, may be just as great.

Transferring Cultures

Darwin, in the *Voyage of the Beagle*, tells of delivering two young people, Jemmy and Fuegia, back to their savage and naked clan on Tierra del Fuego. Although the children had been exposed to British culture for only a few years, they had learned to speak both English and Spanish, were neat in their dress and table manners, quick with their minds, and favorites with the crew.

It was interesting to watch the conduct of the savages when we landed toward Jemmy Button: they immediately perceived the difference between him and ourselves, and held much conversation one with another on the subject. The old man addressed a long harangue to Jemmy, which it seems was to invite him to stay with them. But Jemmy understood very little of their language, and was, moreover, thoroughly ashamed of his countrymen.

The picture Darwin draws is memorable and tragic—the terrified children in their neat British dress being forced back to a bleak and primitive life on one of the most forbidding islands on earth. Kind people in England had felt that they would be happier there, but, innocent of the culture concept, they were inflicting a cruel punishment on Jemmy and Fuegia. Either the children should not have been kidnaped in the first place, or once taken, they should have been adopted for life.

Here is Fung Kwok Keung, born Joseph Rinehart on Long Island, New York. Scheinfeld describes how he was taken to China at a tender age and brought up as a Chinese boy. He comes back to America as a young man, and we find him before the blackboard painfully learning English in an "Americaniza- tion" class. "He had become so thoroughly Chinese in manner, speech, habit, and outlook that he was distinguishable from members of the race only by his features."[2] This is not some- thing strange and abnormal; it will *always* happen when a baby is transferred to another culture.

[2] A. Scheinfeld, *You and Heredity.*

New Perspective on History

The culture concept gives us a new perspective on history as well as on ourselves. A culture is a process of gradual change, without beginning or end. "The spectacular rise and fall of certain civilizations," says Linton, "should not blind us to the fact that most cultures have never fallen." Our own American culture, for example, can be viewed as a continuum extending back unbroken through written history, through archeological time, through the unrecorded dark, to the very dawn of the race. If the chain had once been broken, you and I would not be here.

Individuals are born and die, the culture slowly shifts under the pressure of climate, new invention, internal need; the *group* moves east or south, over Bering Strait, down the Mexican plateau, down to Tierra del Fuego. But always the children are protected, loved, and taught; always the group closes in against its natural enemies; the cord is unbroken for a million years. The group is deathless and timeless. The individual may not be able to adjust to outside realities; the group eventually must.

With our accent on the individual in America, we are normally little aware of the society in which we have our being. In war and disaster the realization breaks through. A forest fire, a child lost in the New Hampshire woods, a flood on the Ohio River, a hurricane in Florida, a plane crash in the Rocky Mountains—and the community swings into action without thought of payment or prestige.

The culture concept gives us the closest fit to the truth about mankind yet discovered by the scientific method. Truths discovered by other methods do not concern us here. History as customarily written, from Herodotus to the present day, seldom focuses on this truth, but rather on kings, generals, popes, presidents, prime ministers, prophets, the great men who rise out of the group, often to torment it. "While the popular view is that the leader makes the times," says Ogburn, "a realistic view emphasizes the exact opposite."

Formal history, with its Caesars and Napoleons, tends to be a record of the abnormal, the geniuses, sports, freaks, and misfits, the glandular cases of mankind. It stands the social pyramid on its apex. The culture concept puts it back upon its base. The kings and the warriors are dramatic, true enough, but the real story concerns the society which sheltered its children, accumulated invention, and wrung a living from nature down through the ages.

TIMETABLE FOR REFORMERS

The culture concept focuses a strong lens, too, on measures for economic and social reform. What, after all, can even the most inspired agitators and propagandists do to a society embedded in the gigantic toils of age-old patterns? They can do something, but not as much as they think they can. Kluckhohn and Kelly point out that many social planners neglect the facts of culture. They think they can somehow wipe the slate clean and start afresh. It is impossible. "Every human being is born into a world defined by already existing cultural patterns." The red government of China, one suspects, is now learning this stubborn truth.

The idea that a group can suddenly be emancipated from its past habits is no more sensible than the idea that a man who flaps his arms rapidly enough can fly. If the group could change as fast as some reformers hope, it would have dashed itself to pieces some time in the Old Stone Age. The group's main task is survival through reproduction and nourishment. The young can be protected, and a food supply secured, only in the momentum of established procedures.

One of my strongest impressions when I visited the U.S.S.R. ten years after the "ten days that shook the world," was how little things had probably changed. Where was this great revolution they talked about? The streets, the shops, the houses, the peasants in the fields, the factory workers, all looked like the photographs taken in czarist days. A Baedeker guide of 1907 described the railroads and local officials of 1927 with apparent accuracy. Power had shifted at the apex, but the base of the social pyramid seemed almost unmoved. Perhaps the common people *felt* differently from their predecessors; but who could tell? I doubted if 5 percent of their day-by-day behavior had been altered by the revolution. But is this not what one would expect in the light of the culture concept? The news we get in the headlines, the accounts by historians, scarcely touch this monolithic continuity.

The adoption of the Weimar Constitution in Germany in 1919 was an attempt to make Germans as democratic as Vermonters, in defiance of a thousand years of German cultural momentum. Naturally it collapsed and in the ensuing vacuum Hitler found his opportunity. There should be a lesson here for those vocal Americans who want to make "democracy"—on the Corn Belt model—the price of aid to hungry people East and West. Can we expect the reforms in Germany after World War II to last longer? It is possible that the people's sufferings did in fact weaken the culture and make it more responsive to change. We must wait for history to give the final answer in Germany. So too in Japan, where some postwar reforms were politely accepted and later abandoned. No reform can bear fruit unless it is grafted successfully to the living tree of culture.

An understanding of the culture concept produces a curious paradox. A given institution in one's culture—say the United States banking system—comes to seem at once weaker and stronger. One can no longer stand in awe of it as an eternal verity, for one knows it is man-made and bound to change with external circumstances. The gold standard has already ceased to be an eternal verity. But for the short view the institution commands increased respect. If one kicks it too hard, one is extremely likely to break some bones.

All this sheds quite a different light on the fears of those congressmen who believed that social science meant wild reforms, strange -isms and -ologies. We find that the social scientists have described the most massive brake on wild reforms possible to imagine; more effective than whole armies of FBI agents and secret police. The senators can relax.

THE FORMATIVE YEARS

The saying that if the church has a boy until he is six he will be a good communicant for life, has strong support from social scientists. The demonstration that any healthy infant can adjust to any culture—if he is not discriminated against because of the color of his skin—emphasizes the vast importance of the earliest years. Five branches of social science are joining today to drive home this conclusion—the anthropologists, linguists, sociologists, psychologists, and psychiatrists.

The *anthropologists* say that since Cro-Magnon days, at least, children of any nation or race have had practically the same inborn equipment. But from birth every experience helps to shape a child to the culture in which he finds himself. Even by the age of three or four he has learned hundreds of habits, and received thousands of impressions, which he will not consciously remember later in life, but which already stamp him as a member of Eskimo or Japanese or American society.

The *linguists* demonstrate that by the time he is six, a child has absorbed the structure of his language, and that this structure will shape his whole system of thought throughout his life.

The *sociologists* emphasize the institutional and community aspects of the culture.

The *psychologists* study the responses of young children, aided with all manner of laboratory equipment—cameras, sound tracks, one-way windows. They analyze the vital process by which an individual becomes a culture-carrier.

The *psychiatrists* emphasize emotional influences on children, showing how early experiences may mold an individual's character, and perhaps produce a mental breakdown in later years.

Scientists talk more and more about the vital importance of security and affection, the feeling of belonging, in early years. A lack of emotional security in childhood may bring serious results, examples of which can be seen in any mental hospital and in outbreaks of juvenile delinquency.

OPTIMISTIC NOTE

Finally, the culture concept gives us hope that many of our problems can be solved. If people were bad by virtue of their "blood," or their genes, or their innate characters, there would not be much we could do about it. But if people are basically all right, and a given problem lies primarily in an adjustment of culture patterns, or an adjustment *to* culture patterns, a good deal can be done about it.

Theoretically, a society could be completely made over in something like 15 years—the time it takes to educate a rising crop of youngsters. But such a theory assumes that parents, nurses, teachers, have all been reëducated themselves—which, as Euclid used to say, is absurd. But it helps, I think, to know that the trouble does not all come from an erring and invariant human nature packaged at birth. It comes mostly from culture patterns built into the plastic human nervous system. Culture patterns do change, and can be changed.

These are some of the stimulating vistas which anthropology and sociology open to the inquiring layman. My image of the V-2 photograph taken from 80 miles up may not be so exaggerated after all. If we let this knowledge flow into our minds, the world can never look the same again. Furthermore, it is not a doctrine, a philosophical system, a prophet's message, it is *social science*$_1$, where reasonable proof has been established.

The laws of culture are something like Boyle's law of gases. An individual person, like a molecule of hydrogen, is unpredictable. But there is a definite pattern which the whole group will follow, and which can be statistically described. We know, for instance, how many will be born, how many will marry, how many classrooms will be needed in the years ahead. If an observer charts the pattern, he can predict behavior with reasonable probability.

I have repeatedly put the idea of culture to work on my personal problems, and used it to help evaluate the news that comes over the air waves every morning. It throws a flood of light on matters which had puzzled me before. It helps explain some of the difficulties in American foreign policy, troubles in Korea, China, Israel, the roots of McCarthyism, the limits of "coexistence" between East and West, the real barriers to world peace, barriers to a universal language, to world government.

It has clarified my ideas on how to bring up children, why they have to be disciplined—not because they are "naughty," but to prepare them for the environment in which they must live. It has broadened my ideas about schools and education, about meetings, participation, democracy. It has given new insight into the importance of symbols and ceremonials, such as weddings, funerals, parades, ticker tape rides up Broadway. I used to sniff at some of these displays, but I sniff no longer. It has made me, I think, a better judge of novels, stories, plays. Has the author run off the track imposed by the culture? As an example, it seems to me that Steinbeck runs off the track from time to time in his otherwise delightful *Cannery Row*. Too many people break too many rules to make a viable society—like those head-hunters in New Guinea. The culture concept has certainly reinforced for me the cardinal importance of religion in a society.

Finally, when one becomes aware how he personally is culture-bound, by a curious paradox he is freed a little from his bonds. He can look over the walls of his own culture and see the other peoples of the world behind their walls. He can for the first time in his life begin to understand people of an alien culture. How strange that science should be the cause of a deep ethical experience!

8

The World of George Adams

Another way to bring the culture concept home is to take a neighbor in one's community and try to find out the cultures which have molded him. Warner and Lunt in their excellent *Yankee City* series have done this in statistical and scholarly detail, but we will be content with a more impressionistic survey.

Here, for instance, is George Adams, an imaginary character who runs a garage, filling station, and milk bar in Middleburg, Connecticut. On the Warner and Lunt six-class scale, he would be a member of the lower middle class which, when bracketed with the upper middle, contains the most energetic and dependable citizens in the community. He is thirty-seven years old, five feet nine, weighs 158 pounds, and was a bombardier with the 16th Air Force in the war. He is a Legionnaire, an Elk, and an active member of the Middleburg Volunteer Fire Company; he goes to the Congregational Church half a dozen times a year. Junior is four, and the baby is eighteen months. His wife taught seventh grade in the Hill School before he married her.

George, a Red Sox fan, likes to watch ball games on TV, and loves to go trout fishing in the spring. He is a Republican in town politics, but twice he voted for Franklin Roosevelt. He is well regarded in Middleburg, for at one time or another his wrecker, a 1930 Pierce Arrow, has pulled nearly everyone in town out of a ditch.

What kind of person is this George Adams? What shaped him? How did he get to be what he is? We know that he must be the product of a group and the culture which goes with it. What group and what culture? Here we encounter a hierarchy of attachments and loyalties. George is not the product of a single culture, as the Greenland Eskimo is (or was), but of a whole ring of cultures, one inside the next. His group, meanwhile, is now so large that it covers a continent—though we can also distinguish a number of subgroups to which George belongs.

He identifies himself loyally with Middleburg, with Connecticut, with New England, in a declining scale. His major loyalty, however, is to the United States of America, with its 3,000,000 square miles and 165 million neighbors. This has now become his community, his We-group, in the most binding sense of the term, as it is mine. It is so by the test of a common culture as well as by national sovereignty. The concrete highway, even more than the railroad, has broken up the old local patterns. To many GI's overseas, "home" meant a place where you can get a good ice cream soda, decent service at a filling station, beauty shops, ice water, TV, acceptance of a majority vote, sports writers who make sense, and big league baseball.

The nation has also become George's *economic* unit in these days of fresh vegetables from California, lumber from Oregon, and oil from Texas. In the times of Obadiah Adams, deacon of the Methodist Church, blacksmith of Middleburg, and George's great-great-grandfather, loyalty to the town came first; Connecticut also claimed a fierce loyalty, but New York State was practically a foreign country, separated by a tariff wall. America, reaching way out to the wilds of Ohio, was a pretty vague concept to Obadiah. He never went 50 miles from where he was born in all his life. His economic region lay within that radius; even the iron for his horseshoes came from the Connecticut hills. He knew the face and name of everyone in town, and many in the region.

George has heard much about rugged individualism. He may think he is on his own, above the crowd, responsible only to himself and to his God, but the facts do not bear out his assumptions. In Middleburg there are many things he might feel impelled to do, but cannot do, because the folkways forbid it. For instance, he may not talk aloud in church, or grow a beard

—unless he is an artist—or strike a woman, or eat with his fingers, or take off all his clothes in public on a hot day, or wear brown shoes with a tuxedo, or bright colors at a funeral, or appear at the Elks' Hall with a patch on his coat. His freedoms are strictly relative. George can choose his necktie from the rack, but he wears a necktie at the appropriate times. Certain foods highly prized among many peoples, such as eels, snails, certain kinds of grubs, he does not think fit to eat. Although his hunger is physical and common to all men, the way he will satisfy it is cultural.

Superstitions have declined somewhat since Obadiah's day, but George still avoids walking under ladders, he would rather not sign a contract on Friday the thirteenth, and wants no black cats to cross in front of him. He is perfectly sure, too, that Ellery Sanford can find water every time with that willow wand.

Where did these codes and beliefs come from? They started coming to George very soon after the doctor slapped him on the back, and he let out his first yell. They came from parents, teachers, schoolmates, relatives, truck drivers, drill sergeants, ministers, policemen, storekeepers, the drug store gang, from nearly everyone who crossed George's path during his impressionable years. Think, for instance, of all the people who taught him to talk, including the voices on the radio.

Where did *they* get the codes? From the generation which inducted them. There was nothing floating in the air; codes always come from people or written records. A few of the simpler habits, like drinking from a cup, or sitting on a chair rather than on the ground, may have been handed down unchanged for 20 generations. Altogether we can identify at least five major cultural rings from which most of George's behavior is derived.

   1. To begin with the broadest, he is a product of *civilization*. For more than 6,000 years the group he belongs to has practiced a widespread division of labor and city living, based on the development of a storable grain. This marks off his behavior from nature peoples who never had cities, writing, architecture,

or mathematics. At the same time it connects George with the peoples of India, China, Persia, and other areas where civilization as defined has been long in evidence. To him personally it means, among other things, living in a house, going to school, eating cereals, paying taxes, using money.

2. Next comes *Western civilization* as distinct from other civilizations. From this source George gets the Christian religion, many of his standards of right and wrong, the decimal system with its priceless zero, nationalism and the sovereign state, modern science and technology, tinkering with machines, music in the diatonic scale, the free market—now, alas, much corrupted with monopolies and government controls—property rights, pecuniary emulation, and military conscription, to name a few.

3. The next smaller ring is *Anglo-Saxon culture*—that part of Western civilization in which English is spoken. Here George learns his language—*the most important single element in his entire cultural inheritance*. Without language the group could not communicate and would rapidly break up. Here too George learns to vote and believe in habeas corpus, the Bill of Rights, political democracy, the idea of progress, and romantic love as the proper basis for marriage. He acquires a streak of Puritanism and the ability to cover up his emotions. He is taught to disapprove of people who shout and weep and wave their hands. For a grown man to cry in the presence of others is humiliating and disgraceful. George stands nearer the Iroquois than the Latin peoples in this respect, but nearer the Latins in his public laughter.

4. Next comes *North American culture*, which George shares with most Canadians, somewhat less with Mexicans. Here he picks up many words and place names and a few customs—like canoeing and corn roasts—which derive from the Indians. More than half the 48 states have Indian names, including his own Connecticut. He has been heavily influenced by the frontier pattern, for even New England was the frontier a few generations ago.

This pattern helps to reinforce George's individualism and a certain social irresponsibility, especially toward public property and resources. "Cut out and get out," move on West, was the frontiersman's idea. The Pacific has long since been reached, but the irresponsibility remains, a cultural lag. It is shown in the fabulous wastes of topsoil, timber, grasslands, natural gas—wastes which mean nothing whatever to George, but which communities in Europe could not tolerate. It is shown in the political immaturity and awkwardness of most Americans when faced with international contacts. There is nothing in their culture to help them cope with such situations.

Other patterns which North America gives to George include: the great motor car complex on which he makes his living, Hollywood, radio and TV habits, the comics; mass production, bathrooms, a sublime belief in education; service clubs, baseball, the success story, the ability to laugh at himself, juke boxes, jazz bands, and a propensity to spoil his children. Notice that we are mixing up material things with customs and attitudes, but so they are mixed in the cultural stream.

5. *New England* is the last ring. Though most of George's habits were learned there, its unique contributions to his way of life are few, far fewer than in grandfather Obadiah's day. George is more tolerant of Negroes, coming from an abolitionist area, than many Americans. New England has given him some favorite dishes, such as clam chowder with milk; a nasal twang to his speech; a disposition to be close-mouthed, to be thrifty and count his pennies, and to be critical of the neighbors; the moral virtue of early rising, hard work, and a full woodpile.

A man brought up in New England usually stands 18 to 20 inches away when talking face to face with a man he has just met. If it is a woman he will back off four inches, making the distance about two feet.[1] If a stranger begins to talk within eight to 13 inches, George's hackles rise, and the stranger should be ready to duck. If George had been reared in Cuba, however, he would feel perfectly comfortable at 13 inches, and uncom-

[1] E. T. Hall, Jr., "The Anthropology of Manners," *Scientific American*, April, 1955.

fortable at 20. "Latin American office visitors will climb up on desks or over chairs . . . to establish a spatial context in which interaction can take place for them."

An Arab thinks no more of being 30 minutes late than George does of ten minutes: the time ratio is roughly three to one. "See you later," means nothing to George beyond a polite good-by. But if he should say the words to an Iranian and fail to look the gentleman up later, it would be a serious insult.

THE OLD MAN OF THE SEA

We have given only the roughest indication of the items in each ring of George's background. A full account of the habits he has learned, and follows largely without taking thought, would require a library. Consider for a moment, or better, try to list, the unthinking customs you yourself follow in a single day—from the time you get out of bed in the morning until you snap off the light at night. There are literally thousands of them.

Sinclair Lewis begins his most celebrated novel with a play-by-play account of his hero's cultural patterns. Babbitt is awakened on his sleeping porch by the new patented alarm clock, with chimes. He proceeds to the ceremonials of the great American bathroom, duly tiled and ornamented with untouchable guest towels. He descends to the family breakfast table, with its dry cereal and its disputes; then on to the garage and the pleasure of starting his new car; and so to the problem of parking near the office. It is a brilliant and hilarious description of the culture of the American business man in a Midwestern city, some years ago.

It is obvious that most of George Adams's habits and systems of belief come from Western civilization, from the Anglo-Saxon culture, and from North America. The first has been in existence at least since Socrates, say for 2,500 years; the second since Chaucer, say 600 years; the third since Captain John Smith, say 300 years. But Indian additions reach back much further; Indian corn probably antedated Homer.

George perforce tries to reconcile these far-flung influences. Wherever he goes he carries this great cultural load—like the Old Man of the Sea. Nobody can get at him, talk to him, tell him anything, except in relation to this burden. When he met Chinese, Burmese, or Dutch during his overseas service, he judged them by these standards, built into his nervous system as the transmission is built into a car. If he happens to take a tourist cruise in the Caribbean, he will judge Haitians, Cubans, Virgin Islanders in a similar way, and unless he is aware of his reaction, it is unlikely that he will judge them fairly. Because their culture rings are somewhat different, many things they do will vary from what he does in similar circumstances, and he will blame them for it. At times the blame may flare into anger. (In Chapter 10 we follow this idea in some detail along the Rio Grande.)

In Washington recently I was told the shocking story of a United States paymaster dealing with Arabs on a Point Four project of technical assistance in the Near East. He had been accustomed in previous assignments to pay the help on Friday, and he proposed to keep right on doing so in his new location. Friday, however, is a holy day, when good Moslems are not supposed to touch money. The agent pulled out his .45 and forced some of them to take their pay—holy day or not. Later he complained bitterly because the "lazy beggars" had left the job never to return. Such tragic misunderstandings could not occur if Americans—and Arabs—had a working knowledge of the other fellow's culture.

If we compare George with such a person as Laughing Boy, the Navaho hero of Oliver La Farge's novel, we see a strange and significant contrast. George is caught in a whirl of cultural rings, and an interdependent society far beyond the face-to-face range, which make his way of life more complicated and uncertain than that of Laughing Boy. George can seldom be so sure what is the right thing to do as the Indian learned to be. His loyalties do not run to a single tribe, a definite cosmology, a straight and narrow path in life's journey.

George has not belonged to anything wholeheartedly since he left the Air Force. He is worried, despite the breezy way he comes out to fill up your tank. He had to borrow so much money to start his business, and prices have been so high. He is not sure what is in store for him and the family. He does not see clearly where he is going, or the country, or the world. The H-bomb, now, and those Russians and the Chinese Reds, and the next depression . . .

Laughing Boy's world was steady as a rock; but sometimes George's world seems to be coming apart.

9

Common Patterns of Mankind

"Those who know no culture other than their own," says Linton, "cannot know their own." In this chapter we will look at 33 behavior patterns which social scientists have found in nearly all societies. After he penetrates the surface differences between peoples, the student strikes the mother lode of human similarities.

The similarities begin, of course, with biological structure— how human beings are equipped to see and hear and eat and reproduce. Julian Huxley points out some less obvious biological traits. The human species is unique, he says, in its *variability*. Man has a far wider range than any other large creature, and has maintained his dominant type without splitting into sub-species. The evolution of animals generally is divergent, but in man, after some divergence, the various branches come together again, "until the course of human descent is like a network." There is no such divergence among men as among dogs, or even horses.

Huxley emphasizes how Homo sapiens alone has evolved true language, giving him unique powers to think and to pass what he learns in one generation to the next generation in a cumulative spiral. Perhaps, says Huxley, culture is displacing evolution. Instead of building biological resistances to tropical climate, for instance, we exterminate malaria mosquitoes with DDT, invent pith helmets and air conditioning units. Instead of nature's changing us, we *change nature* in the interest of survival. If this theory is ultimately verified, it will give the culture concept even greater significance. As it stands, it shows the intimate connection between biology and anthropology.

The common culture patterns which we are about to describe, while based on hundreds of field studies and research in comparative cultures, are still provisional and may be modified by later scientific work. At least they are a good deal more dependable than the homilies of folklore—such well-worn tags as "You can't change human nature"; "Spare the rod and spoil the child"; "Satan finds some mischief still for idle hands to do"; "Divide up the wealth and it will soon be back in the same pockets."

THE FIRST FIELD STUDIES

Let us go back a bit and see how it all began. In the 1840's, Lewis H. Morgan, a young lawyer in Rochester, New York, became interested in the language and customs of the neighboring Seneca Indians. This study presently led him into the family organization of the Six Nation League of the Iroquois. He defended the Indians in a lawsuit against a company which was trying to cheat them of their land, and as a result, in 1847, he was adopted into the Seneca tribe under the engaging name of "Ta-ya-da-o-wub-Rub."

A law case in Michigan gave Morgan an opportunity to study the kinship system of the Ojibwa. From there he extended his investigations into kinship systems in various cultures around the world, and published several books on the subject. He became the father of cultural anthropology, with an influence on many successors, including Boas, Wissler, Rivers, and Kroeber. Said Wissler: "Morgan . . . dealt first-hand with data on primitive peoples. . . . He made objective observations, using chiefly data on relationship systems and marriage. The former may be said to have been discovered by him, and first used in a scientific way. . . . If he did not inaugurate anthropological field work, he was one of the first to make a thorough study of the social life of a tribe." We have here a scientific ladder reaching back more than a century. By 1936, enough material had accumulated to enable Linton to make his definitive inventory.

THE CROSS-CULTURAL INDEX

Meanwhile, George P. Murdock began to compile the Cross-Cultural Index at Yale. He and his staff have assembled records of several hundred cultures, past and present, and indexed them under such headings as law, housing, financial methods, funerals, education, and so on. If you take, let us say, a lively interest in marriage ceremonies around the world, a trip to New Haven would give you a comprehensive story. You would not need to wade through all the books and documents to find out about wedding customs; the record would be there ready for you in the Index.

At this point our earlier metaphor of a storehouse of scientific knowledge becomes concrete. The Index is a storehouse which you can go and look at with your eyes—scores of file drawers, containing a million entries, with more continually being added. The Index was used by the Navy in the war preliminary to the invasion of the Marshalls, the Marianas, and the Carolines. It saved many costly mistakes as the Marines got ashore and began to deal with the local inhabitants as well as the Japanese defenders. It told our troops what to expect.

UNIVERSAL NEEDS

The first task of every human society parallels the first task of all other living creatures—namely, to adjust to the environment and survive. The *task* is thus a universal, but the *performance* is infinitely varied. Geography, climate, available raw materials, the rate of invention, sheer accident, all help to determine whether people eat raw fish or coconut meat or deep-dish apple pie; whether they live in tents of animal skins, or ice huts, or log cabins, or steel skyscrapers.

Here is a classification of needs and functions which seem to be universal. They are found in every society so far studied and are satisfied by thousands of different customs:

1. Language—the most important of all.
2. Status of the individual in the group. Who outranks whom?

3. Family and other social groups.
4. Methods for dealing with food, shelter, clothing, and other vital materials.
5. Government and law. These can be very informal but are always there.
6. Religion and ethics.
7. Systems for explaining natural phenomena—magic, mythology, and lately science.
8. Rules regarding property, who owns what: methods for barter and trade.
9. Art forms—the dance, stories, songs, poems, architecture, handicrafts, and design.

Although every human child will require a means of dealing with these needs and functions, no child knows the answers intuitively. Every detail must be taught him by the culture. Many customs are taught to every individual in the society, others to selected children. Certain boys are trained as potters or carpenters, others as medicine men or doctors. Girls are usually trained differently from boys.

Observe that no reading, writing, or arithmetic is necessarily included in the above list of primary needs and functions, nor any "liberal arts" courses. The list shows the elements of every child's *real* education, what he must have for living his life—in contrast with the formal education taught in the schools of Western civilization. (When we get the two curricula a little closer together, perhaps not so many child-years will be wasted in school.)

We will now look at some common behavior patterns, grouping them under such headings as "the family," "crime and punishment," and numbering them consecutively. Most of them I have compiled from Linton's *Study of Man.*

What use are they? Here is an example. Suppose you are worried about the condition of the family in America today. The divorce rate bothers you, or the unfortunate manners of the young, or the difficulty in making life tolerable for the aged.

Before joining a spirited crusade to do something about it, it would be a good idea to find out some of the conclusions that social scientists have reached concerning the institution of the family. On this most important human group of all, a lot of information has been collected. Morgan started his studies with the family structure of Indian tribes. Maybe your crusade should never start, or should take a different form. One of the first things that you would find out is the toughness and durability of the family—as well as its flexibility.

THE FAMILY

1. Homo sapiens has apparently always lived in permanent families, though the form changes greatly from tribe to tribe. The complexity of the form does not vary with technological progress. The most intricate systems known are those of Old Stone Age cultures in Australia, while the American family organization "is as simple as among the Great Apes."

2. The idea, favorite among cartoonists, of the old man with his bristling beard, his knotty club, his fallen rivals, and his woman dragged by her hair, is unknown to science. It was probably a Victorian myth, constructed to flatter the British family of that time, especially Papa in Dundreary whiskers. He was supposed to be the pinnacle of human evolution, reached by incredible exertions up a long ladder of progress from the cave man. Research has shown, however, that our remote ancestors were less barbaric than the cartoon. They did not habitually murder one another and they were generally monogamous and kind to their wives.

3. The principal function of the family is to protect the young. "It remains the most effective mechanism for the care and rearing of children," says Linton. Practically all societies leave these duties to the family group. The association between mother and infant is everywhere most intimate, as with other mammals. This means that baby farms and group nurseries, however sanitary and progressive, are no substitute for a mother's love and care. Legislators are beginning to realize this in de-

vising modern social security systems where "family allowances" are granted directly to the mother, rather than to social workers. We are dealing here with the majority of mothers; a few abnormal women, of course, are not fitted for the task.

4. A family includes able-bodied adults of *both sexes*, everywhere, though they may not always be the true parents. The presence of one or two males is important in child-rearing, for without it, boys are handicapped in learning the masculine roles they will be expected to fill.

5. The family always practices division of labor. The mother has her duties, the father his, the children theirs, grandfather his. This is being modified in the changing American family of today. Father is trying his hand at many tasks hitherto reserved for mother, and vice versa.

6. The family functions as an economic unit, within which nobody is regularly paid for performing his duties.

7. The family cares for the aged as well as for the child.

8. The superior physical strength of the male makes him everywhere the formal ruler of the family and of society. The free-swinging Amazons, alas, appear to be another myth. "It is questionable whether there is any society in existence which is actually dominated by women."

9. Monogamy is the usual form of marriage. It may, however, coexist with other forms in the same society. Polygyny is widespread, and polyandry not uncommon.

10. The Victorian idea of marriage based on romantic love, now brought to supercolossal heights by Hollywood, is found in few societies. Marriage involves such an intimate joining of whole families who may have been strangers, that families in most societies have felt obliged to control it. The chances of a successful home in which to rear children appear to be at least as good in an arranged marriage. Romantic love, of course, occurs everywhere, but marriage based on it is usually regarded with reserve. Often the romance is worked off by means of premarital unions.

11. Marriage probably never developed from capture. Group

marriage is another Victorian myth. Wife-lending, however, is fairly common.

12. All societies recognize divorce, but *no* society approves it. The ideal marriage everywhere is for keeps.

13. Some types of incest are taboo in every known society, with the strongest prohibition against marriage between mother and son—the Oedipus tragedy. Father and daughter marriages are permitted in at least one society, while brother and sister marriages have not been too rare, especially in royal families, such as the Pharaohs.

14. Big families are the human norm, and there seems to be sound sociological as well as biological reason for it. Children educate each other and learn to get on with one another in large families. This may not, however, mean many children per mother. Often "the family" is a small clan with several mothers, and the children all running together.

15. Marriages across cultures are always difficult. (Many World War II veterans and their overseas brides discovered this universal.)

CRIME AND PUNISHMENT

16. Every society provides definite punishments for infringement of its rules, of which *ridicule* is one of the most severe and effective. Some societies, indeed, have no other form of punishment at all. If you have ever broken a social code and been laughed at in front of a crowd, you know the impact of this penalty. Jail rather, or even death! It is said that a Chinese gentleman will go to any length to avoid loss of face. So will George Adams.

17. Stealing within the community is everywhere a very serious offense. Stealing from the out-group, however, from "those foreigners," is often regarded more leniently. A face-to-face band always cares for all its members; nobody is allowed to be in dire want—beggars come only with civilization. Furthermore, to steal is extremely hazardous in a small group, for the thief can be easily traced. The first offense is usually for-

given, and the lesson pointed out. But when a band member is caught stealing the second time, he is punished severely, sometimes by death.

Some Economic Universals

18. No society has ever been found with *complete* communal ownership of property. Private property in personal belongings is universal. Primitive communism thus appears to be another myth.

19. At the same time private property in the natural resources of the group is rare in primitive societies. No individual has exclusive "rights" in fishing areas or hunting lands on which the livelihood of the group depends. Such property is held jointly, and must be passed on intact. One of the greatest breeders of conflict between the early settlers in America and the Indians was that the Indians followed this more normal definition of property in natural resources, while the settlers followed the special Anglo-Saxon custom. When they "sold" land for a few knives and beads, the Indians thought they were transferring hunting rights only. They were naturally bewildered and angry when the palefaces began to exercise exclusive ownership. The Europeans, on the other hand, felt that the Indians were liars and cheats for not living up to their signed agreements. Another tragic example of cross-cultural misunderstandings that lead to bad blood and war.

20. Free giving is a high virtue in many societies, while the desire for profit is often absent. Thrift and frugality, instead of being virtues, are often considered the reverse. Wealth is frequently used for conspicuous consumption rather than for increasing the stock of capital. The Kwakiutl Indians of Vancouver hold prestige contests at feasts called *potlatches*, in which a man tries to shame his rivals by giving away or burning up valuable goods. Veblen played on this theme of conspicuous consumption in *The Theory of the Leisure Class*.

21. Some individuals are acquisitive, and so "all societies have had to develop techniques to insure a share of the necessities

to all members." Otherwise the greedier members try to monopolize necessities. All societies place limits on the acquisition of property. A recent technique to limit acquisitiveness in American society is a graduated income tax climbing well above 80 percent.

22. No human culture has remained long at the stark survival level on which classical economists most often base their hypotheses. "Economic Man" in economic theory, who always acts on the principle of the lowest cost, the largest take, and maximum efficiency, can be found only in books. Flesh and blood men elaborate the necessities, and begin to look for non-economic satisfactions as soon as they rise above the level of bare subsistence. *Indefinite elaboration is one of the most striking of universals.* Even the Old Stone Age people etched designs on their axes. Where is the economic justification for an Egyptian pyramid, a Maya stela, Chartres Cathedral, or the Washington Monument? Think of the progressive elaboration from a shepherd's pipe to a symphony orchestra! Economic theory which leaves out this universal behavior pattern is useless.

Patterns for Group Members

23. Every normal person needs response from his group. Hermits and recluses are abnormal everywhere.

24. The individual needs recognition. Somewhere in the society he must think he has a useful place, even though a modest one, and that he is filling it adequately. This is demonstrated in the status structure of every society studied, and is of the utmost significance.

25. Prestige is a major motive for individual action, stronger than money in most societies. In American society we have, until lately, combined the two—that is, defined prestige in terms of money. The great depression, more leisure, and the graduated income tax, have relaxed the pecuniary standard a little in favor of other forms of prestige.

26. The individual constantly feels the need for a leader. He wants somebody whom he can trust in charge of his group.

27. The individual shows a deep need in every society for friends of the same sex.

28. He needs a way to work off frustrations. Continually obeying the rules of the culture burns him up from time to time, and to preserve equilibrium, if not sanity, he must let off steam. Americans have no recognized method for doing this, but other societies provide an official Saturnalia, fiesta, or Walpurgis Night, when taboos are ceremonially suspended, and the sky is the limit. Our nearest approach is perhaps the annual convention of the American Legion.

29. In the Victorian era it was fashionable to complain that "uncivilized" people—such as African Negroes or Mexican Indians—did not think logically, and were, therefore, hard to deal with. Only in recent years has it been made perfectly plain that civilized people do not think logically either. The record of the social scientists demonstrates that man is not habitually a logical creature. Shaw once observed that we only use our reason to support our prejudices—but that may be a little strong.

The record also shows that W. I. Thomas, the sociologist, was not far wrong when he wrote of the "four wishes" of mankind a generation ago. Every individual, he said,[1] needed from his group four things: *response, security, recognition, and new experience.*

Universals of Government

30. Linton makes a sharp distinction between "group," "government," and "state." A group or society he defines as any collection of people with a social structure. As we have seen, it is the transmitter of culture to the young, and varies in size from the face-to-face band of a few hundred, to all the people in George Adams's continent. The leaders of the group or society are by definition the government, official or unofficial. No society has ever been found without a government—which seems to leave the philosophical anarchists high and dry. The

[1] In *The Unadjusted Girl.*

state, however, is something different. It is the term for a society and its government *organized as a sovereign power, prepared if necessary to wage war*. This gives the state a number of unpleasant powers—unpleasant to the peace and comfort of the individual.

Without war, or the threat of it, we might not have an institution corresponding to "the state" at all. If war is a universal, it follows that the state is one too. But war has not been conclusively established as a universal culture trait. Some societies, like the Arapesh of New Guinea, apparently have never engaged in it.

31. A well-knit, face-to-face band—say among the Plains Indians—holds formal government to the absolute minimum. There is not much for the big chief or the elders to do, for every member knows his place, his duties and rights, and disciplines himself so well that he needs little governing. The most successful nations, observes Linton, are those whose citizens feel toward their country in somewhat the way nature peoples feel toward their tribe. If citizens have this feeling, almost any form of government—monarchy, theocracy, democracy—will work. If they lack it, the finest constitution will be of no avail. Looking around the world today, it appears that the Swedish people have such a feeling. The English have it in their native isle. The French have less of it. The melting pot must bubble a while longer before we get it in America, where a hundred pressure groups still are crying, "Me First."

STATUS AND ROLE

Prepare now for a surprising universal! Quoting Linton:

32. "Individual talent is too sporadic and unpredictable to be allowed any important part in the organization of society." Social systems which endure *are built on the average person*, who can be trained to occupy practically any position adequately, if not brilliantly. If roles had always to be filled by Napoleons or Lincolns, they would often not be filled at all. But the social scientists concede that in periods of rapid cultural

change, like the present, many talented people come to the fore. This conclusion upsets some of our most cherished ideas about leadership, yet its logic is hard to answer. The facts, of course, are only too clear. Practically all societies, for nearly all of the time, *do* have mediocre leaders. Just look around the town.

33. Status can be either *ascribed* or *achieved*. You are born to a social position, or you fight your way up to it. In feudal societies status is mostly ascribed; the son of a noble becomes a noble at birth; the son of a serf remains a serf. In America the accent is on achieved status—which is a technical expression for the success story. Any boy can be president, although it helps to be born in a log cabin. (The popular saga fails to remind us that up to now no Catholic boy or Jew or Negro has been elected president—but this too may change.)

Ascribed status reduces competition, rivalry, and conflict. The citizen is easy in his mind, for he knows where he belongs and is comfortable there. One reason for tension and worry among Americans is the drive to achieve a higher place. Wave after wave of immigrants comes to a city, lands on the bottom with the most menial jobs and lowest pay, and then begins to fight its way up—Irishmen, Scandinavians, Germans, Italians, Poles. In New York, the Puerto Ricans are now on the bottom, even below the Negroes in Harlem. They will not stay there, for the culture bids them climb. The process, though it generates plenty of tension, is an essential part of the American way of life. We do not accept an ascribed status.

Let me repeat that the above 33 universals are the result of a rough and ready analysis, drawn largely from Linton. Qualification may well be in order as new facts come in to the Cross-Cultural Index. But when all qualification is made, and the proper scientific caution expressed, the anthropologists' contribution is bound to stand out with luminous clarity. What they have given us is a comprehensive and compelling affirmation of the brotherhood of man.

10

Cultural Chasm

In this chapter and the next we will tell two stories of the culture concept in action. The first reports a skillful analysis of the cultural chasm between English-speakers and Spanish-speakers in the American Southwest. The second story concerns a camp of Japanese-Americans, transplanted from their homes on the Pacific Coast during World War II, and how a social scientist helped to prevent a bloody uprising.

Medical personnel in Texas, New Mexico, Arizona, California, have had a difficult time dealing with two-and-a-half million Spanish-speaking people in the area. A social scientist, Dr. Lyle Saunders, with the help of Dr. Esther Brown of the Russell Sage Foundation, studied the situation for some years on the spot, exploring the clash of cultures, and the great trouble which comes when neither group understands the language, customs, and belief systems of the other.[1] Such things as the following are continually happening:

The Spanish-speaking couple who failed to report to the proper medical authorities the birth of a child, and its death one hour later, and who themselves buried the infant in a box in their yard, were not bad or heartless people. They were, of course, picked up by the police when their deed became known. But they do not deserve punishment. Instead they need an opportunity to acquire an understanding of our ways. They did what all people do in the tiny, remote Mexican community from which they came. They did what for them seemed right, what was customary, what they had learned to do from the people among whom they had lived most

[1] See his book, *Cultural Difference and Medical Care.*

of their lives. But in the United States it was not right, not customary.

A cultural chasm indeed—what is right and proper in one society becomes a crime in another.

There are three main groups of Spanish-speakers in the Southwest: (1) Spanish-Americans, who first settled in the Rio Grande Valley some years before the Pilgrims landed on Plymouth Rock. (2) Mexican-Americans who have become United States citizens. They speak the soft Mexican Spanish, but their children are increasingly bilingual. The culture of this group is a mixture of Spanish and Indian. (3) "Wetbacks," who have waded the Rio Grande to become migratory laborers, illegal immigrants, and most welcome to United States farmers with crops to gather.

Dr. Saunders' study describes the interrelations between the "Anglo" or English-speaking culture, and the Mexican or Spanish-speaking culture. The findings, intended for the use of medical personnel in the Southwest, are also valuable for similar borderline medical programs anywhere in the world. The World Health Organization, UNESCO, projects in technical assistance, Rockefeller Foundation projects abroad, are already using them to advantage. Beyond that, the findings are dramatic and revealing for anyone trying to look over the walls of his own culture.

CASE WORK

Doctors and social workers in the Southwest find themselves repeatedly baffled by such situations as these:

A mother who clearly loves her child waits until he is critically ill before calling a doctor.

A patient with t.b. who walks out of the hospital to attend a family wedding.

Children, already retarded in school, do not appear until months after school opens.

A child, dying of leukemia, is taken from the hospital by the family and placed in the care of a *curandera*, or local herb-doctor.

Such cases are hard for "Anglo" professionals to understand. The natural reaction is to call names—"stupid," "ignorant," "childish," "irresponsible," "lazy," from which it is only a step to "genetically inferior." But to the Spanish-speakers, Anglos often seem to be crazy strangers, talking a harsh gibberish and making a fetish of bathing, of being on time, wearing outlandish clothes, their men degrading themselves by doing women's work, and showing alarming ignorance of the real nature of illness and disease.

What the Anglos often overlook is that medicine is a social activity. There are always at least two persons intimately involved, patient and therapist, and their relation takes place within a social system. Medicine in every culture is, and has been for thousands of years, a vast complex of knowledge, belief, skills, roles, ideologies, attitudes, customs, rituals, and symbols, "interlocking to form a reinforcing and supporting system."

When the young doctor down from Ohio laughs off Juan's behavior as ignorant and irresponsible, the doctor really is the ignorant one. Juan is operating within a powerful and complicated system, which has rules about disease and its cure just as deep-seated as in the medical schools of Ohio, and far more ancient. There are at least 46 cures for rheumatism in Mexican folk medicine, some of them very elaborate therapies. Useless? Probably. *But Juan does not believe them to be useless, and it is his belief which the Anglos do not allow for.* He holds to it as firmly as they hold to cortisone.

Seven Differences

Analysis of the cultural chasm between Anglos and Mexicans reveals seven major differences:

1. Language.
2. Attitude toward time.
3. Attitude toward change and "progress."
4. Attitude toward work.
5. Accepting one's fate. Resignation.

6. Relation with one's group.

7. Attitude toward formal organizations.

Language

Language forms the deepest cleavage. Anglos make little attempt to learn Spanish, though the Mexicans are all expected to learn English. It is possible to live out one's life in sections of El Paso, San Antonio, Los Angeles, without knowing a word of English. This creates a vicious circle of misunderstanding. Anglos tend to shout, hoping to make themselves better understood. When the response is only a terrified *no comprendo*, the Anglo concludes that of course the chap must be stupid; he can't understand plain English and ought to go back where he came from. If the chap happens to be a Rio Grande villager, his ancestors got here in 1598.

Dr. Saunders quotes the linguist, Benjamin Lee Whorf, showing how the language one learns as a child shapes his thinking throughout life. Our perceptions are organized around verbal symbols; what a person "sees," the meaning it has for him, is tied to the structure of his language and group experience. In English, a clock *runs*, but in Spanish *el reloj anda*, "he walks." This simple difference has enormous implications. If clocks run, there isn't a minute to lose! If they walk, we can take our time.

In Spanish, a worker does not miss the bus, the *bus left him* —the culprit is the bus, not the person. Spanish is replete with this kind of construction—buses leave people, objects lose themselves, automobiles wreck themselves, dishes break themselves by falling away from people. The English-speaker reaches into his box of categories and proceeds to label the Spanish-speaker as "lazy" and "unreliable."

The cultural characteristics of any people are not haphazard. They are all of a piece and built up over the centuries. The function of culture, as we have seen, is primarily utilitarian, to enable the group to survive. Every trait has, or once had, relationship to other traits and some relevance to the environment. New layers can be deliberately added, but old ones cannot easily be taken away, although they may gradually erode through the process of cultural lag. When people move they take their culture right along, as much a part of them as the hair on their heads.

Time

To understand the Mexicans, says Saunders, we have to look to the old environment as well as the new. In the old environment, either along the Rio Grande or in Mexico, time moved slowly, the corn field was tended, the fiesta celebrated; changes were few. A past without written records is misty, and the future offers no particular promise—"neither anticipated with joy, nor feared."

In the villages the rhythm of life was seasonal rather than diurnal. What one did on a particular day did not matter much; what one did during the year mattered a great deal. There was no money, no boss, no time clock, "no pressure to develop any particular concern with time." This rhythm, of course, is found in handicraft cultures all over the world. Only recently has Western culture pushed pins into citizens, bidding them remember that time is money, clocks *run*, and they must get a move on if they expect to climb the ladder of success. Anglos are oriented toward the future, Mexicans are oriented toward the present and the remembered past. To them, the Horatio Alger story is meaningless, the American success saga a form of mild insanity.

The young doctor says to his Mexican patient: "What day would you like to come to the clinic next week?" How does Juan reply to this strange question? He stammers, runs his sombrero through his hands—not from stupidity, but because he does not think about time in that way at all.

Change

A major belief among Anglos is that change is good and "progress" inevitable. There was little progress along the Rio Grande for 300 years, the villagers had almost no experience of change. The future, if they thought about it at all, was an extension of the present. Uncertainty, perhaps danger, would come with the new and untried. This is also true in many Russian villages, villages in India and China and Africa.

Work

Dr. Saunders picks up a story from Bennett Cerf to illustrate the attitude toward work. A businessman from New York is strolling along the platform of the railway station in Albuquerque. He sees a group of Pueblo Indian men relaxing in the sun. What a waste of manpower! He goes up to one of them and asks with some asperity why he isn't working.

"Why should I work?"

"To earn money," says the businessman.

"Why should I want to earn money?" asks the Indian.

"So you can save it, and some day you will have enough so you can retire and won't have to work any more."

"I'm not working now," says the Indian.

When I first went to Mexico I was told that the people were congenitally lazy, and a good many of them did seem to be sitting in the sun. But as I stayed on, collecting material for a book, I realized that Mexicans could work as hard as anybody else, carrying prodigious burdens on their backs, toiling incredibly to cut down the jungle for a new milpa, *if they felt that the work was important*. They seldom worked just for the sake of working, or from a moral compulsion. With Americans, work is tied to personal success; with Mexicans it is tied to the demands of the environment and the rhythm of the seasons.

Resignation

A Mexican is more likely than an Anglo to resign himself to whatever fate brings. This again reflects the ancient village pattern—"a remembrance of men and women who were born, resigned themselves to suffering and hardship along with occasional joys, and died when their time came." There are plenty of never-say-die *caballeros* in Spain and in Mexico City, but most villagers see life in more philosophical terms. They may not be dedicated to the main chance, but often they seem to have achieved an enviable human dignity.

Death is regrettable but inevitable, and so the Mexican does not call the doctor when the baby dies. To die at home, furthermore, is much better, he thinks, than in a strange, impersonal place called a hospital.

Here is Maria with a serious case of t.b. But she feels quite well. So she cannot be ill, she thinks. If she is not ill, how can she transmit sickness to her children? These Anglo medicos are very foolish. She does not hear the doctor's words saying she is sick; they simply do not come through. The medical concepts which make the words meaningful are unknown to her. She "knows" about sickness, and in terms of her "knowledge"—deep and ancient and complex—she is not sick.

In Conclusion

Western ideas of medicine are unquestionably sounder than village ideas. Scientific medicine is bound to prevail in the end. But it will win out sooner, with far less frustration, if Anglo medical workers can be given a working knowledge of the culture concept. In due time, perhaps, the children of Maria and Juan will understand it better too.

About 70 or 80 years ago, biology came in to help Western medicine, revolutionizing the theory of infections, among other things. Today the social scientist is offering medicine another important aid, in such studies as Dr. Saunders'. Students in medical school, he says, should begin with courses on the culture concept, while all large health programs, where more than one culture is involved, should include social scientists for planning and for constant consultation.

Medicine is a social complex, as we have seen; but too many American doctors assume that it is only a business between doctor and patient, without reference to environment, cultural beliefs, and local customs. The Anglo often concentrates on symptoms, forgetting people. "During the first year in medical school the student's contacts are with dead people."

Looking at a man with the naked eye, he is an individual. Looking at him with a microscope, he is a biological specimen. Looking at him from the long view, he becomes a unit of society, bound into its culture with bolts of steel. The doctor needs all three perspectives to do justice to his great mission.

11

Revolt in the Desert

A serious handicap of the social scientist is the lack of laboratory conditions where controlled experiments and measured observations can be carried on. Researchers often dream of an isolated spot where they would have the power to vary conditions and pinpoint behavior.

Such an opportunity came to Dr. Alexander Leighton, psychiatrist and anthropologist, during World War II. With a small staff, he was assigned to observe one of the relocation centers for Japanese-Americans. At Poston in the Arizona desert, men, women, and children were obliged to live under great tension and insecurity for many months. Various experiments might have been made, but Dr. Leighton chose to concentrate on the patterns of group tension itself. Later he reported his findings in a penetrating book, *The Governing of Men,* which has value for administrators and executors in many kinds of human situations.

The camp was guarded by the Army and administered by the United States Indian Service. Leighton was delegated to watch its development, advise the administration, and search for valid conclusions. He asks:

. . . What in all this is recurrently human? What are the laws of individual behavior, what are the perennial social forces at work here? . . . What general characteristics of human nature are in action, a knowledge of which would prevent such sudden diseases of society as this? The breakdowns of man's organizations of himself and his fellows are not events isolated in evacuation camps. They cover as much of the earth as is covered by the human race, and questions that run deeply into the fate of mankind in a shrinking world are involved.

Japanese people coming to America to settle on the West Coast had different culture rings from the ancestors of George Adams. They had centuries of civilization back of them, to be sure, but not Western civilization, not Christianity, not Anglo-Saxon culture, and above all, not the English language. By 1940, however, they were well on the road to making the adjustment; to becoming "acculturated," as the anthropologists say. Their children were at home in both worlds.

In their ranks were tuna fishermen from Terminal Island, Judo instructors, lawyers, celery farmers, rose gardeners, a Y.M.C.A. leader, "Texas Mary" (the ornament of a Salinas saloon), wholesale produce merchants, a Baptist minister, research workers, butlers, bums. At 7:55 A.M. on December 7, 1941, Pearl Harbor was attacked. Instantly life for every one of these people became difficult. On January 2, 1942, Manila fell, and it became more difficult. Said the Los Angeles *Times:* "A viper is none the less a viper wherever the egg is hatched." On February 15, Singapore surrendered, and life became critical. Ten days later, when a Japanese submarine shelled Santa Barbara, the limit was reached in the opinion of the authorities. The Japanese on the coast had to go inland to special camps, where they were held under observation by the government to forestall mob violence against them. On March 18, President Roosevelt created the War Relocation Authority to handle the mass evacuation.

Poston sits in the burning desert near an old mining town. In summer the temperature sometimes climbs above 120° in the shade. Here, as the spring of 1942 progressed and the sun mounted higher, 9,000 evacuees were assembled in a new community. The government did not plan to punish them for what had been done at Pearl Harbor, nor was the idea to pamper them. They were to be as self-sufficient as possible, to earn a little by raising some crops for the outside market, and to live a very simple life in Army barracks on the hot desert floor until the war was over.

In the camp were three well-marked classes of Japanese. The *Issei*, who had been born in Japan and could never become American citizens. The *Nisei*, born in the United States and ipso facto citizens, mostly children of *Issei*. The *Kibei*, who were *Nisei* that had gone to Japan from America, and subsequently returned. Many of the *Issei*, after being treated like lepers on the coast, wanted Japan to win the war, though they did nothing overt about it. Most of the *Nisei*, however, despite the treatment they received, remained loyal to America. In complete disregard of these distinctions, demagogues in the Far West repeatedly made headlines by whipping up agitation against *all* people of Japanese descent, proclaiming that "a Jap is a Jap," and none could be trusted.

Meanwhile, the administration of the camp was split into two kinds of staff members, called by Dr. Leighton "people-minded," and "stereotype-minded." The former were full of good will, which was fine; but some of them tried to operate on the blanket assumption that "we're all human beings"—which was not so fine. We *are* human beings, right enough, *but our cultures are different*, and if this crucial fact is ignored we misjudge what is happening.

The stereotype-minded were at the other extreme. They looked on their charges as "Japs" first and people second—if indeed they were not to be classed among the higher apes. Motivations were allegedly different from those of "white men." The stereotype-minded thought the Center ought to be an out-and-out concentration camp. Since they were thinking of slogans rather than people, they gave no attention to incentives, but relied on punishment and fear. Shoot a few Japs and the rest would come around, was the general idea—"the only treatment the yellow so-and-sos will understand." This attitude was held by the least educated of the staff, and those least informed about the reasons for the Center. One of the top officials, a man of fifty, "honest, forthright, and inflexible," came from the deep

South. We will call him Mr. Z. He had no difficulty in transferring to the Japanese his whole built-in belief system about
Negroes—a lower order of being to be kept in its place.

The hot months of 1942 dragged on. The divided policy of
the Poston administration, shortages in many promised supplies,
the unknown future, all combined to develop among the people
of the community various acute needs—physical, social, psychological—and all related to a feeling of insecurity and fear. One
task of the administration was to discover those needs and
meet them, and so keep the community from disintegration.

This kind of situation is an acute test for any administrator.
He should know that strong fear inside a group is likely to lead
to strong anger, which in turn may lead to violence. The people
at the Center were full of fear. They had no worthy status, no
sense of belonging, no idea what was going to happen to them.
They had lost most of their property, and had nothing to hope
for.

A local self-government council had been set up, but it did
very little and, as the people progressively lost hope, it became
the target for their grievances. There was no real integration,
no rank and file leadership in the whole camp. Toward the end
of the summer, neighborhood groups began to form spontaneously, with each block of barracks as a political and social unit.
The "good of Poston" was too nebulous an incentive, but many
members began to pick cotton in earnest when it was known
that the proceeds would be used to improve their own blocks.

As in all human communities, members varied from responsible
upright citizens to bad actors full of hate. Within narrower
limits, so did members of the staff vary. The degree of coöperation and responsibility was also affected by government policy
at Washington. Abrupt changes and reversals of policy were
frequent, and they bewildered people and hurt morale.

By October, 1942, it was clear that the struggle to build a
going community had been lost. The Center was visibly disintegrating, and dire things were in the wind. It was cool in
the evenings now, and people stood on the streets around the

fires which they had built against the chill, recounting their grievances. They spoke bitterly of the poor food, the terrible heat of the preceding summer, the hospital equipment which had never come, the mosquitoes, the wretched pay of fifty cents a day.

Around the fires, ugly rumors began to spread. Premonitions and prophecies began to be heard; Ouija boards were brought out. A situation out of control usually encourages magical solutions. Crackpots, demagogues, trouble makers, had a receptive audience around the fires. Gangsters were not only tolerated but admired as men who got action. . . . Action!

The administration consulted Dr. Leighton, and he sought to interpret what was happening. People, he said, were trying to adjust to a society that had no framework and no stability. They were trying somehow to exist without security or hope.

By the middle of November, their strong inhibitions against aggression and violence began to crack. Meanwhile, small elements of new social organization, the nucleus of a new structure, were appearing in the fluid confusion. The lack of harmony was almost unbearable. When would the little bonfires turn into one great conflagration?

During the night of November 14, a thirty-year-old *Kibei*, a rice broker and reputed swindler of Japanese farmers, was attacked in his sleep in the bachelors' barracks and beaten almost to death. Fifty suspects were rounded up, and two of them held for further investigation by the FBI, one a former university student, the other a Judo instructor; both were popular. Their families tried to obtain their release. A meeting was held in the block where the two men lived, and a delegation was appointed to see the project director. The director said that the FBI had the matter in hand, and he could not interfere with the investigation.

Then a curious thing happened. The handful of people who threatened violence unless the men were released became suddenly the catalyst which exploded the frustrations and grievances of the whole camp. There was a spontaneous walk-out—not so

much on behalf of the prisoners, as on behalf of long accumulated resentments and hopelessness. As one striker said: "I
didn't know what the issues were and I don't imagine anyone
else did either—there were so many conflicting issues. Everyone
took up the torch in defense of his particular peeve."

The administration was on the spot. Should they call in the
Army and quell the strike with force? This would certainly involve bloodshed, for some strikers were offering to die for their
cause, while soldiers outside the gates, mostly raw recruits, were
eager to charge in. Should the administration try, on the other
hand, to weather the crisis and use the emotional energy the
crisis released to build a better community? If the Army came
in shooting, the hope of anything better than a concentration
camp was gone. The Berlin and Tokyo broadcasters, furthermore, would have a field day equating the attack with the Four
Freedoms! The majority of the people at the Center, it must be
remembered, were *American citizens,* American born, whose
loyalty had never been disproved.

When the strike exploded, the staff split down the middle.
To the stereotype-minded, the matter was simple. Mr. Z had his
formula ready: The Japs (considered all to be identical) were
raising hell, and it was the duty of good Americans to go in
there, slap them down, and put them in their places. If this
involved shooting irons, it involved shooting irons. The whole
disturbance was the result of previous coddling and lack of
discipline.

Mr. Z had followers, though not all so outspoken. Some of the
staff saw the situation in pure Hollywood colors, with plots,
secret agents, Axis machinations, buried food supplies for invading armies, all complete. The melodrama mind, Leighton says,
was exceedingly dangerous at this juncture. It was primarily a
product of fear; but "out of the figments of the mind springs
actual catastrophe." Thus the top administration had to deal not
only with tension in the community it was trying to govern, but
with emotional breakdown in its own ranks.

On the other side were the "people-minded" staff members,

some of them sentimental, some of them realists. They tried to canvass various alternatives. Breaking up the crowd that milled around the jail where the two suspects were held would not halt the strike. If the Army took over there was no way to force residents to work. Frustrations and grievances would be driven underground, only to become worse.... So the "people-minded" reasoned.

Not even the most tender-hearted of the staff entertained for a moment the idea of letting the two prisoners go free, as the crowd demanded. "Face seems to be important in all societies. ... Orientals have no monopoly." The alternative to summoning the Army was some kind of negotiation which tacitly implied that the strikers had a case. The strikers by this time were represented by a so-called Emergency Council, mostly elder *Isseis*.

The top administrator was attending an important conference outside the State and could not, at this critical juncture, be reached. We cannot envy the assistant director, who, after a stormy staff meeting between these two schools of thought, stood looking out the window at the gray November desert, trying to decide what to do. If he said "yes" and let the Army take over, he had a perfect escape for himself, but the Center was finished. If he said "no," perhaps the mob would go on the rampage, looting and burning, as Mr. Z so confidently prophesied. After a long time he turned back from the window and said "no." He would ask the Army to establish patrols *outside* the area, but not to take charge of the camp.

Every administrator, Leighton remarks, must be prepared when the time comes to back himself against the world, and if necessary take the consequences of losing. It is no field for the faint of heart. True, the moment does arrive when the administrator stands alone, but how much better, when that time comes, to be backed by knowledge! For a few hours at Poston it was touch and go, but the decision turned out to be the right one. When the people felt that the administration was ready to negotiate in good faith, the hotheads lost their following. The strike ended with a mass meeting in front of the jail.

It was a cold night and the fires were all burning. Speakers praised the work of the community's Emergency Council, the law and order which it had maintained during the strike; they looked toward the bright future of Poston as a self-governing community. The director, recently returned from his conference, made a warming speech. The strike was nobody's fault, he said. "It's not the administration up there and you people down here, but we're all working together." The meeting ended with three *banzais* and the crowd went quietly away, its tensions relaxed. In some quarters there was even a feeling of jubilation, of liking everybody, including the administration. The fires were put out; the rubbish was cleared away.

One of the prisoners was released outright, after the FBI concluded its investigation. The other, the Judo instructor, was paroled pending examination by the regular civil courts of Arizona. Subsequently the case was dropped because of insufficient evidence. Self-government really developed out of the Emergency Council and a sounder community with indigenous leadership was born. Although other troubles arose from time to time thereafter, no more strikes and no more mass frustrations were found at Poston.

LESSONS FROM THE CRISIS

The crisis and its settlement had focused attention on certain fundamental *needs* of the community "on behalf of which," says Leighton, "the strike had been only an imperious cry for attention." The story of the uprising, dramatic as it is, is merely the prelude to the conclusions which went into Dr. Leighton's notebook as a social scientist. Some of them will impress you as simple common sense; others are clearly exploring new areas in human relations. "I am certain that in the Relocation Camp experience, my hands, groping blindly below the surface, touched here and there on a real body of constants and laws in human living."

He begins his analysis with two constants which we have already encountered:

Principle 1. In all the different peoples of the world there are universal basic characteristics inherent in human nature. *Principle 2.* There are profound differences in belief, sentiment, habit, and custom among the various communities, tribes, and nations which make up mankind.

These two linked principles summarize the culture concept. They are accepted by practically all modern scientists who have seriously studied the nature of man and his society. The more naïve of the "people-minded" administrators at the camp accepted the first but were not sufficiently aware of the second. The "stereotype-minded" embraced the second in its most extreme form, and denied the first. So both groups missed the mark, though Mr. Z and the "shoot-'em-down" school were the more seriously afield.

Here are other useful conclusions and recommendations arising from the study:

Do not think of people as racial, national, or class stereotypes. Get up close and look at them, particularly at the children.

Group stability is helped by situations which give economic security, by work which is thought to be important, by outlets in sports and recreation.

All people everywhere create social organizations, given time enough. Very recent immigrants are thus at a great disadvantage. Human groups cannot carry out actions for which they have no social organization.

Remember that your own staff is composed of human beings, too, reacting in ways similar to the people under them.

Keep the communication line open, both from the administration to the group and from the group back to the administration.

Never make threats or lay down rules you cannot enforce. Do not take a strong stand on a weak position. This sounds a little like "don't kiss a buzz saw," but administrators and legislators and Secretaries of State are doing it all the time.

Most individuals, most of the time, prefer peace and quiet. The administrator can always count on this massive inertia. He can also count on a sense of humor. He can count on the relatively long time it takes for aggressive feelings to rise to the point of violence. In Poston it took almost six months.

A sure warning of breakdown is a rise in rumors and magic. Never dismiss complaints as trivial; they may be storm signals.

Following an outbreak of aggressive action, people have a feeling of relief and well-being, of liking everyone. *This is the worst possible moment to deal out punishment.*

Finally, if an administrator finds he cannot control his prejudices, he had better get into another line of work.

ROLE OF THE SOCIAL SCIENTIST

When Dr. Leighton and his associates came to Poston, the administration was making decisions off the cuff after informal staff conferences. The communication lines were not good in either direction. After he had collected sufficient first-hand information, he began to tell the top managers about it—to their apparent astonishment. "We thus became aware of what would seem to be a basic principle in the application of social science to a fast-moving administration program, namely, that the research staff have direct access to policy-makers, and participation in policy meetings."

When the strike ended in November, the social scientists had been in constant attendance during the critical hours. *They did not make the final decision;* the man at the window did that. But they put the major characteristics of the situation before him, so that he could make his decision on the basis of understanding instead of passion. Mr. Z supplied the passion. . . . In these two men, Mr. Z and the Assistant Director, do we see two worlds, the one we have known, and another which may come?

FROM STONE TO STEEL

Here is another story about social scientists observing a community in the midst of change. A single small change, from a stone ax to a steel one, shook this particular community to its foundations, and came near to destroying it.

On the subtropical north coast of Australia lives a tribe of native hunters and fishermen called the Yir Yoront. Like most primitive Australians, long cut off from other cultures, the tribe enjoyed great stability. Customs and beliefs were standardized, and before any change was accepted, a myth had to be invented which proved that one's ancestors did things that way, and thus the change was really no change at all.

Up to the turn of the century, the tribe was still living in the Stone Age. An important tool, a short-handled stone ax, was used to build huts, cut firewood, and make other tools for hunting, fishing, and gathering wild honey. The stone heads came from a quarry 400 miles to the south, and were obtained from other tribes in an annual intertribal fiesta. The handle was fitted with great skill and care and attached with bark and gum. The completed article—or artifact—was far more than a tool. It had become a symbol, a totem, a sign of the owner's masculinity, to be cherished and handed down, and loaned only with the greatest circumspection. The stone ax was not only useful, it was a kind of keystone in the belief system of the Yir Yoront.

About 1900, steel axes began to filter in along the tribal trade routes. They were welcomed at first as more efficient; one could cut down a tree much faster. By 1915, missionaries were distributing the steel axes as gifts and rewards. If a man worked especially hard he might get an ax, and so might his wife or young son. The missionaries hoped by this means to induce people to plant and fence gardens and improve their diet.

The idea was excellent, but it overlooked the culture concept. The steel ax destroyed a most important symbol in the belief system of the tribe. A man lost his importance and dignity; his very masculinity was threatened without his stone ax. Women and children, now possessing axes themselves, became independent and disrespectful. The entire system of age, sex, and kinship roles was thrown into confusion. The old trade relations were disrupted and the intertribal fiesta was robbed of significance and charm. Stealing and wife lending increased. The ancient totem system was shattered, for it could not be decided whether the steel ax should be a totem of the Sunlit Cloud Iguana Clan, as the stone ax had been since time out of mind, or the totem of the Head-to-the-East Corpse Clan. . . .

Anthropologists, studying the situation in the 1930's, found that the culture had not broken down so completely as in the case of certain other tribes more exposed to western influences, but it was shaky and insecure. The major reason was the change in the composition of one artifact, from stone to steel, and a change technically for the better.

Lauriston Sharp, who tells this story in a collection about technological change, leaves it here, but the editor[1] points the moral in a list of questions. Before introducing a new artifact into an established native culture, missionaries and others would do well to ask: "What will it replace? What other tools and techniques are likely to be affected? Who will benefit and who will be hurt? What symbols and totems and beliefs will be upset?" Hundreds of native cultures around the world have been wrecked and undone by well-meaning Westerners for want of an Alexander Leighton.

Well-meaning Westerners are themselves now threatened by the new electronic artifact of automation. Who will benefit and who will be hurt? What symbols and totems will be upset?

[1] Spicer. See Bibliography.

12

Scientists Look at Race

Despite their color, the Japanese-Americans at Poston behaved the way any human community would behave under severe stress. As we follow Dr. Leighton's account, we almost forget the racial differences; to Mr. Z, however, these were paramount. But the scientist helped to prevent an explosion by treating the situation as a human problem in group tension.

Race prejudice is a cultural phenomenon. One is not born with it; it has to be learned. It has come to our Western culture in relatively recent times, a modern form of the age-old suspicion of the out-group, the foreigner, the person who is different. Religious prejudice has declined in the West as race prejudice has increased.

In the ideal community nobody would need to instruct children about races or warn them against prejudice. The adult would act without bias, and the children would automatically follow. But in George Adams's New England, as well as below the Mason-Dixon line, the pattern of prejudice is established, sometimes stronger, sometimes weaker. The children see the snub, feel the antipathy, hear the ridicule, and presently they are locked into the pattern too, ready to pass it on to *their* children.

THE BIOLOGY OF RACE

The story of Adam and Eve in the book of Genesis has been vindicated in part by biology. Its main point is now generally accepted as true: namely, that there is only one human family. All of us now alive, the whole two-and-half billion of us, are the descendants of a comparatively small group of common ancestors. In Genesis, the dates are wrong, and we find quite a few poetic trimmings, but the idea is sound. If each of us could trace his family tree back for enough generations, we should all find the same great-great-great . . . grandfather.

Our most remote forebear, according to Linton, was probably a small tree-dweller, ancestral to both men and apes. Succeeding generations became larger, with relatively bigger brains. During the Miocene Age, some members became too large for trees and took to the ground, still on all fours. Gradually they developed carnivorous habits and began to stand erect. Their brains grew still bigger, and late in the Pliocene Age, one branch reached the subhuman level, in the form of a very primitive gentleman indeed. He gave rise to a number of species, one of which finally developed into modern man. Language, the most human of all our traits, began then. This species overran the earth, and in due course began to differentiate into the various races which we know today—brown, yellow, and white.

If we could piece together the story of how a small group, starting probably in Central Asia, gradually spread and migrated around the globe, it would make the American conquest of the West seem like an afternoon stroll. How did these remote ancestors of ours get from the mainland to Japan, to the Philippines, across the watery wastes of the Pacific to one island after another? How did they make their way from the mouth of the Nile down to the Cape of Good Hope? What was their rate— a hundred miles a year, or ten miles a century? How did they eat, and keep the family together?

Even more astonishing, after crossing Bering Strait into Alaska, how did they reach Tierra del Fuego, 10,000 miles away, over some of the most savage territory on the planet? How did they get to Australia, and why was that continent then sealed off for 20,000 years, leaving the people there culturally frozen in the Old Stone Age, still using stone axes in A.D. 1900? Did an easier route exist, perhaps on islands later swallowed by the ocean?

It has taken scientific teamwork of a high order to get the

facts of race together. The *historians* have studied recorded migrations, the *sociologists* have studied group organizations, the *biologists* have studied anatomy and genetics; some *anthropologists* have studied culture, and others have taken many measurements of skulls and shinbones; the *psychologists* have studied intelligence. Their joint findings have been checked and cross-checked, and they have come to the overall conclusion that "all the peoples of the earth are a single family with a common origin."[1]

Take, for instance, the human foot. All human feet have practically the same structure, with intricate bones and muscles and joints. It is clearly impossible for this combination to have arisen twice in two independent species. All humans have the same tooth and jaw structure. They are capable of similar physical tasks—running, striking, lifting. They are capable of similar mental tasks—acquiring a language, counting, abstracting, using logic, argument, persuasion. They all gather into bands and groups, and develop cultures which contain many parallel patterns and universals, as we have seen. No other creature passes on a culture to the next generation.

Scientists find that the only demonstrable *racial* differences, which are over and above individual differences, are in a few superficial bodily characteristics—the texture of head hair, the shape of the nose, eye color, skin color. White people are the hairiest, perhaps because most of them live in colder latitudes. Negroes have the darkest skin color, certainly because this gives them protection against the rays of the tropic sun. All races have some primitive and other less primitive characteristics. The thin lips of the white man, for instance, are nearer those of the ape, the thick lips of the Negro further away.

Skin color is determined by two chemicals, *carotene*, which gives a yellow tinge, and *melanin*, which gives a brown. These colors, combined with the pinkish tinge from blood vessels showing through, provide all the skin shades known. Every human

[1] Benedict and Weltfish, *The Races of Mankind*. A good short survey, based on Boas' *Mind of Primitive Man*.

being has some of each—unless he is an albino, which means he lacks *carotene* and *melanin* completely. Albinos are found in all races. Skin color "is not an all-or-nothing difference," says Ruth Benedict, "it is a difference in proportion . . . due to the amount of these chemicals present in your skin."

Height is no reliable characteristic of race. The Shilluk Negroes, near the sources of the Nile, average 6 feet 2 inches, while not far away the brown pygmies average 4 feet 8 inches.

Head shape is similarly unhelpful. In West Africa we find long heads, along the Congo round heads. American Indians are both long-headed and round-headed. In Asia Minor, where human mixtures rise to a kind of frenzy, there are long heads and round heads among close relatives.

Blood differences are nonexistent between the races; no chemist can tell from a blood sample to what race its donor belongs. He can tell whether it is type O, A, B or AB; but these blood types are found in *all* races. Your son and a Maya Indian may both be type AB, while your father's type may differ from your own. Folklore has developed a great mystique about "blood," and how some people are "pure" and some are "mongrels." The truth is, says Gordon Allport, that "most men are mongrels." At the outbreak of the Civil War, however, a Kentucky editor clarified everything by declaring that it was a war to the death between the pure "Angles" of the South, and the decadent "Normans" of the North.

Differences in the size of the human brain today tell us little about race, nothing about intelligence. The world's largest brain belongs to an imbecile. Some geniuses have relatively small brains. As in the case of a blood sample, no scientist can tell by examining a brain alone to what race the owner belonged. The average brain size in cubic centimeters differs slightly by races, but it has not been proved that this affects intelligence until the variation becomes substantial. Back of Neanderthal man, differences in brain size are important.

Curt Stern, writing in the *Scientific American*,[2] says that

[2] October, 1954.

while there remains a group of believers in the mental inferiority of the Negro, the majority of students today holds this proposition to be unproved. All intelligence tests are loaded with cultural conditioning, but one extremely significant fact that has emerged from these tests is that the *range* of measured intelligence is as wide among Negroes as among whites. One little colored girl has scored an IQ of 200, and many Negro children score 140 on the Stanford-Binet scale.[3]

All races can interbreed everywhere, and with remarkable industry have done so. Your typical European is a dizzy mixture of Slav, Mongol, African, Celt, Saxon, Teuton, Semite, and other strains. "So far as we know there are no immutable laws of nature that make racial mixture harmful," says Benedict. Have you a picture in your mind of the Scandinavian people as predominantly tall, blue-eyed blondes, with long heads and long faces? If you stood on a street corner in Stockholm with a notebook and counted, you would find that only about 15 percent of the passers-by fitted this description.

All races except the Australian aborigines have developed high civilizations from time to time. There were Negro empires and states in Africa when large sections of Europe were sunk in barbarism. The people of China were reading Lao Tze when the original Britons were painting their bodies blue and yelling in the fens. The Maya Indians were better astronomers and sculptors than their Spanish conquerors.

The "character" of the different races turns out, as we might expect, to be a result of culture, not biology. American Indians in New Mexico pueblos were mostly placid, peace-loving, and unemotional, while in the horse culture of the plains, Indians of the same stock were "frenzy-loving Dionysian warriors."

The three primary races—the Caucasian, Mongoloid, and Negroid—exhibit no significant difference in height, weight, anatomy, blood, intelligence, or character. They all have the same normal temperature of 98.6° F., the same life span under

[3] In a ten-year study by Allison Davis, some Negro children at the University of Chicago's demonstration school outranked children of professors.

similar conditions, the same muscular prowess. All are vulnerable to certain diseases and cured by similar methods. Individuals
within each race, of course, differ greatly, and subgroups differ
in certain characteristics, like the Negro giants and pygmies.

NONBIOLOGICAL OR MYTHICAL RACES

Many other "races" are identified verbally, argued about, and
fought over. On analysis, however, most of them turn out to
be national or religious groups with little or no biological difference. "Aryans" are properly people who speak languages derived
from the Aryan language group. "Jews" are properly people
who subscribe to the Hebrew religion, and practice certain ceremonies like the Seder on Passover. The so-called "Jewish type,"
with hooked nose and black hair, is a Mediterranean variation of
the Caucasian race, and includes many Arabs, Armenians, Turks,
Levantines, Greeks, and South Italians, as well as Jews.

Hitler and his kept biologists got into some weird difficulties
with their "Aryan" doctrines. The Hungarians were obviously
not members of the master race, but when they joined Hitler's
Axis, they had to be accommodated somehow under the main
tent. The solution was to call them "non-non-Aryans." The
Arabs and the Japanese presented further complications. In due
time the savants in Berlin became so involved in this racial
mythology that they had to assert that the Jews, far from being
simple "non-Aryans," did not belong to any race at all, but
formed a mongrel community thenceforth to be called "Anti-
Race."

"A plotting of racial characteristics," says Linton, "on the
basis of their degrees of evolutionary advance, shows such an
uneven balance between the various races and breeds, that we
are forced to conclude that all of them stand at about equal dis-
tances from their common ancestor." Perhaps the real reason for
the long domination of Europeans over the so-called backward
races was reflected in the famous couplet:

> Whatever happens, we have got
> The Maxim gun and they have not.

The inaccuracy of most talk about racial differences becomes apparent when one turns to the evidence which scientists have accumulated in the past generation or two. Neither science nor the book of Genesis has had much effect, however. The Christian ethic of the brotherhood of man, as well as the story of Adam and Eve, turns out to be substantially in line with the latest findings in blood chemistry—*but the word does not get around*. What is the trouble?

Polls show large majorities of Americans believing that the intellectual inferiority of Negroes is inborn. Thus while real biological differences are slight, believed-in differences are transcendent. "Race, so to speak," says Robert Redfield, "is a human invention." It is not to be found in the blood count, but it has an enormous place in the culture. We have gone far enough in our exploration of social science to know what that means. It means an intangible force against which argument has little effect.

When a white tenant farmer south of the Mason-Dixon line joined a posse to keep Negroes "in their place," he was not necessarily either a brute or an enemy of society. He was following the accepted customs of the tribe, doing what he had been brought up to do. To him it was right and proper that Negroes should give way to whites. This he began to learn almost before he could walk. George Adams learned it, too, but less tenaciously.

In the deep South—for reasons too complicated to go into here, but partly tied up with the frustrations of the War between the States—a caste system has been developed almost as rigorous as that of India. In India it is religion, here it is race, on which one's rank is founded. To change the system suddenly would be as shocking to Southerners as the sudden elimination of Brahmins would be to Indians. Mark Twain in a magnificent passage reveals the conflict in Huck Finn after Huck saves the Negro Jim from being captured as a "runaway Nigger" before the Civil War. Huck feels that he has committed a major crime;

his whole moral code lies in ruins. "I got to feeling so mean and
so miserable I most wished I was dead."

Perhaps the only way to modify a caste system, in a culture
where it has been established, is to change beliefs in people's
minds. That is not done overnight. It probably can never be
done solely by appeals to reason, or by reading the Bill of Rights
in public parks.

PREJUDICE VS. DISCRIMINATION

It is important to understand the cardinal distinction between
race *prejudice* and race *discrimination.* Prejudice is a culture
pattern not susceptible to frontal attack, and not to be reasoned
about except within narrow limits. Discrimination, on the other
hand, is a specific, material thing, like keeping Negroes out of
schools, washrooms, restaurants, and making them ride in the
rear seats of buses.

Discrimination can be attacked, particularly in a country
where democratic traditions in other respects are strong.[4] A
specific Jim Crow practice can be selected for attack, and if
the strategy is well devised, the discrimination can be, and has
been, eliminated. Negroes are now being admitted into many
colleges in the South. As a discrimination is reduced, there is in
turn a reduction in prejudice. It develops, furthermore, in the
best way, by use and wont rather than by arguments and propaganda. "If the do-gooders in race relations would waste less
time fretting about prejudice and devote their efforts to the
reduction of specific, vulnerable cases of discrimination, real
progress could be made," says Donald Young.

Branch Rickey, manager of the Brooklyn baseball team, engi-
neered a famous example. He put a Negro, Jackie Robinson,
on first base in 1947 for the first time in big league history, and
backed him to the limit. It took great tact on Robinson's part
to survive the first two or three months and avoid a fight with

[4] Rigorous Jim Crow practices in the American South are of comparatively
recent origin, beginning about 1880. See Woodward, *The Strange Career of
Jim Crow.*

some of the players born in the South. By August, however, he was an accepted institution, batting, fielding, and base running with great brilliance. Other Negroes were then signed by Cleveland and St. Louis. John Chamberlain asked Rickey if he had fought for his first baseman to solve a sociological problem. "No," said Rickey, "I brought him up for one reason: to win the pennant! I'd play an elephant with pink horns if he could win the pennant."

This brings up the whole question of social engineering for better race relations. We will concentrate on the Negro problem in America, but the implications are world-wide. Most Southerners sincerely desire to see race relations improved. What methods are available in this direction? Leighton's book about Poston provides important suggestions, and Young has offered more.

Suppose the mayor of a city wants to guard against a race riot; suppose the president of a big steel company wants to introduce Negro workers into his mill; suppose a labor leader wants to persuade the rank and file to accept Negroes into the union? Social scientists can help plan his campaign.[5] They say that trouble always takes place at *some point* in the social structure—on a bus, at a factory gate, on a housing project, in a school. The social engineer studies these points and consults the growing literature about them. A War Department manual for white officers who were to lead Negro troops in World War II was prepared by a team of sociologists, psychologists, and anthropologists. Police handbooks now in use analyze the tensions that lead to race riots, and serve to alert police officers stationed in parts of a city where Negro and white communities merge—often a danger zone. Such technical studies are worth many manifestos about injustices and unconstitutionality.

The United States Armed Services are conducting a great program to abolish discrimination, aided by social science research. It was found that white soldiers who had no experience

[5] Donald Young's "Techniques of Race Relations." *Proceedings* of American Philosophical Society, November, 1947.

with Negro soldiers in World War II voted more than 90 percent against being brigaded with them. (Samuel A. Stouffer designed the polls.) Those who had limited contact were 67 percent against it. Those who were used to Negroes in the same regiment but not in the same company were 50 percent against. But white soldiers who had fought side by side with Negroes in the same company were *86 percent in favor of continuing the arrangement!*

"When I first heard about it," said a platoon sergeant from South Carolina, "I'd be damned if I'd wear the same shoulder patch with them. After that day when we saw how they fought, I changed my mind. They're just like any other boys to us." Elmo Roper, in summarizing Stouffer's findings, says that whites and Negroes got along well in the Army at the front because they had a common enemy, and had to depend on each other in battle. Nobody was conducting a moral crusade or appealing to the Constitution; far from it, American soldiers, with various percentages of *melanin,* were trying to win a war against stiff opposition.

These studies helped to hasten antidiscrimination programs after the war. A reporter at Fort Dix, New Jersey, found the Army program working well after six months of trial.[6] There had been no flare-ups, though the first days were rather tense. Negroes and whites were brigaded together, ate and played together; in some cases Negro officers had white enlisted men under them. The reporter asked a white private whether the Negroes in his platoon were good soldiers. "I never thought about it," he said. "Like everybody else, I guess, some good, some lousy."

Col. L. L. Gmeiner, the deputy post commander, summarized the situation at Fort Dix:

These young soldiers, put into large camps for the first time, have to learn to live together and work together. Under pressure of military necessity, we have found that they accomplish this adjustment in about two weeks.

[6] New York *Herald Tribune,* May 21, 1951.

The rigorous discipline of the Army makes an antidiscrimination program easier. Civilians usually take far longer than two weeks in learning to live and let live. United States public schools, in some localities, following the Supreme Court's decision of 1954, may require years. But the Army experience has abundantly verified social science theory.

EXPLODED BELIEFS ABOUT RACE

We used to think that the "Negro mind" could not aspire to much education above a vocational course, as taught in schools like Tuskegee and Hampton. Now we know that such a limitation is as false as it is cruel. Negro education should follow the regular American educational pattern, varying with individuals and economic opportunity, not with race.

We used to think that the Negro was particularly susceptible to delinquency and crime. His moral brakes were weak, and he just could not help himself when temptation crossed his path. Now we know that his brakes are as well lined as anybody else's, and that the trouble is cultural, not racial. If Negroes have a high crime rate, the social scientist investigates the slums in which they were reared, and the emotional security they got as children.

We used to think that Negroes were gifted with a special sense of song, rhythm, and dance. Now we know they are no more innately musical than the inhabitants of Aroostook County, Maine. If Negro children, or white children, or Balinese children, are brought up to sing and stamp their feet, they will sing and stamp their feet. Many Negroes are good at blues, but no better than Eddie Condon or Bix Beiderbecke.

Derogatory stereotypes ("big, black, buck nigger"), and sentimental stereotypes (Aunt Jemima with her pancakes) both harm race relations. Playing up Joe Louis, the boxer, as representing a special race of superathletes is very harmful. "Such credits imply a biological theory of race differences just as surely as do unfavorable stereotypes," says Young. The reaction to the brilliant career of George Washington Carver or Ralph Bunche should be "Why not?"—rather than the more general "Who would have thought it possible?"

Interracial tactics should be designed—we are still considering engineering—to let whites and Negroes become more and more used to each other along Main Street; in stores, hotels, trains, parks, theaters, buses, and other public places, acting like anybody else. The young soldier at Fort Dix had the right idea: "Like everybody else—some good, some lousy."

It is bad tactics to suppress news unfavorable to Negroes. Twisting statistics to show their achievements is not sound engineering either. The unvarnished truth will be found a more effective agent in the slow process of cultural change than slanted stories. Negroes are no worse, *and no better*, than the rest of us. Born not far from George Adams, I never solved the race problem for myself until I began to look at Negroes the way I looked at dark Italians or blond Scandinavians—different complexions from mine, otherwise *people*; not to be pitied or fussed over because of their race any more than Tony the fruit dealer or Greta Garbo.

Harping on conflict and injustice can be harmful too. The right to protest injustice must be maintained, but to indict a whole region for injustice, day in and day out, is to challenge retaliation. Every sensible observer sees that the Communists' campaign to raise a black rebellion in the South is a perfect formula for putting the clock back to carpetbagging days. Fewer realize that harping on "incidents," like the trial of the Scottsboro boys, has a similar, if less violent, effect. One of the stupidest things to do is to send agitators from the North down to protest an incident in the South.

There are more than 100 national organizations working on race relations today, not counting federal agencies. Most of them lack any means of measuring the effects of their propaganda. They send out leaflets and broadcasts and hope for the best. "The dearth of appropriate research and consequent lack of a proven base for action is one of the most conspicuous features of existing intergroup programs," says Robin M. Williams, Jr.

How much good will and how much good money is wasted on projects that ignore the known laws of human relations? How much of it boomerangs, to make a bad condition worse?

Race prejudice involves a prejudgment of individuals on the basis of a stereotype—"a Jap is a Jap," "a Nigger is a Nigger," —Mr. Z's trouble at Poston. It involves also a set of evaluations. A prejudiced individual brings to the issue certain beliefs about traits in others, favorable or unfavorable. It is interesting to note that an unfavorable prejudgment does not always rate the victim as inferior. In anti-Semitism the stereotype is sometimes the other way around—"the Jews are too smart."

HISTORIC DECISION

Negro children living in Negro districts are usually retarded in language compared to white children, but Negro children in mixed neighborhoods are practically equal. Segregation tends to slow down intellectual development.[7]

The United States Supreme Court made history—and gave Moscow propaganda a serious blow—when, in 1954, it ruled against separate public schools for white and Negro children. Most schools in the North have never had this separation—the schools and colleges I attended in Massachusetts almost always had Negroes in the classes—but the ratio of Negroes to whites is low compared with the South.

Now segregation is to be ended. After the Court spoke, certain border communities were first to end it, including Washington, D.C. Some states in the Deep South have tried to postpone the day. So drastic a cultural change always carries the possibility of serious trouble, and provides a rich field for demagogues to exploit.

Social scientists promptly moved to meet the challenge. Forty-four scientists, headed by Alfred McClung Lee of Brooklyn College, set up a committee of consultants to assist local communities in making the change. Robin M. Williams, Jr., and Margaret W. Ryan edited a book, *Schools in Transition: Com-*

[7] See Gordon Allport, *The Nature of Prejudice.*

munity Experiences in Desegregation, which describes the experience of 24 communities in giving up segregated public schools. "Where desegregation has been tried," the editors report, "the typical outcome has been eventual acceptance." Only in Cairo, Illinois, was violence reported, and that without bloodshed. Nowhere did the opposition remain organized very long after the change had been made. Citizens got used to it, like the soldiers at Fort Dix.

The scientists observe, however, that it is an uneven, shifting transition, not a sudden, massive change. General rules can help, but "there is no substitute for careful local diagnosis"—a survey of local conditions and tensions before any action is taken. Prejudice among the children themselves in the 24 communities studied was found to be slight. . . . "If the parents did not interfere the children got along all right."

A NOTE ON SOUTH AFRICA

In the United States, after a long and disgraceful period, citizens with a different *melanin* content are being accepted as fellow human beings. Lynching is becoming as obsolete as the duel,[8] while signal advances can be noted in the armed services, Southern universities, in restaurants, theaters, public transportation, big league baseball, labor union membership, employment opportunities (F.E.P.C.), and now in the public schools. Victory is far from won, but the curve is definitely up and has been mounting since the war.

In South Africa the curve is definitely down. In the United States whites outnumber the colored races, but in South Africa the reverse is true; Negroes, plus Indians, far outnumber the whites. Fear and insecurity are much greater among the whites —a major reason for the downward curve. Both prejudice and discrimination are bred of this fear. Negroes are excluded from many occupations, or admitted only to serve their own race. Unequal pay for equal work is the rule, with a large differential in favor of the whites. Negroes must live in designated areas,

[8] No lynchings recorded in 1952, 1953, 1954.

usually reeking slums. They cannot own land, and have no freedom of movement; passes must be shown if they travel. In the cities they must observe a nine o'clock curfew. They cannot vote.

Yet, Edmund Brunner points out, the white population is increasingly dependent on the Negroes for its standard of living. Whites in factory and industrial work are declining, Negroes increasing; and the rate is even more rapid in agriculture. The black man's brawn becomes a makeshift in place of machinery, but at a high economic cost, despite his low wages.

Careful studies show no evidence of inferior mental ability. The few Negroes who reach the universities—about 5 percent of the total enrollment—do well and some win honors. The nonwhite senior class of the McCord Zulu Hospital Nurses' Training School, in Durban, has for several years made the highest average score of any nursing school in the Union, on the final standardized examinations, set and graded by the government.

Bitterness among the majority is increasing, and this in turn breeds more fear and more repressive measures among the minority—a vicious circle if ever there was one! A heavy social cost is thus laid on top of the economic cost, and all the trend curves seem aiming for disaster. Here, as elsewhere, the social scientist finds himself confirming Abraham Lincoln when he reportedly said: "You can't keep a man in the gutter without getting into it with him."

13

Laws of Social Change

For three days after the bombing of Hiroshima, newspaper men approached many physicists, chemists, and zoologists in the University of Chicago with the question: "What does it mean to society?" Only at the end of the third day did it occur to one of the reporters to ask a social scientist. The moral does not need pointing. It is the chief reason why I am writing this book.

The social scientist whom the reporter finally consulted was William F. Ogburn of the department of sociology. It would be difficult to find a man better qualified to deal with the effects of new inventions. He is the major interpreter of the broad concept known as Social Change. For many years he has been running curves into the future, based on how people have behaved in the past, and has arrived at certain general conclusions about both the curves and the behavior.

Ogburn, together with Franz Boas and W. I. Thomas, helped to establish about 25 years ago an important landmark in the history of social science. They extended the culture concept into sociology, psychology, and other disciplines. Many earlier scientists had tried to explain the evolution of society by analogy with Darwin's theory, in terms of heredity, natural selection, and variation. The hypothesis was that social institutions progressed only as men's brains progressed. The modern white man in his white tie was contrasted with the savage in his nose ring. The *Queen Mary* was compared with a sailing barge, a parallel development.

This was all very pleasing, but there was a catch in it. As the years went by and more was learned about genetics, it became increasingly difficult to explain how the human cortex could have progressed so rapidly. The development of the *Queen Mary* took less than 100 generations—a span too short to allow much change in the brain or in the genes of ship designers.

How then *could* one account for the *Queen Mary?* Ogburn, pondering this question, measured the brain case in the skull of a Cro-Magnon man, who lived 12,000 years ago. He found that it contained about as many cubic centimeters as that of modern man. More tests were made, and the conclusion was established that the brain case and facial characteristics of the Stone Age men of France—the artists who etched those dynamic buffaloes on the walls of caves—were no more primitive than those of the faculty of any university you care to name.

Was the mind of Cro-Magnon man as powerful an instrument as our own? Did it have the same 15 billion electrical connections in its switchboard? The evidence seemed to run in that direction. So scientists began searching for another hypothesis, and found it in the culture concept. Even if we hand down no more mental ability to our children today than our ancestors did 12,000 years ago, we do hand down the laws of thermodynamics, analytical geometry, and how to split the atom. Our children today have an enormous cultural storehouse to work with.

THE LAW OF GROWTH

When to this conclusion is added the demonstration that material culture grows like compound interest, things begin to fall neatly into place. The theory of the evolution of the brain can be discarded in favor of a theory which fits the facts more closely. Invention, exponential growth, and cultural development account for the *Queen Mary* quite satisfactorily.

In Ice Age days the material culture transmitted from generation to generation was limited in amount, and changed very slowly. Gradually new inventions in weapons, foods, clothing, equipment came into use and the rate of change increased. If the number of inventions from our Cro-Magnon ancestors to the present could be plotted on a chart, the resulting curve would rise first slowly, then more and more steeply, approximating a compound interest curve.

What an exponential rate of growth means has been dramatized in the story of the farmer who brought his horse to be shod. The blacksmith said he would charge one cent for the first nail, two cents for the second nail, four cents for the third, and so on until the job was done. That seemed reasonable to the farmer, and he accepted the offer. But the farmer had not fooled around with exponential curves. For eight nails in each shoe, or 32 nails altogether, the bill came to just $42,949,672.95! (You may take your pencil and prove it—as I did when I first heard the story.)

Ogburn has assembled a number of these curves, and they all point in the same general direction. He took Darmstaedter's ponderous record of inventions from 1450 to 1899, and plotted the number over four and a half centuries. He took the number of patents issued in the United States and Great Britain; he took various records of discoveries in physics and the other natural sciences. All show exponential rates of growth.

Harvey C. Lehman, in a recent paper,[1] has carried on the analysis. He plotted contributions to chemistry, genetics, geology, mathematics, medicine, pathology, entomology, and botany for the past three or four centuries, on a 25-year time scale. They all show the typical compound interest curve. In chemistry, for instance, 688 contributions out of a total of 1616 noted since 1500 A.D. occur in the *last* 25-year period studied—1875 to 1900. There is no diminution in any of these subjects after 1900. Even contributions to subjects like economics, political science, education, philosophy, music, show similar curves. Lehman concludes: "with each succeeding interval, man's creative output . . . has tended to double in amount." The increase has been in the order, per unit of time, not of 1, 2, 3, 4, but of 1, 2, 4, 8—and what a difference, as the farmer found out!

[1] "Exponential Increase of Man's Cultural Output," *Journal of Social Forces,* March, 1947.

The theory behind the graphs is that the larger the number of elements in material culture, the greater the number of possible inventions and improvements. Three elements can be combined in four different ways, but four elements can be combined in ten different ways. (Try it with playing cards.) Therefore, as the number of inventions increases, technological change becomes faster and faster. Man can thus proceed from a damp cave to the Waldorf-Astoria on the exponential law without needing any increase in his intelligence.

Let us reverse the proposition. If H. G. Wells's time machine were in good working order, and if it could carry 1,000 babies from the brightest of modern parents to be reared by Cro-Magnon mothers, it is very doubtful whether they would speed up progress. There was not enough in the storehouse for them to work on in 10,000 B.C. We catch a glimpse of the same idea when we realize that even if Leonardo had evolved the laws of an airplane in flight, he could never have flown it (except as a glider) because no engine had yet been invented to power it.

CULTURAL LAG

It is necessary to distinguish clearly between: (1) material inventions, (2) human behavior resulting from the inventions, and (3) cultural institutions and systems of belief.

Inventions are usually accepted into the culture in two stages. To begin with, people change their day-by-day behavior to accommodate the new device. If it is a useful device, like radio broadcasting, this may happen fairly soon, a matter of ten or fifteen years. Americans are particularly spry at moving over and making room for new material inventions. Then, considerably later on, people change their institutions and belief systems to allow for the invention, and arrange means for controlling its effects. The time between the first and second stages is known as the *cultural lag*.

The invention of the steam engine made inanimate energy practicable in workshops and factories to run machines. There was some opposition by hand workers, but not much. Because the tempo of the machine, not the tempo of the man, now dominated the process, industrial accidents became more frequent. In the United States, it took about 75 years before workmen's compensation laws were inaugurated to offset the accidents. Such laws ran counter to a belief system of prefactory society, namely, that it was the workman's duty to look out for himself. And indeed when the worker had control of the process in his own home or shop, it *was* his duty. This particular cultural lag can be measured not only in years but also in the number of pauperized widows and maimed workers over the period.

The invention of the automobile was joyously accepted by nearly everyone but carriage makers. The cultural lag was relatively brief in America. Laws were passed almost immediately in an attempt to control its speed and direction. The Amish community of Wayne County, Ohio, a kind of cultural pocket, still forbids its members to use automobiles as inventions of the Devil, encouraging the sin of pride.

Andrew Yoder, a member of the community, was, however, confronted with a practical problem. He had to drive his baby daughter twice a week for treatment to a doctor who lived 15 miles away. Finally Andrew could no longer stand the trip in a horse-drawn buggy. He bought a car and learned to drive it—only to be ostracized by the community. He was still allowed to work but was deprived of social intercourse. His own brother would not eat with him. When out threshing he had to take his meals alone. "It was like feeding a dog out of a dishpan," he told a reporter from *Time*. No Amish cobbler would repair his shoes. The cultural lag governing automobiles held firm in Wayne County, if not in the rest of the United States.

By and large, the motor car has brought at least as much fundamental change in the life of the American people as the horse did in the life of the Plains Indians. In such institutions as traffic courts and parking facilities we are still trying to catch up, without much success.

Some of the most perplexing problems of the present time—mass unemployment, inadequate housing, economic insecurity—

are really problems in cultural lag. We have the economic tools available to cope with them, but community feelings will not permit it. Congress votes against it, often with a lofty sense of moral righteousness. Belief systems have not caught up with the facts. One of the most cruel illustrations of this is the full generation which elapsed between the introduction of the child labor law and its final passage. Robert Lynd in *Knowledge for What?* lists other lags, as of 1940:

The ragged disparities in marriage and divorce laws among the several States.

The taboo against discussing venereal disease (now lifting).

The opposition of the American Medical Association to government aid in medicine.

The resistance of almost 90 percent of the press to the social legislation of the 1930's.

ARE WE GOING TO HIT SOMETHING?

Another curious paradox arising from the cultural lag is the ample financial support given by society to encourage more material inventions, and the meager support for social inventions to mitigate their effects.

It is a fearful thing to be aboard an exponential curve—something like an express train out of control. Ultimately, such curves run off the map. A penny at compound interest grows in a few centuries to a ball of gold the size of the planet. Nature often permits such curves to start, as in the multiplication of fruit flies, but she never maintains them for long. They always hit something and shrink with great suddenness.

Are we going to hit something? Ogburn is too careful a scientist to say. He does point out, however, that when an invention like the atomic bomb comes along, social scientists should be urged to do their utmost to find a social invention to cope with it. He does not believe it is possible deliberately to halt the rate of material invention. Can you imagine Congress passing a law to "halt progress"? The answer to the tensions caused by growth curves seems to lie in encouraging steeper curves in social invention.

A social change, when measured statistically, is called a time series, and is described by zigzag lines which move over time, with a sweep or trend in one general direction. An appropriate equation, fitted by the method of least squares, runs through the middle of the zigzags and indicates the trend. We do not know why these trends rarely change their direction, although they are undoubtedly connected with culture patterns and probably with methods of education. Whatever the explanation, social trend lines in hundreds of cases show remarkable inertia. There is a lesson here for social engineers. If a trend cannot be changed radically, it is better to accept it and adjust your program to it. If you are determined to change it, prepare to see the shift take place slowly. Or else analyze the connection between the educational system and cultural change. So far, to my knowledge, no one has adequately realized this problem. Perhaps John Dewey came closest.

The exponential law casts a heavy shadow on the Great Man theory of progress. This theory holds in essence that without the giants of the past we would still be living in Mesopotamian mud huts. The exponential law, on the contrary, indicates that what determines new invention is not a giant intellect so much as the number of elements in the culture. Thus when physics reached a certain point of development in the seventeenth century, and a dynamic mathematics was needed to carry on, both Leibnitz and Newton invented the calculus. If neither had lived, calculus would have been invented by somebody else. History is filled with simultaneous inventions of this kind. We can expect more and more of them as knowledge accumulates.

If Columbus had died of plague before he discovered America, some other explorer would soon have found it. Why? Because the techniques of ship-building and navigation had reached a point where a man could sail into the unknown with a fair chance of getting back.

THE INVENTION OF RADIO

Over the years Ogburn, together with other scientists, has developed many variations on the theme of Social Change. He has shown how the interrelated parts of modern culture are changing at unequal rates with consequent strains. He has traced the succeeding waves of new behavior which follow important inventions like the automobile and the radio. He has pushed trend curves boldly into the future to find out what the probable effects of a new invention are likely to be.

Take, for instance, his work on radio. In *Recent Social Trends* he lists 150 effects, of which 12 are in the direction of cultural diffusion, tending to "standardize" listeners. Some may deplore this tendency; others realize that a more homogeneous people may have less internal strife. Here are some effects of radio listed by Ogburn:

Regional differences becoming less pronounced.

Penetration of city musical and artistic culture into rural areas.

Distinction between social classes lessened.

Isolated regions brought into contact with world events.

Illiterates brought back into community life.

Concentration on fewer languages.

Canada, the United States, and Latin America drawn more closely together.

One item on the list reads: "Interest in sports increased by radio." True enough; who can forget those first championship boxing matches over the air! Not content with this single statement, Ogburn goes on to outline 15 derivative effects of radio in the area of sports, a kind of secondary wave. Among them:

Big matches emphasized to the neglect of local matches.

Reputation of star athletes further inflated.

Reputation of star football coaches also inflated, plus an increase in their salaries.

Recruiting of players in rural areas greatly increased.

Colleges with high scholastic standards put at a disadvantage.

Reduction in special sports editions of newspapers.

Sixty-one effects following the invention of x-rays have been chronicled by Ogburn; 23 following rayon; 150 following the automobile—including a change in the whole pattern of courtship in America. The young man with the convertible has displaced the young man with the bouquet.

This is all very interesting and possibly all very scientific, you say, but what can one *do* with such studies? Ogburn offers us a monumental answer to that question, too. The United Air Lines retained him to predict the probable effects of the invention of the airplane over the next ten to twenty years, and his report runs to more than 700 pages. We are reminded early that there are some 50 variables to be considered in plotting the extrapolation. No one can know exactly what the place of civil aviation will be in 1970 or 1980, but an estimate based on trend curves looks like a safer probability than one based on a blind guess or on wishful thinking. Managers of airports, airplane companies, commercial airlines, federal, state, and city officials, real estate interests, all must now plan for the future on *some* basis. Meanwhile, the investments involved, both public and private, are enormous.

"ELEMENTARY, MY DEAR WATSON"

Sherlock Holmes, philosophizing on Boyle's Law of Gases, said to his friend Watson: "While the individual man is an insoluble puzzle, in the aggregate he becomes a mathematical certainty. You can never foretell what any one man will do, but you can say with precision what an average number will be up to. Individuals vary but percentages remain constant." Social scientists, using this statistical approach, can give community leaders invaluable advice about future problems.

The life expectancy of American males (or females) can be predicted with great accuracy, although it is impossible to foretell when $Adam_1$ or Eve_2 will die. Using probability theory, furthermore, margins of error can be calculated, indicating how far off a prediction may be—say plus or minus 4 percent. The Royal Society, we remember, started actuarial science three centuries ago. The United States Census is not a vast mass of undigested figures as many people seem to think, but a helpful guide to programs for housing, schools, public services.

In 1955 there were about 15 million persons in the New York metropolitan area. The Regional Plan Association, using census figures, predicted upwards of 19 million by 1975—an increase of 28 percent. This in turn called for a new survey "very much more imaginative than has been displayed in the past to plan for this massive addition," and providing more transportation facilities, recreation centers, sewers, shopping centers, schools, and parking lots.

SCHOOLS AND HOUSES

Suppose we concentrate for a moment on schools—not desegregation this time, but classrooms, teachers, and textbooks. The National Citizens' Committee for the Public Schools, headed by Beardsley Ruml,[2] predicted 12 million more children of school age in the population by 1965 than there were in 1954. This would bring the total school population to 48 million youngsters, a 33 percent increase, at a cost of $3.5 billion more in 1965. For the whole nation to match the educational plant of New York State (tops for the country, though still inadequate), would cost $17.1 billion more in 1965. No fewer than 950,000 new classrooms would be needed by 1965, at a capital cost of $32 billion.

The building boom in houses which began after World War II is still booming. Are we building too many houses? For the whole United States, says Edmund Brunner,[3] that is not a difficult question to answer, and here is the way to go about it:

We know how many persons there are in the United States in each age group. Therefore we know how many are under twenty-one, and the probable number—based on past performance—who will leave school, enter the labor force, and marry, year by year. We know how many families will be formed, and how many "dwelling units" they will require. We know how

[2] Report summarized in *Time*, December 13, 1954.
[3] Memorandum to the author.

many units burn up, or are torn down, every year, and how many new ones are now being built. Putting these figures together, it does not take an electronic brain to calculate how many units will be needed in the years ahead, and whether we are overbuilding or underbuilding.

On similar principles, scientists can calculate the probable size of the labor force ten years hence, the food requirements of future populations, the need for doctors, nurses, and engineers, the number of old people and their percentage of total population—the last a growing figure and full of thorny problems. Brunner estimates that population increases should solve the "farm problem" in the United States in another ten to twelve years, as agricultural surpluses are progressively consumed by urban eaters.

When social scientists in the mid-1930's looked at the 1930 census figures, says Brunner, they found that the United States had reached an all-time high in youth population, sixteen to twenty-four years of age. So they promptly urged a big housing program, especially as construction had meanwhile slowed down during the depression. They predicted that if this were *not* done, families would be doubling up by the 1940's, with a heavy strain on human relations. The program was not undertaken. American families were crowded as never before, often ready to tear each other apart—exactly as predicted.

FAMOUS CURVE

Another statistical law which vitally affects human behavior is the frequency distribution curve. Biologists use it too, for it applies to all living things, as well as to many human characteristics and problems.

Take the height of men in the army. Line them up—the figures, not the men—the tallest at one end, the shortest at the other. The probability of a soldier being near the middle is great, of his being at either end is small. If we now plot the number of soldiers at the various points on the scale we will get the familiar bell-shaped curve.

The curve is a great help in making predictions about schools, desks, hospitals, markets, army uniforms and boots to be ordered, all manner of things. It is useful in plotting IQ's, and is even employed in marking examination papers.

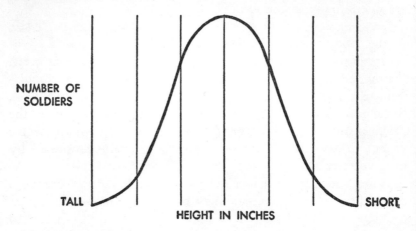

NUMBER OF SOLDIERS

TALL   HEIGHT IN INCHES   SHORT

It is also, I may add, the greatest destroyer known to man of the bad habit of overgeneralizing. With the frequency distribution curve in one's tool kit, no one can continue to say that all Mexicans are lazy, that all Swedes are blond, that all Russians are untrustworthy, or that all United States senators rival Socrates. Some do and some don't, as the anthropologists observe. Plot them on the curve.

As modern living grows more complicated large plans for the future become more mandatory. Social scientists, like Ogburn and Brunner, with curves based on vital statistics and other dependable data, render an indispensable service. "Planning," somebody has said, "is intelligent coöperation with the inevitable."

14

In Darkest Middletown

In my library I have a "Middletown" shelf of a score of volumes, which I enjoy collecting as others collect ship models. The collection started in 1929 when I reviewed Robert and Helen Lynd's *Middletown* and found it new and exciting territory. Later, in a book about Mexico, I compared Middletown with Robert Redfield's study of Tepoztlan, an Aztec town on the Mexican plateau. This cross-cultural survey of mine, strictly an amateur performance, served to bring out some of the striking differences between handicraft societies and those of the machine age.

Clark Wissler said, in his introduction to the original *Middletown*: "We are always hearing that the study of society must be made objective. . . . The realities of social science are what people do." Here then, for the first time, is a study of the things people do in a normal American small city, observed as social scientists would observe a town in darkest Africa. There had been plenty of earlier urban surveys in the United States and Britain, but they were primarily concerned with coal miners, or working girls, or with wages, housing, the cost of living.[1] The Lynds tried to comprehend the whole community. "A new field of science has been opened up," said Dr. Wissler, "the social anthropology of contemporary life."

There were 38,000 people in Middletown—which everybody now knows is Muncie, Indiana—when the Lynds arrived with their small staff in 1924. The great boom of the 1920's was fairly

[1] Famous pre-Middletown studies were *Life and Labor of the People in London,* by the Booths, and the *Pittsburgh Survey* of the Russell Sage Foundation. Rural sociologists had also made studies of American small communities, beginning with Warren H. Wilson's *Quaker Hill.*

launched, buoyed up by the soaring automotive industries. Middletown had been chosen among many candidates because it was as American as a baked apple. Manufacturing was diversified, with the glass jar business prominent. Farmers came in from the rich surrounding corn lands to Saturday market at the county seat.

There were 42 churches in town and 6,300 automobiles. Said a factory worker from the South Side: "I'd go without a meal before I'd cut down on using the car." Said a police court judge after a difficult day: "The automobile has become a house of prostitution on wheels."

The Lynds stayed for nearly two years, studying the town in action under six main headings: (1) getting a living, (2) making a home, (3) training the young, (4) using leisure, (5) going to church, (6) joining up. Before they got through, 454 active clubs and associations had been identified, including, along with the Chamber of Commerce, the Lions, and the Elks, an Ad Club, a Kill Kare Klub, and the Sew We Do Club for well-to-do matrons.

The Lynds gathered material by first-hand interviews, by questionnaire, by analyzing newspapers, by direct counting. They also obtained all relevant United States census figures covering the town, together with state and city statistics. When we finish reading the section on getting a living we know as never before the economy of the 1920's. We realize in an intimate, graphic way how the boys and girls that we see playing in the school yards of Middletown are later to be indiscriminately tumbled into the 400 occupations which the city affords. We see the shops, offices, factories in which they are to work; the machines they are to operate; the houses, bungalows, and shacks in which they are to live and raise their families; the stores in which they will buy their goods; the advertisements which will so often predetermine their wants; the editorials, sermons, service club speeches which will nourish their belief systems; the income groups into which they are bound to fall with the precision of a life expectancy table.

In the Nineties

The Middletown survey, furthermore, compares the 1920's with the 1890's. Wissler calls it "a new kind of history." The authors try to reconstruct the community as it looked a generation earlier. "A small river wanders through the town, and in 1890 when timber still stood on its banks, it was a pleasant stream for picnics, fishing, and boating, but it has shrunk today to a creek discolored by industrial chemicals and malodorous with the city's sewage."

Workingmen in 1924 still attend lyceums and listen to some of the old lecture topics—"Milton as an Educator"—but businessmen have given up this type of "culture" altogether. The singing societies of the nineties have disappeared, save for one working class exception. The Apollo Club, once favored by the bloods of the town, has long since collapsed. Where are 300 schoolboys to sing Gounod in the Opera House? The Art Students' League was organized in 1892, and members went sketching along the clear waters of White River. The Art Club of 1925 listens to lectures on the Gothic Period and never handles a brush or tube of paint. Music, like poetry and the other arts, is almost nonexistent among the men of Middletown in the era of Calvin Coolidge. In the light of Linton's universals this shows how abnormal Main Street has become.

Everyone rides in a car, goes to the movies; more and more people are turning on the radio. One salty old character came back to Middletown for a brief visit in 1924. "These people," he complained, "are afraid of something." The Lynds point out that amid an ideology celebrating the ruggedest kind of rugged individualism, nobody along Main Street dared to be different. Again and again the word "bewilderment" creeps into the text. Citizens are bewildered about their jobs, about money, about the new "gob feeder" in the glass factory, which can make glass bottles a hundred times faster than a hand blower; they are bewildered about marriage, religion, the growing role of government; about their children, about their very souls.

The old traditions survive—many survive today for that matter—but even in the twenties there is little blood in them. A pecuniary economy and mass production call insistently for new systems of belief, but these have not yet crystallized. The lag grows longer. Back of the Buicks and the backslapping, one feels in the Lynds' account the confusion of a generation which has lost its way.

Down, Down, Down

The Lynds went to Middletown to check their findings in 1935, after ten years had gone by—four more years of boom, then six of depression. They wrote another report on it, called *Middletown in Transition*. At a time when employment is near capacity, it is almost incredible to recall how far the nation dropped in the great depression. By 1933, Middletown's storekeepers had lost 57 percent of their business compared with 1929—yet there were 6 percent more stores struggling to survive. Building construction fell to 5 percent of 1929 while factory payrolls were cut in half. Motor car sales dropped 78 percent, but gasoline sales only four percent; the cars were old, but people kept on driving them. Loan sharks did a thriving business. When General Motors tore the machinery out of their big plant and left town, it looked as though the end had come. A full quarter of Middletown was on relief.

Yet for two years following the stock market crash, the leaders of the town refused to admit that their symbols of progress —self-help, bigger motor cars, bigger bank accounts and land values—could ever be tarnished. Not until General Motors shut its plant did they face reality, and then only for a brief interval. In 1934 the first federal farm relief checks, like gentle rain on parched ground, began to irrigate the Saturday market, as farmers drove in to cash them. Soon Middletown's leaders recovered their standard credos . . . "When Mr. Landon is elected president—as the *Literary Digest* poll shows he is sure to be—everything will be safe and sound again."

Across the tracks[2] on the South Side, however, the workers had pretty well abandoned their predepression ideas, and were organizing unions as never before. The great sit-down strike era is close at hand, and we must remember that for every three townsmen on Main Street, there are seven workers across the tracks.

THE MIDDLETOWN CREDO

In a chapter entitled "The Middletown Spirit," the Lynds preserve for the curious historian the credo of Midwest America in 1928. No fewer than 172 beliefs are categorically set down. As I scan the list today, I should estimate that about 100 of these beliefs have been rendered obsolete in whole or in part by the march of events. Some, of course, were specimens of cultural lag even when most fiercely held. Here is a sample lot:

That economic conditions are the result of natural order and cannot be changed by man-made laws.

That we always had depressions and always will.

That men won't work unless they have to.

That any man willing to work can get a job.

That business makes all our employment.

That the open shop is the American way, and labor unions are foolish, if not wicked.

That all strikes are due to troublemakers.

That the individual must fend for himself and in the end gets what he deserves.

That the small businessman is the backbone of America.

That women cannot be expected to understand public problems.

That the American form of government is the final and ideal form.

That government is bad and politicians are the lowest form of life.

[2] "Across the tracks" is an important symbol in the American culture, dividing those who have arrived from those who have not.

That high tariffs mean protection to the American wage earner against the pauper labor of Europe.

That taxes are always evil.

That Christianity is the final form of religion.

That preachers are rather impractical people who wouldn't be likely to make good in business.

That you can't change human nature.

What happened in Middletown from 1929 to 1939 defied almost every canon of this credo. Main Street deplored federal aids for community survival and ridiculed them in a vast folk literature of stories about "boondoggling."[3] At the same time it clawed like a drowning man for more federal relief. Its belief systems were thus in direct opposition to its tangible behavior—creating a kind of community schizophrenia.

So Middletown learned nothing from a world war, a crazy stock market boom, and a depression which made beggars of a quarter of its people? No, it is not so simple as that. Middletown, like every community, must have a suit of symbolic clothes. If no new styles are on the market the old will have to do. Middletown—at least the North Side—still wears the ancient garments, but the simple faith has gone. Below the surface, Middletown is in profound ideological turmoil and transition.

PLAINVILLE, USA

Running along my book shelf, we pick out *Plainville, USA*, by James West. The author, an anthropologist, knew exactly the kind of town he wanted to study. After a long search he found a rural community of under 1,000 people in the Midwest which fitted his specifications. He made the analysis alone, between June, 1939, and August, 1941, as part of a larger study on acculturation, financed by Columbia and directed by Ralph Linton.

Plainville is a far less complicated community than Middletown. There are no factories, and marginal farming is the principal way to make a living. Yet the same contradiction is to be found out here on the prairies as along the Wabash. *People do*

[3] Foolish and wasteful make-work programs.

not believe in what they are in fact doing. During the great
depression Plainville shifted from an individualistic to a welfare
economy—it had to or starve—but almost nobody approves of
it. Charity and relief in 1940 have become functions of the federal government, except for a little private charity still carried
on by one church. All the federal agencies are utilized to the
fullest extent, yet they are denounced constantly for "ruining
this country," "making people unwilling to work," "meddling
with other people's business. . . ."

A whole new form of rural social organization has been insti-
tuted under the government's agricultural program—subsidized
prices for crops, soil conservation work, farm credit, rural elec-
trification, government-promoted cooperatives, and the rest.
The older system of farm operation, social aims, and personal
security is disintegrating, but reaction to the new pattern is
turbulent. Nowhere have I seen the agricultural revolution
which has struck America since 1933 more vividly described.

Mr. West's working methods are interesting. He made the
rounds of "several notable loafing centers," collected gossip and
news at every opportunity, attended church bazaars, basket
dinners, funerals, baseball games, pie suppers, public auctions.
He taught in the high school as a substitute when a teacher was
sick, and joined a number of clubs and organizations. Afternoon
and evening were often spent in interviews. These interviews
varied from a total of two hours to several hundred hours per
person. He took life histories of eight adults, ranging from
30,000 to 75,000 words each. He hired high school students
to record their "autobiographies," some running to 50,000
words, under the general style of "I Remember."

He ransacked the county courthouse records, and those of
the AAA, FSA, and other federal agencies; he combed files
of the weekly newspaper back to 1885. He read genealogies
and the *History of Woodland County.* He sums up this material
with the surprising statement: "Even in an isolated community
like Plainville, there exists so vast a body of relevant printed
and other documentary material, that no one could read it all

in a lifetime." Mr. West's freestyle interviewing contrasts with the structured interviews of rural sociologists, where in some cases every respondent is asked the same series of questions.

DEEP SOUTH

Beside *Plainville* on the shelf is *Deep South*. Four social scientists, trained at Harvard, lived for a year and a half in the 1920's in a southern city of 10,000, studying its culture. More than 5,000 pages of typewritten notes form the basis for the book, together with statistical records of the town and the surrounding countryside. The investigators were two married couples, one couple white, one Negro, who thus had unparalleled opportunity to check events from both sides of the color line.

Deep South, by Davis and Gardner, describes the plantation system, both before and after the Civil War. We are shown the romantic memories which are preserved in the belief systems of the upper class, and also the tangible facts of history and sociology.

Ruth and Josephine took up the fight and went back generations telling each other things about their families, digging up things that nobody wants to hear about. That is the way people do here. If they once get mad with you, they don't just be mad with you—they go back as far as they can—telling stories on each other's ancestors.

The greatest insult possible in "Old City" is to defame one's "original ancestor," the cotton planter who founded the family. No attention is paid to *his* forbears—they can be burglars or pirates—it does not matter. The whole belief system of the upper class comes to rest about the year 1840. Nothing since then amounts to much. Naturally this emphasis affects all the town's behavior—10,000 people walking slowly backward. "A very old woman may be said to be a symbol of the upper class group. . . . The ritual and deference surrounding her attendance at a group gathering—generally limited by her great age to afternoon tea—is suggestive of royalty." She is the cherished link with the past, the closest living symbol of "the old days."

In the old days the planter aristocracy was recognized as

superior to all white freemen, who in turn were superior to all black slaves. This pattern was destroyed in the Civil War, but after some floundering in the dark days of reconstruction, "a new social system in Old City and its countryside began to evolve. It, too, organized the relation of Negroes and whites among themselves and with each other." It divided the occupations carefully, too—Negroes getting the more unpleasant tasks.

CLASS AND CASTE

A curious and interesting change gradually took place. Nobody should write seriously about race relations in America without mastering this change, for it extends throughout the deep South. The investigators call it the emergence of a *class and caste system.*[4] Educated Negroes, such as doctors and professional people, "recognize themselves and *are recognized* as being different from the laborers and domestics who now work for both whites and Negroes." The following diagram helps to visualize the system:

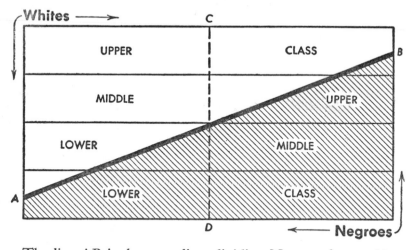

The line AB is the caste line, dividing Negroes from whites. No Negro may ever marry a white person. Other rules may be broken, this one never. A caste system by definition forbids

[4] We referred to it earlier in Chapter 12 when discussing race.

intermarriage across a caste line, and considers any offspring of mixed unions illegitimate.

But on the Negro side of the line, as well as on the white, classes form—upper, middle, and lower. The white middle class has standards similar to the Negro upper class; the white lower to the Negro middle class. People can marry across *class* lines, and can move up and down across the lines. It is not easy or frequent, but it does happen. This mobility is what distinguishes a class from a caste system. In the latter one is frozen, in the former he can move.

Before the Civil War the line AB was not skewed but *horizontal;* there were no Negro professional people, no Negro upper class. Slaves were in the subcellar, considered a different species altogether. Will the line AB continue to revolve until it approximates CD? Then the races would be truly equal, though still separate.

OTHER MIDDLETOWNS

There are many more books on the shelf. Here is *Preface to Peasantry*, a study of two Black Belt counties by Arthur F. Raper, particularly interesting for its description of how the New Deal came to darkest Georgia. To jump 5,000 miles north, here is *Arctic Village* by the late Robert Marshall. By profession a forester, Mr. Marshall determined IQ's and other data about every person in a small Alaskan town, including the Eskimos. He lived there all winter, writing notes in his shack at night.

Here is *Small Town Stuff* by Albert Blumenthal, a keen analysis of a mining town in Montana; *Small Town* by Granville Hicks, the most readable of the lot but the most personal. Here is *Wilton: A Study of Suburbanization* (from where I am writing I can almost throw a stone into Wilton); *Elmtown's Youth*, and a dozen more.

DOCUMENTARY

Let us take down *Home Town: The Face of America* by Sherwood Anderson, and look over the photographs. This is a special kind of scientific record, one which may have a considerable future. Instead of a man with a notebook, we have a man with a camera. Anderson's prose is, as usual, admirable, but the pictures tell us even more.

To get these pictures, Roy Stryker of the Farm Security Administration dispatched expert photographers all over America with instructions to record what people were doing—no posing, no retouching, no tricks; the straight documentary story. More than 35,000 negatives were collected. *Home Town*, accordingly, is not an account of a specific community, but a generalized picture of small-town life in the 1930's—Main Street, the Methodist Church, Town Meeting, Back of the Tracks, the Civil War Monument, the Church Supper, the Drug Store, One Room School, Front Porch, Saloon, Movie House, Shacktown, Poker Game, Filling Station, Service Club Lunch, Revival Meeting, Town Constable. . . .

We have in this Stryker collection a kind of visual sampling report—telling more, in one way, than any table of figures. . . . Cornfields in Iowa to make a farmer's mouth water, dust and drought in Colorado to dry anybody's throat, pictures of sunny rural peace, terrible pictures of rural poverty. The weathered faces of men, the faces of women sagging with household drudgery, the pinched faces of children, the cow barn, the farmer's tools, the sharecropper's rags—"they are all here, photographed in their context, in relation to their environment. In rows of filing cabinets they wait for today's town planner and tomorrow's historian."

YANKEE CITY

So we come to the published volumes of the Yankee City series—the most ambitious Middletown to date. It is the costliest, most searching and technical of them all. Thirty scientists worked on it over a five-year period from 1930 to 1934— though they were not all working at once.

W. Lloyd Warner, back from a three-year study of Stone Age peoples in Australia, was appointed director. With him were associated scientists from Harvard, Chicago, and Yale, and

Paul S. Lunt was his first lieutenant. The Crane Memorial Fund underwrote the project.

Two regions in America had been selected as having the most stable local cultures—New England and the South. A city was chosen in each region for intensive analysis. Of the southern project we have already caught a glimpse in *Deep South*. The northern one was far more ambitious. The city chosen was Newburyport, Massachusetts, once a great clipper-ship port at the mouth of the Merrimack river. Now its seafaring activities have declined to a little clamming along the mud flats, but factories making shoes, silverware, and other products keep the people employed in normal times. The old China trade families on Hill Street, each in its stately colonial mansion crowned by a captain's walk, rival the plantation families of Old City in pride of ancestors. The whole town, on the rising ground above the river, displays an architecture more gracious than America has built for a hundred years.

When the social scientists moved in, there were 17,000 men, women, and children in Yankee City. When they moved out, they carried punch cards for every citizen, with notations showing age, sex, class, status, occupation, clubs, religion, political affiliation, housing, health, income, expenditures, property owned, education, magazines read—and Heaven knows what. By running the cards through a machine, they could classify everyone in town in every conceivable manner. No community of this size ever had such a going over.

The research staff was particularly interested in the class structure of Yankee City. Who outranked whom—in the family system, in the factory, in ethnic groups like the Irish, Jews, Poles, French Canadians, Negroes? It was concerned with housing, property rights, sources of income, clubs and cliques, churches, schools, and the political framework of the town. . . . It is all there, in immense detail.

In the middle sections of Volume I we find a novel experiment in social science. Here are a dozen very human short stories, drawn from the punch cards and the notebooks, but with fictitious names. One of them begins like this:

Mr. Charles Watson, the superintendent of the cemetery, squatted on his haunches while he supervised the pick-and-shovel activities of two workmen. It was hot. . . . A shoveler stopped his work and lit a cigaret. "Why the hell can't Phil Starr leave his old man and old lady rest in peace? Why they've been down in this grave thirty years. And now, by God, he's digging them up and running all over town with them. I say once they're buried, let them stay buried."

And another:

Going home after he had said goodnight, Sam Jones crawled in bed beside his wife, and the springs sank in the middle. Three small children were asleep on a mattress in the corner of the room. Two adolescent daughters slept on cots next to the wood stove in the kitchen. . . . It had suddenly turned bitter cold. The kitchen table was still littered with the remains of the evening meal.

These stories have an effect like the photographs in *Small Town*; they tell about people in a vivid human way and put flesh and blood on the cold statistical tables and the charts.

The Six Classes

The research staff had not been long in town before a cherished hypothesis was upset. They began their labors believing that the fundamental structure of American society was *economic*—rich on top, poor on the bottom—and that the richer you were the more prestige you had. But evidence began to accumulate which made it difficult to accept this simple thesis. Six classes were finally identified by the people of the town themselves. "She's one of those Hill Street snobs. . . ." "He runs around with the Riverbrook gang. . . ." There were borderline cases, of course, but after thousands of interviews, nearly everyone in town was placed in one of six classes as follows:

1. Upper upper   3. Upper middle   5. Upper lower
2. Lower upper   4. Lower middle   6. Lower lower

It was found that the rich were not necessarily on top, nor the poor necessarily on the bottom. The richest class was the lower upper, while some of the old families in the upper upper class were poor as church mice. Also it was interesting to note that many of the clammers in the lower lower class, who lived in shacks along the river, were descended from the same Anglo-Saxon forebears as the great folk on Hill Street. When fate beckoned they had preferred clammin' to smuggling.

This, observe, was a class system, not a caste system. Observe, too, that it bore little relation to the Marxist "class struggle." People moved up and down from class to class, but mostly up; and occasionally they married across class lines. The upper uppers were without exception old Yankee stock, but the Irish were breaking into the lower upper, Jews and Italians into the upper middle. It is an exhilarating sight to see steerage immigrants from the old country land first in the lower lower, and then ascend as in a slow elevator, class by class, while a misfit from Hill Street flashes by them on his way to the bottom.[5]

New York City has long exemplified a similar process. The latest wave of immigrants—beginning with the Irish after the starvation time of 1848, and continuing with Germans, Jews, Italians, Greeks, Slavs, and so on—starts on the bottom, with the worst housing, the least attention by all city services except the police, the minimum of prestige. All earlier waves of immigrants, including the original Dutch and the English, look down on them as the dregs of humanity. Gradually they ascend, sometimes to the highest levels—making a shambles incidentally of the New York *Social Register*—as new waves come in under them.

The books on my Middletown shelf may not always represent social science₁ as defined earlier, but the research staffs use many of the latest scientific methods, and their techniques continually improve. A survey of intergroup relations begun in

[5] American class structures are further analyzed in Warner's *Democracy in Jonesville*.

Elmira, New York, may turn out to be the most rigorously scientific of all.[6]

Meanwhile the information gathered and the conclusions drawn can be helpful to everyone interested in improving his town's performance—mayors, judges, chiefs of police, city planners, social workers, school boards, traffic engineers, housing authorities. The scientists take the town apart, but carefully and with due respect, allowing the rest of us to see for the first time its intricate, closely woven structure, and what makes it run.

John P. Marquand used some of the "Yankee City" material in writing what many believe to be his best novel, *Point of No Return*. Is it too much to expect that social science research will give novelists and playwrights both a rich mine of new material, and a closer check on the credibility of plots and characters? Instead of another course in How to Write, the aspiring novelist might take one in anthropology.

[6] Conducted by Cornell Studies on Intergroup Relations, under an eight-year grant from Rockefeller Foundation, scheduled to be completed in 1956.

15

Managing Men

The massive changes in human relations that have come over many large American firms in the last generation were highlighted for me in a recent conversation. I was talking to the vice president of a huge corporation, and he told me about the three presidents he had served under since he joined the company, fresh out of college, in 1909.

"My first boss," he said, "was a complete autocrat. He made all the big decisions, and would have fired any of us who raised a question. He knew all the answers, and we did what we were told, yes sir, right down the line of management. Like the Army." The second president was an autocrat too, but he didn't believe in himself with the sublime conviction of number one. On big decisions he would ask for advice occasionally, and didn't claim to know all the answers. Once in a while you could talk to him as a human being.

"The president we have now," he went on, "has the ultimate power, of course, but none of us thinks of him as an autocrat. He goes in for open communication, group decisions, decentralization of authority, even opinion polls of workers. He has more experts on human relations around the shop than you can shake a stick at. Once it was only lawyers. Then came the engineers and accountants. Now the place is crawling with industrial psychologists."

"Is this shift typical of other businesses too?" I asked him.

"Yes," he said, "some executives go gladly, some grumble, but we're all headed in that direction."

"And how about these industrial psychologists? Do they know all the answers?"

"Well, most of them never met a factory payroll, but they have something management wants. They can put you wise to angles you never thought of before. It's probably being over-done, and there are some quacks—take that Dr. Y with his Freudian motivations; but we'll never go back to the czardom of my first president. For one thing, the company has almost three times as many employees as it had in 1909. When an organiza-tion gets as big as that, you've got to use some science if you're going to manage it at all."

The Factory as a Social System

Businessmen abroad are puzzled by these changes. In Europe, the chief concern of management is to manage money, mate-rials, machines—and if possible markets. In the United States it is increasingly the management of men, and so becomes ever more deeply involved with the behavior sciences. Worker and boss in Europe are still heavily influenced by the class struggle concept—what one side gains the other side loses. Over here, a more flexible class system, plus the mass production idea of expanding markets—with gains for both worker and stock-holder, and even consumer—have provided scanty nourishment for the Marxian philosophy.

Indeed some executives have gone beyond the managing of men to the managing of a social system. F. S. Roethlisberger of the Harvard Business School puts it this way:

I should like to suggest that the manager is neither managing men nor managing work, but that he is managing a coördinated set of activities; he is administering a *social system*. That is the human relations approach as contrasted with any approach which implies that people at work can be considered separately from their work.

This puts the culture concept into industrial relations. When a factory is thought of as a social system—a functioning com-munity like Middletown or Plainville—the behavior of workers

and managers makes sense. When it is regarded as an exhibit in
the class struggle, or in paternalism, or as a kind of zoo stocked
with Economic Men, the sense goes out of it, and about all the
investigator can do is to cuss human nature and argue whether
the boss or the worker is the more to blame.

Somebody has said that you can lead good men through the
fires of hell, but that you can't drive them across the sidewalk.
The autocratic manager got the work out, but at a cost. He
thought most people "dumb," distrusted "human nature," and
believed firmly in Economic Man, i.e., that the pocketbook
motive was supreme. Business existed solely to make a profit
for its owners, and notions of public service were tosh. He had
no conception of democratic leadership, of staff decisions, or
workers' participation. Unions were anathema, and he never
tired of declaring that "what we need around here is more
discipline." One often found a picture of Napoleon on his
office wall. Beatrice Webb, investigating labor records in Britain
many years ago, kept finding the statement: "Water plentiful
and labor docile"—which suited Mr. Big right down to the
ground.

Napoleons are not extinct in America, especially in little
business, but the problems of our giant corporations, now operating in harness with giant labor unions, have grown altogether
too much for them. Mr. Sewell Avery may have been the last
of the Great Tycoons.

NEEDED: MORE SCIENCE

The American Management Association, composed of executives in many industries, is now deeply committed to more
science, and fewer Napoleons in the front office. "Most individuals readily agree," said Lawrence A. Appley, president of
the Association, "that as much should be known about the
people of an organization as about the operations. . . . The great
danger lies in the assumption that all that needs to be known
about people is already known by those who know it. That assumption is loaded with dynamite—and has blown up in the

hands of many a management." Mr. Appley argues for more research in human relations. After a visit to the tremendous laboratories of the General Electric Company at Schenectady, he hopes that some day he will see "the same fine facilities, the equivalent talent, the excellent environment for research, devoted to human resources."[1]

American businessmen—and some union leaders, too—are already spending millions of dollars a year on social science research and consulting work. Here is a list of problems on which management wants help, and is willing to pay handsomely for it:

1. *Incentives.* What makes the workers work? The carrot and stick idea is an indifferent answer. Will profit-sharing systems help?
2. *Two-way communication.* How can we get our story down to the rank and file? How can they get theirs up to us?
3. *Decision-making.* How can vital decisions be made most reliably? How tie them effectively to the facts? What about group decisions? What about decentralizing decisions—pushing them down the line? What kind of decisions can be pushed down the line?
4. How can we *pick executives* with less uncertainty?
5. How can we mold various *levels of management* into a better team? How can we hold more effective executive *meetings?*
6. How can we deal more intelligently with powerful *unions?*
7. What can we do about *absenteeism?* About *safety?*
8. How can we *train foremen* better? And new *employees?*
9. How shall we handle *technological displacement* due to automation, or to any large shifts from handwork to machine?
10. What are the best methods for administering *pension systems* and *fringe benefits* generally? (Work for economists, psychologists, and medical experts, combined.)
11. How should we read the *economic weather map,* and adapt our business to it? Inflation, deflation, what is the outlook?
12. How do we come to terms with the *community* which surrounds our factory? Does it control the social system inside the factory?

[1] The General Electric Company has purchased a large estate at Crotonville, N. Y., for a laboratory in human relations to rival its engineering laboratories.

These are large questions. Social scientists are far from solving all of them, but their knowledge keeps growing. We can only select for discussion a handful of illustrations from the expanding field. Suppose we begin with the most famous piece of scientific research so far done in labor-management relations. The story has often been told, but I find it a useful bench mark.

THE HAWTHORNE EXPERIMENTS

Elton Mayo, who fathered this study, was born in Australia, lived for a while in England, and then became a professor at the Harvard Business School, where he taught and worked for 25 years. He died in 1949. He might have been a physicist, an entomologist, a surgeon—he had that kind of mind. He wanted to know, and he doubted what was known. No one who met him can forget his stimulating talk and blazing blue eyes. Mayo was not the originator of research in labor-management relations; he stood on the shoulders of other men, for instance, Carleton Parker and Clarence J. Hicks. Even Frederick W. Taylor, with time studies of bricklayers and steel workers, had put some knowledge of human relations into the storehouse.

Here is a group of six girls, sitting in a small room in a large factory in the town of Hawthorne, near Chicago. On the bench before them are small metal parts in trays, to be assembled into a telephone "relay"—which looks something like a pocket whistle. Their nimble fingers fly. When a relay is completed, every minute or so, it is dropped into a chute and automatically counted. The production rate of each girl, and of the group, can thus be figured per hour, per day, per year.

In the back of the room sits a man with a notebook, watching everything that happens, day in, day out, for five years, beginning in 1927. (He has substitutes from time to time.) The girls do not resent him, they come to like him and often tell their troubles to him. They learn to trust him as a kind of father confessor, and he respects their confidence. He represents the Western Electric Company, and the Harvard School of Business Administration, which are jointly making the experiment under Mayo's direction.

In experiments for the Fatigue Institute in England, during World War I, Mayo had worked with factory employees before. He found that they often produced more munitions in a ten-hour day than in a twelve-hour day. This was contrary to common sense, but not to human nature—which may tire and run down when worked too long. The girls at Hawthorne were a test group, being compared with a control group assembling relays in a larger room. The object of the experiment was to determine the effect on output of various changes in hours, in wages, rest periods, piecework, and so on. The assumptions were that higher wages would increase output, shorter hours decrease it—the usual common-sense assumptions.

Before the experiment was a year old, these preconceptions had been seriously undermined. What was the matter with these girls? Why didn't they behave the way they were expected to behave? Being scientists, the investigators continued to keep a faithful record of what happened even if they were in the dark as to what caused it. The mystery story developed like this:

The first seven weeks were devoted to establishing a base period. The girls averaged 2,400 relays a week each, and worked a regular 48-hour week, including Saturdays, like the rest of the plant.

They were then put on a piecework basis for eight weeks. Output went up.

They were given two rest pauses, morning and afternoon, for five weeks. Output went up again.

The rest pauses were lengthened. Output went up sharply.

Six rest pauses were tried and output fell off slightly. The girls complained that their rhythm was broken.

Then back to two rest pauses. Output went up again.

Hours reduced for a seven-week period. Output went up.

So it continued, trial after trial, each one lasting for some weeks. Whatever new factor was introduced, the number of relays coming through the counters increased, with the one exception noted. The research staff began to lose sleep as their assumptions disintegrated. Some force they could not measure was pushing output up, no matter how they shifted hours, wages, rest pauses.

They prepared then for a supreme test. Take away everything given to the girls over all the periods, and go back to where the experiment started—48 hours, no rest pauses, no hot lunch on the company, no piecework, no Saturday holiday, nothing. The supreme test lasted 12 weeks. *Output jumped to an all-time high—3,000 relays per week!*

The scientists were as disorganized as their assumptions. They had tried to return the girls to the original conditions of the experiment, but the original conditions had disappeared. The experiment had transformed the group; the girls no longer possessed the characteristics they had started with. What was this mysterious X which had thrust itself into the experiment? The staff began looking for it all over the factory.

They finally found it in the girls themselves. The workers' attitudes had changed. The mysterious X was the way the girls now felt about their work. By putting them in a little friendly society of their own, by consulting them often, the scientists had caused a psychological change in these young women and given them a new sense of their status and value. The girls were no longer cogs in an impersonal, pecuniary machine; they were helping in a small way to direct the machine. So their output went up no matter how conditions were changed under them.[2] The investigators concluded that this happened because the girls were recognized, because they felt *important*. They had found work whose purpose they could clearly see and their interest was deeply engaged. So they performed their tasks faster and better than ever before in their lives.

Since the invention of the steam engine most factory managers had regarded workers as "hands"—a part, and on the whole an unreliable part, of the cost of production. "Labor" was a commodity, to be bought and sold like pig iron. Sometimes, by way

[2] Of course, if physical conditions had been changed beyond tolerable limits, output would have been affected.

of contrast, a paternalistic manager treated his workers like little children, to be given candy and petted. The Hawthorne experiment broke down these illusions and proved that the way to make workers work hard and willingly lay in two basic and allied principles: *First,* make the worker realize that his work is important, and that he is important. *Second,* accept the fact that a factory is part of society. Under its roof society must function in its accustomed ways. Bands and teams and groups will form. They must be allowed for, respected, and if possible utilized.

FOURTEEN MEN

The research staff then set up their instruments in another room in the Hawthorne plant where 14 men were engaged in "bank wiring," which means attaching wires to switches for certain kinds of telephone equipment. Nine men are wirers, three are solderers, two are inspectors. In another frame of reference, four are Czechs, three Germans, three Yankees; two are Poles, one is Armenian, and one Irish—an average Chicago ethnic cocktail.

These men have somehow become a team, a little society, inside the Hawthorne plant of 20,000 workers. Unlike the group of relay girls, however, this society does not increase output— which is one reason it is being studied. Not only was the team formed spontaneously, but natural leaders have arisen. The managers of the plant are sublimely unaware of the strength and toughness of this outfit. The 14-man team is not opposed to management but comparatively indifferent to it, having more important matters to attend to. It is strictly a cultural phenomenon, not an economic one. The men are not concerned with the amount of money they get nearly as much as they are concerned with how their wages compare with Tom's and Jerry's. Relativity is what counts with them.

The company has recently adopted an incentive pay plan: the more work an employee does, the more he earns. It is a fair plan, and contains no speed-up provision. Management assumes it will increase production. It does nothing of the kind. The team members hold to a flat 6,000 units a day, no more, no less —though they could readily turn out 7,000 units without fatigue. If some member gets ambitious, the gang slaps him down. There is no apparent relation between an individual's ability and his output. The team does not appear to act in accordance with its pecuniary interests at all. Why?

More racking of brains for the research staff. Why don't workers earn more money when they have a fair and honest chance to do so? The answer seemed to be that the men in the bank wiring room were more interested in maintaining their group relations than in cash. They were afraid, too, that a speed-up might be hidden in the plan. This was a result which neither the incentive plan nor the management was prepared to cope with. Yet any management which ignores the feelings, sentiments, belief systems of the workers is operating in the dark.

The great plant at Hawthorne was found to be full of similar informal groups and teams, powered by leaders whom nobody in authority had ever selected. They exerted a rigid control over "rate busters"—who turned out too much work; over "chiselers"—who turned out too little; over "squealers"—who told on group members. The life of a squealer could be made very unhappy indeed.

It was found that efficiency engineers had tried in the past to break up informal groups, hoping to free individuals for greater production. This policy looked well on paper, but when it was put into effect, time and again production went down. The engineers had unwittingly deprived the worker of the thing which chiefly gave meaning to his work, and without which his full coöperation was impossible. He wanted to "belong."

AIRCRAFT PLANT TEAM

During the war, social scientists made a study for the government of labor-management relations in California aircraft factories. Why, they were asked, were labor turnover and absenteeism so high? This is what they found.[3]

[3] Reported by Elton Mayo and G. F. F. Lombard. See Bibliography.

"John Briggs" is a team leader in Department Z. Nobody appointed him, he just is, and every worker in that end of the shop knows it. One day John goes to the supervisor to present a grievance for one of his team members—a little matter, easily straightened out. The supervisor, who is having an off day and dislikes John anyway, fires him without even hearing the grievance. A team leader is lost who the management did not even know existed.

John had been building up production in Department Z the way a good football coach builds a random collection of rookies into a striking force. The research men discovered that he was boosting morale and could relieve the foreman of many problems of minor discipline—a real tower of strength. And now he is walking out the gate, burning with resentment at the supervisor and the company. The team he led has lost its structure. In the front office, the chart makers presently begin to wonder why output in Department Z has taken a nose dive.

It is useless, the scientists say, for management to ban informal groups. They will form anyway; they seem to be as natural as falling in love. Well-informed managers now are utilizing this drive, and even organizing groups deliberately. It was found in this California experiment that most absenteeism and labor turnover came from workers who did not make a team, who perhaps had no chance to do so. Thus they had no social life in the factory, nothing to involve their interest and loyalty. Again and again we come back to the first principle of the behavior sciences: man is a social animal.

You can readily see what has happened in these experiments. Scientists are at last uncovering some of the basic theory of human relations on the job. Before Hawthorne, we had a little common sense, no underlying theory, and a great deal of plain, loud dogma from both managers and workers. Now we are beginning to understand what makes workers work, and to test the knowledge in controlled experiments.

A Million Foremen

The new understanding was applied on a grand scale in the Training Within Industry program during World War II.[4] Under the War Manpower Commission, more than a million foremen were taught methods for handling workers under them, based on the recognition that they were human beings in a social structure. In one simple technique, the foreman may straighten out a situation in the factory by letting Bill tell him about the trouble at home. This is a long way from the old-time foreman who was asked:

"How do you handle a new employee?"

"I jest stand there . . . and stare him down to kinda show him how dumb he is."

"And then?"

"Then I spit. . . ."

The Job Relations Course in the TWI programs gave every foreman a little blue card with these printed reminders:

Let each worker know how he is getting along.

Give credit when due; tell him while it's hot.

Tell people in *advance* about changes that will affect them. Tell them why.

Look for ability not now being used.

People must be treated as individuals, not numbers on the payroll.

In any given problem, *first get the facts*, then weigh and decide, and only then take action. Afterwards be sure to check results.

This problem-solving technique for foremen, you will note, is based firmly on the scientific method.

[4] See report edited by Walter Dietz and Frances Kirkpatrick.

16

The Cause and Cure of Strikes

On a cold March day at the bottom of the great depression, 1,500 workers walked out of the dozen shoe factories in Newburyport, Massachusetts, almost without warning.[1] They struck with such impact that every factory was closed tight; not a man remained at his bench. The principal industry of the town shut down, at a time when work was very hard to get, and remained shut for a month. In two weeks' time the strikers were completely organized and began picketing effectively. Two weeks later the managers recognized the union. Arbitration by the state board was then accepted, and gave the workers nearly everything they had struck for.

The managers were dumfounded by this rush of events. Again and again they had said that their employees were too sensible to go on strike. Yankee City workers had never been thoroughly organized, and union men from the shoe factories of Haverhill and Lynn complained that they couldn't be organized—they were too obstinate and independent. Some of the workers themselves just before the walkout had told the research staff there would be no strike. Then the impossible happened!

Foreigners and Yankees of ten generations, men and women, the very old and very young, Jews and Gentiles, Catholics and Protestants—the whole heterogeneous mass of workers left their benches, and in a few hours wiped out most of the basic production from which Yankee City earned its living. Not only did they strike and

[1] Volume 4 of the Yankee City series is devoted to this strike.

soundly defeat management, but they organized themselves and joined an industrial union. . . .

EXPLANATIONS

How could this have happened? To find the real causes required months of study. Explanations, however, were freely offered within ten minutes of the walkout. Everyone naturally asked the reason, and everyone had his own private answer. It was the *depression*, said a manager; *low wages*, said a worker; a *plot of the rich*, said a Greek shoe cutter; a *red plot*, said a superintendent; *union agitators*, said a Hill Street gentleman. . . . "Each man, owner and worker and townsman, spoke his own brand of economic determinism."

Plenty of noneconomic determinism was offered, too, and many scapegoats. "It's the foreigners," said the Irish-Americans, thinking of recently arrived Greeks, Poles, and Armenians. "It's the Irish," said some of those whose forebears had landed earlier. "It's those New York Jews"—meaning the financial syndicate which now owned the shoe factories.

The research staff worked overtime, interviewing managers, workers, union organizers, tradesmen, city officials, government arbitrators. "All of them told us why the strike had happened. Each told us but part of the truth; no one knew all of it." In every account, important characteristics were left out.

If social science is to be of any worth to us it must be capable first of all of adding significance and meaning to human behavior which will give us deeper insight into human life, and explain more fully . . . why human beings act the way they do.

Among the questions in Newburyport were these: In a community with few previous strikes and no successful ones, why did the workers suddenly walk out *en masse*, hold their ranks firmly, and win their demands? Again: How could a strong labor organization rise in a town where unions hitherto had hardly achieved a toe hold? What, in short, were the *real* reasons for the strike, as contrasted with the alleged reasons so freely offered?

It did not take long for the scientists to agree that one real reason *was* the depression. Yankee City, like Middletown, in Indiana, had been hit hard. A clerk in the local relief office reported: "Last Tuesday I saw 360 people here, and yesterday 240. . . . We have two doctors, a minister, lawyers, businessmen on relief—people you'd never believe could be on our books." Citizens were breaking up furniture to burn in their stoves; some were literally going hungry.

Depression, low wages, rapid style changes in shoemaking, waiting around the shop without pay, all had contributed economic reasons for the explosion. But they did not explain nearly enough.

Tracing Back

So the scientists began delving into the past. They constructed an economic and social history of Yankee City since its founding in 1635. They built a technological ladder, showing inventions and changes in shoe manufacturing. With the help of John R. Commons' study,[2] they reconstructed the labor history of the industry; and with a book by Emile Durkheim, they worked out the development of machines and division of labor which led to the mass production of shoes.

When settlers first came to the Merrimack Valley they made their own shoes, as one of the winter tasks. Then came the itinerant cobbler with his tools, to process the hides which the family had cured. He would live in the house with them for weeks, while he measured feet from baby to grandfather, and shod them for the coming year. His pay was mostly board and lodging.

About 1760, the so-called "ten-foot shops" were set up to make shoes to order for the local folk. A customer who went to be measured "bespoke" his order, and the shoemaker pro-

[2] "American Shoemakers, 1648-1895," *Quarterly Journal of Economics,* November, 1909.

duced the complete article. Later the first entrepreneur, or capitalist, appeared. He hired workers to make shoes and then he sold them in the immediate neighborhood. Specialization began; some workers made soles and some made uppers, but there were no machines.

So we come to the great change. In 1852 a machine for stitching uppers was invented, and within a decade many other tasks had been mechanized. The saving in labor costs per pair of shoes was fabulous, sometimes up to 90 percent of the old hand cost. Where an expert hand laster could process 50 pairs a day, the lasting machine spewed out 700 pairs. The shoes themselves changed only in detail, but the process of manufacture shifted from a single skilled trade, carried on by a craftsman from start to finish, to a process involving hundreds of operations per pair, most of them done by machine. Workers no longer owned their tools; they had no part in designing the machines they were asked to operate, and no way of predicting what operations would next be mechanized. At a stroke they lost both their security and their pride.

By the time the last old shoemaker died, financial interests in New York had bought out the local factory owners, and the final link of control within the town was broken. Shoemaking in Yankee City had become a strictly impersonal operation for a distant market. New York interests might speed the factories up or close them down; nobody in authority seemed to care.

So the "American Dream" dimmed and faded out in the shoe factories of Yankee City. Warner's men had finished reconstructing the story and come to the end of the trail. They understood now why workers had marched out as one man on that cold March day and joined the union. The same evidence indicated one reason why the American labor movement has grown from two million to 16 million members in recent years. Unions restore some of the pride and self-respect which machines have taken away.

Shoes used to be made by people who wore them themselves,

or took pride in their skill, or both. They are now made by people who rarely wear the shoes they make, have no idea what happens to the output, and have lost their skill and the status which went with it. From a dynamic and absorbing human occupation, mass production has revolutionized shoemaking into an impersonal, monotonous routine. So Newburyport shoemakers in 1933 were under tension not only economically but *emotionally*. Their work had ceased to give meaning to their life.

ON THE BELT

Shoes today are made by machines which the worker feeds, but mass production has taken a long step beyond that. In the conveyor system, used for automobiles and other durable goods, the machine sets the pace of the job. The worker briskly attaches the windshield wiper as the car goes by. This presents us with the problem of the *robot*, the mechanical slave, the man on the belt. He has long been pointed to as a major liability of the machine age, but only recently have social scientists found out what the menace really amounts to. Some managers allege that there is no menace at all, the robot enjoys the job. What are the facts?

Here is an automobile plant in New England, employing 1,800 workers. About a thousand of them are on various assembly lines —chassis, body assembly, final assembly after the dramatic "body drop" onto the chassis, and various subassemblies. A team of social scientists from the Institute of Human Relations at Yale, headed by Charles R. Walker, have selected a group of men as a quota sample of the total force on the line. These men are given intensive interviews at their homes, with both management and union endorsing the investigation. The results are set forth in *The Man on the Assembly Line*, by Walker and Guest, published in 1952—a small book which is making industrial history.

What did the scientists find? They found that nine men out of ten did not like their work. Most of them preferred some for-

mer job in a smaller concern. They stayed on the belt because
of the high pay and job security. But absenteeism and labor turnover were higher for them than for other workers in the plant,
and some said they could not take it much longer. One out of
ten either liked his work, or was indifferent to it. "If you can
daydream," one worker said, "it isn't so bad."

GRIEVANCES

What did the majority object to? They hated being paced by
a machine rather than by their own working rhythm. "The work
isn't hard, it's the never-ending pace. . . . The guys yell 'Hurrah!'
whenever the line breaks down, you can hear it all over the
plant!" Again, they were bored beyond endurance. "The job is
so sickening, day in and day out plugging in ignition wires. I
get through one motor, turn around, and there's another motor
staring me in the face."

They said that they had no opportunity to develop personal
skills, which made them feel inferior and stupid. "One of the
main things wrong with this job is that there is no figuring it
out for yourself; no chance to use your brain."

They said that the job was in a kind of mental twilight zone;
they had to pay attention, but not *enough* attention to interest
them. A job which left the mind completely free was better,
but a job which absorbed the mind was best of all. The craftsman in them was in revolt—like the shoe workers of Newburyport.

Perhaps the biggest grievance, however, was that each man
worked alone. Assembly lines, as commonly run, break up the
natural teams and groups which always tend to form in industry,
and which can do so much, as Mayo discovered, to make factory
work more tolerable and human.

These automobile workers had few grievances against foremen,
equipment, the plant. The light was fine, the washrooms clean.
But their unhappiness was reflected in the bitter things they said
about "the company," off there in Detroit somewhere. They had
to blame somebody. Frustration, as another group of scientists
at Yale once concluded, usually leads to aggression.

Can the Belt Be Humanized?

The scientists found the men ready with suggestions to improve their lot. Two appeals stand out: give us a chance to use our minds; give us a chance to work together. Both are close to basic human nature and no culture can deny them indefinitely without risking an explosion.

Rest pauses, they said, might help. Instead of waiting for the line to break down, why not stop the damn thing for a few minutes morning and afternoon? "It would be something to look forward to." Any opportunity to *change pace* would help. It was suggested that they be allowed to "work up the line," attaching, say, defrosters, rapidly—and then relax for a few minutes, thus beating the remorseless rhythm. Instead of one nut, screw in half a dozen, giving more *variety*. "I'd like for once to do a whole fender." A whole fender may be too much to ask, but the poor chap might do more of it than he does now.

Once set, the pace of the conveyor cannot be changed much, but workers would feel better if they were *consulted* about it at retooling time. If they had a hand in the process, they said, they would not resent it so much.

Instead of learning the job at only one station on the line, the men suggested, learn the job at five or ten stations, and take turns doing them—this week at Station 6, next week at Station 17. This is the principle of *rotation*, and not so impractical as it may sound. "Utility men," who substitute for sick or absent regulars, learn to handle a lot of stations, and feel much better about the job than the regulars. The scientists found one foreman who had organized his whole crew this way, and the rotation worked so well that management considered extending the practice.

Many observers, both in and out of industry, have said that variety cannot be introduced into the conveyor system without abandoning the central idea. Mr. Walker does not bear them out. The robot can become a good deal less of a robot without sacrificing the moving line. But the big problem of social relationships inside the plant needs much more research. How can teamwork, which is essentially circular, be combined with the belt, which is essentially linear? The conveyor is in conflict with a cardinal social principle.

The Yale scientists have demonstrated that there is a crack in the door. More research may well push it open. Industrial engineers have shown how physical materials can click in a moving line, delivering a Buick every 45 seconds. Social scientists, in consultation with workers, have now to show how human beings can click at stations along the way and retain their humanity. Mass production may never rival a ball game as entertainment for those who work at it, but it can become more tolerable if it allows for the laws of human behavior as well as the laws of physics.

CONDITIONS OF INDUSTRIAL PEACE

We have looked at some of the causes of labor unrest, and listened to a few constructive suggestions. Have any large companies really solved their labor problems? Is there a tested formula for stopping strikes?

No, there is not. In totalitarian countries you can shoot strike leaders, but that does not make the rank and file work any better or cure their grievances. Some American corporations, however, have operated for many years without a strike, and social scientists are trying to find out why. An outstanding example is the Standard Oil Company of New Jersey.[3] From 1917 to 1955 it went without a serious strike in any of its far-flung operations. Even though it may have a strike some day, its record cannot fail to remain impressive. When most American refinery workers were out in 1945, Jersey's employees remained on the job.

All this began during World War I, when a series of terrible strikes in the Jersey plants produced pitched battles on the streets of Bayonne, with men killed and the state militia mobilized. Management, at its wit's end, called in an expert on human relations, Clarence J. Hicks, a forerunner of Mayo, Roethlis-

[3] On which I reported in their magazine, *The Lamp*, October, 1946.

berger, and Warner. After a careful survey he advised a change in policy which, for 1917, was revolutionary. He said that if managers wanted to stop strikes, they would have to think about workers as human beings rather than as commodities. He said that executives should not be hired unless they had demonstrated their ability to get on with people.

This was a heresy like telling the Republican Party it should come out for free trade. But the traditional policy had broken down so catastrophically that Jersey's managers were ready to try anything. They swallowed the bitter pill of Mr. Hicks. His specific recommendations included: collective bargaining, the highest wage scale the industry could afford, a full set of what we now call "fringe benefits" for workers, the encouragement of teamwork, better communication between men and management—especially the prompt settlement of grievances.

Since that day, Jersey's management has been in the hands of executives who have followed these policies in good faith, and added more along the same line. The policies were first suggested by a social scientist, and the company has employed other scientists to carry them forward. It has on the payroll, for instance, several expert counselors, who meet with older workers and advise them about the tough psychological problems of retirement at age sixty-five.

One activity which particularly interested me, when I was looking into Jersey's labor relations, is the survey conducted from time to time by Elmo Roper Associates to determine what workers think about the company and their jobs. These consultants first secure the full coöperation of the union, and then conduct a mass questionnaire. When the poll was first proposed, the men were naturally suspicious. Mr. Roper at a shop meeting guaranteed that no names would be revealed, and that the union as well as management would see the results. After a period of uneasy silence a union president spoke up:

"I'm for it," he said. "It's a good idea and here's why. I tell the management what the workers want. They want this and they want that, and I bang the table. So Bill here [the superintendent of the plant], he says no, that's not what the workers want, they want that and they want this. And *he* bangs the table. But neither of us knows a damn thing about what the workers *really* want, and I'm for Mr. Roper finding out!" The questions Mr. Roper asks include:

Does management consider you as a human being or a number on the payroll?

Does it make you feel your job is important?

Do you like your foreman? Does he welcome your suggestions? Show favoritism?

What is your favorite company policy? (Sick benefits get a large vote, also the promotion system.)

Would you rather work for a big company or a small company?

EIGHT PRINCIPLES

In 1947 the National Planning Association, a private research group in Washington, set up an ambitious project—to find the principles of industrial peace. Instead of relaxing and thinking about it, the Association sent field crews of social scientists all over the country to study big companies where strikes were few and labor relations good.[4] Clinton S. Golden, of the Harvard School of Business Administration, assumed command of the project with these classic words: "Instead of looking into the causes of the conflicts we hear so much about, we ought to try to discover how much peace there is and what makes peace."

Twelve companies were analyzed in the field, and 18 more by questionnaire and records, over a period of five years—the most comprehensive study of labor relations ever undertaken. They were all "good" companies, selected deliberately to answer the question: How do the good companies do it?—so that the word could be passed along to the not-so-good companies. All 30 corporations had strong unions, which was also central in the program.

[4] Some of the companies were Crown Zellerbach Corporation, Libby-Owens-Ford Glass Company, Hickey-Freeman Company, Lockheed Aircraft Corporation, Colorado Fuel and Iron Corporation. Now recorded in a book, edited by Golden and V. Parker. See Bibliography.

The story of the research has been published in detail by the National Planning Association. Here we have space only to list the eight "universals" for industrial peace which were found to be operating in all the companies. We can be confident that these same principles also help labor and management to get on relatively well together in America today.

The principles were taken hot and dynamic from actual operations. If you are thinking of starting a nice little business some day—say the manufacture of magnesium wheelbarrows— you could do no better than to plan your labor policies with these eight guides. You may not need them all, you may modify them, but they will start you in the right direction; they are something to predict with, based on careful scientific research.

1. Management accepts the union as here to stay, and begins looking for ways and means to put the union to work to help the company. Rather than a headache, the union becomes an ally. A responsible union, for one thing, can take over the administration of discipline in the shop.

2. Management gives top priority to human relations. Its personnel department is the best that money and brains can obtain.

3. Management recognizes the union as a different kind of social organization from the company itself. Union leaders are responsible to the rank and file, while company leaders are responsible to the man above. Deals with union leaders are accordingly dangerous; management must keep its eye steadily on the rank and file.

4. The union unreservedly accepts the company as a profit-making institution. All thoughts of "taking it over," or raising wages to the point of financial loss, are abandoned. The class struggle is out the window.

5. The union expects management to manage. The union ceases to be a protest outfit and becomes a watchdog outfit. This marks a profound change in labor philosophy. In the early stages of union organization, violence is frequent, bosses are always wrong, name-calling is loud and eloquent. But in these

30 companies the union has grown up, leaders assume that managers are ordinary decent human beings. Ordinary decent human beings, however, need to be checked up from time to time, and the union exercises this function.

6. Both union and management deliberately subordinate drives for power to a search for the *accommodation* of their differences. They do not expect to agree on everything, but they do expect to avoid violent conflict, and to find a modus vivendi, a way to live and let live.

7. Both union and management use the "problem-solving" approach rather than the legalistic approach. Instead of reading the fine print on the contract and battling for their "rights," both sides try to settle problems as they arise, on their merits.

8. Both union and management keep communication lines open, ready to discuss practically anything, any time, anywhere. We noted earlier that the American Management Association is concentrating on this principle, promoting it throughout industry. It has become as live a topic as Taylor's scientific management was a generation ago.

This is all very fine, the skeptic may say, but what is the net result? All the 30 companies were found to be paying relatively high wages, while earning very satisfactory profits. Good human relations, it seems, pay off.

I have given only a hint of what the scientific attitude is accomplishing in labor-management relations in America. My business friend, who described the change from czardom by referring to the three successive presidents under whom he had served, was not talking about an isolated case. The new ideas are making astonishing headway. One finds them not only in private business, but in some government agencies like the TVA, and in many nonprofit organizations—charities, universities, foundations—wherever men and management face one another. The college student who wants to make a career of social science as researcher or consultant will find here a vast and exciting field.

17

The Science of Polling

Polls of public opinion are used increasingly by all the social science disciplines as a research tool, and are now a formidable discipline in their own right. Research centers for training interviewers are operating at Princeton, Columbia, the University of Michigan, Chicago, the University of Washington at Seattle, and in large private organizations like Gallup, Roper, and Crossley.

Customers for opinion research include government at all levels, the mass media, businessmen, advertisers, labor unions, foundations, political candidates. Polls have lately spread halfway around the world. The same question can be asked in Canada, the United States, England, France, Denmark, Italy, Belgium, Australia. Whatever its scientific accuracy, obviously the product would not be in such large supply unless there were a powerful demand for it. The case of Jersey Standard, cited in the preceding chapter, is one example of its use. The study of the robot on the assembly line was done by a special polling technique, so-called "depth interviews."

To the man on the street, the word "poll" usually means the prediction of elections, especially for United States President. These get the most publicity, though they constitute a very small part of opinion research. This chapter is primarily concerned with less sporting matters, but election results need an introductory word.

ELECTION POLLS

The original election polls were "straw votes," where a reporter might ask a few people on the street how they intended to vote. Then came an elaborate tabulation of a great many straw votes, like that of the *Literary Digest* in the 1936 election. The *Digest* sent out millions of return postcards, asking the respondent's preference as between Roosevelt and Landon. Returns indicated that Republican Landon would be overwhelmingly elected. When the actual voting in November showed him overwhelmingly defeated, the *Literary Digest* as a vendible property presently folded.

Messrs. Gallup and Roper, newcomers in the field, correctly foretold the 1936 election of Franklin Roosevelt. They foretold it again in 1940 and in 1944. In 1948, however, they predicted the election of Thomas E. Dewey over Mr. Truman. In the words of Mr. Roper, "We could not have been more wrong." In the presidential elections of 1952, the pollsters retreated to more cautious estimates. Some of them concentrated on measuring changes in public opinion during the campaign rather than venturing flat predictions.

There is a very important difference between straw voting and the sampling technique of modern opinion research. The former has no protection against bias; the latter is scientifically designed to eliminate it. The *Literary Digest* poll contained two serious errors in selection: (1) postcards were sent to people listed in telephone books—who, especially in 1936, were the more well-to-do; (2) most of the cards returned came from those who had the clerical habit strongly enough to fill out and mail them. Republicans tended to have more telephones, and superior clerical habits, so the *Literary Digest* poll was doubly biased in Mr. Landon's favor.

Gallup and Roper used the sampling method, whereby representatives from all groups in the voting population were interviewed, in their estimated proportions. Thus if Negroes were 13 percent of all American voters, the sample interviewed would include 13 percent of colored citizens—and similarly for other major groups, with various qualifications for regions.

Sampling theory is scientific, as we shall see; why then did the pollsters go so wrong in 1948? There has been a good deal of soul-searching analysis, and a number of explanations. The out-standing reason seems to be that the pollsters did not allow for voters *changing their minds* between late summer, when the predictions were announced, and November, when citizens actually voted. It is possible that if the electorate had marked their ballots for President on September 1, Mr. Dewey would have been elected. Both the labor vote and the farm vote were seriously affected by events after September 1, while many Republicans, thinking that the election was in the bag, did not bother to vote. Several local polls that persisted through October caught a large drift away from Dewey in the last three weeks before election.

Certainly one of the reasons for the pollsters' success in 1936, 1940, and 1944 was the outstanding personality of Mr. Roosevelt. Voters were strongly for him or strongly against him, and there was not much change in their feelings between September and November of those years. In 1948, however, Mr. Roosevelt had passed from the scene, and opinions had not crystallized so strongly about either Mr. Truman or Mr. Dewey.

Opinion research was in low repute for months after Mr. Truman's election, but presently it emerged, and today is at an all-time high. It furnishes useful information which can be got in no other way. Even if results are occasionally wrong, the demand is massive enough to overlook some errors. The pollsters, moreover, are not likely to repeat their carelessness of 1948.

SAMPLING THEORY

Sampling theory has been in use, largely for material things, for thousands of years. Instead of counting or tasting or weighing the whole lot, you analyze a sample which represents the whole lot. But unless the sample is truly representative of the whole lot, or "universe," as the scientists call it, the technique is not only valueless but dangerous.

An early illustration was sampling wine by tasting it; a few sips would define the whole vintage. A "universe" of sand, marbles, or other free-flowing material can readily be measured by sampling. When units are not free flowing, they are said to be "clustered," and the sample must then be composed of similar clusters.

Most of us use sampling to save ourselves work, without realizing that we are on the edge of a scientific technique. If, for instance, I want to find out how many words I have written so far in this book, I select half a dozen typed pages at random, count the words on each page, average them, and multiply by the number of pages typed. The result will be close enough for my purposes. I know from previous tests that it will be within 2 or 3 percent of the exact number of words.

If we have any way to find a representative sample, we can determine the total of the universe at a fraction of the cost of a complete census. To count all the words in a book would take many hours. Not only can we get answers to more questions, but we can get a given answer faster; the technique has both coverage and speed. It applies to many aggregates, organic as well as inorganic—nails, bolts, most mass-produced units, trees, grain, sheep—anything which has some uniform characteristics.

The first use of scientific sampling in the social field seems to have been when Halley, whom we met in the Royal Society, employed the mortality statistics of the town of Breslau for 1693, to draw conclusions about the mortality of mankind. Breslau was the sample, and mankind the universe. In 1800 Sir Frederick Eden, using the sampling technique, estimated the population of England at 9 million, and next year the actual census confirmed the estimate. Among the most active uses today are:

Inspecting mass production articles and parts in factories. Johnson & Johnson, for instance, have scores of sampling stations in one of their factories at New Brunswick.

Estimating crop yields—widely practised by the Department of Agriculture.

Compiling economic data, such as the number of unemployed, wages, prices, housing conditions—and thus saving the taxpayers' money. The number of unemployed published by the government every month is calculated on a sample basis. If a complete census were taken, results would be months behind and the cost fantastic.

Health surveys, crime surveys, youth surveys, indeed all manner of social surveys. As I write, the United States Public Health Service is estimating the effects of smoking on health by interviewing 25,000 Americans.

Market research: to find answers to such questions as "What don't you like about Plymouth cars?" "What is your favorite toothpaste?" Also to measure the popularity of radio and TV programs.

The depression of the 1930's gave sampling theory tremendous impetus. The government needed figures in a hurry concerning the number of people unemployed, on relief, eligible for social security benefits, and so on. Time did not permit a complete census; samples would serve the purpose within a calculable margin of error.

World War II carried the technique further. Samples were taken to determine consumer wants, housing facilities, goods in short supply, dealer inventories, public reaction to war measures, characteristics of selectees, employee attitudes in war plants, radio listening habits, quality control of munitions.

"The science of sampling," says Angus Campbell, "has reached the point where it can select unbiased samples of known probable error to represent virtually any universe a surveyor is interested in."[1] In the face of this comprehensive demand, the question of who is going to be elected president or senator or dog catcher is minuscule. We can summarize the development of public opinion research something like this:

First comes *sampling theory*, founded on the mathematics of probability and rigorously scientific.

From it many useful applications have been worked out in *counting material things*—beans, rice, gravel, many kinds of industrial and military inventories.

From it, counts of *human populations* have also been developed, such as the total number of boys subject to the draft, of housewives with electric washing machines, etc.

[1] *Journal of Social Issues*, May, 1946.

Counts of *opinions* are next in line—what people think of the United Nations, the Marshall Plan, President Eisenhower's performance, the Jack Benny program.

Out on the far edge is the prediction of *political elections*—since the trouble in 1948, the boys are going easy on this one. It would suit a lot of us if they would forget the whole thing. But the popular demand for a winning prediction, as in the case of the Kentucky Derby, is great.

Until scientific sampling came along, no politician, leader, reformer, had any objective way of knowing what the people thought about public issues. Leaders relied mostly on intuition, wishful thinking, or pessimism about the intelligence of the rank and file. Congressmen tended to draw conclusions from their mail—which provides a perfectly terrible sample of the congressman's universe! Only angry people, or very earnest and literate people, or people prodded by pressure groups, write letters to Congress. Congressional mail in 1941, for example, ran 90 percent against the draft law. But careful polls indicated a majority of citizens *in favor* of the bill. The bill won by one vote.

WARTIME POLLS

Samuel Stouffer, whom we met at the Harvard Laboratory, directed many of the Army polls during the war. Soldiers were asked what they thought about their food, about their equipment, their uniforms, the entertainment offered, promotion methods in the Army, deficiencies in leadership, methods of discipline, personal plans after the war. The soldiers themselves determined the "point system" of discharge. Subsequently the system never fell below the 70 percent line in soldier approbation. It worked so well that even the Marines took it over. The Army knew two years in advance, and within 3 percent, how many claimants there would be under the G.I. Bill of Rights. The government probably saved millions for the taxpayers by knowing what to plan for in this costly business.

Rensis Likert found out by opinion research that if the

Treasury made it easier for people to refund war bonds, more new bonds would be bought, and *more net would stay bought*. This was contrary to some positive opinion in high quarters, but the Treasury trusted the poll, and made the change, with the results predicted. The Price Control Board kept in close touch with the public by frequent opinion surveys. When a poll showed a bad public reaction to some ruling in, say Cleveland, trouble-shooters were rushed to Cleveland before the grievance grew. Sometimes the ruling was changed, sometimes a better explanation was given of its necessity. . . . What a future in public relations this opens up!

A poll in June, 1946, showed that 78 percent of Americans wanted price controls maintained for a while longer. Presumably they were afraid of inflation without them. Yet Congress killed the agency, on the assumption that competition would reappear after its long hibernation and bring prices down. Congress turned out to be wrong and the people right.

OUTSTANDING ACCOMPLISHMENT

This brings us to an outstanding achievement of the polls. They have given strong statistical proof of the wisdom of the people, and thus vigorously supported the theory of political democracy. Time and again the polls have shown the majority of the people ready for a given change ahead of their leaders, and even farther in advance of Congress. William A. Lydgate, of the Gallup organization, has written a book, *What Our People Think*, packed with evidence. His first chapter is entitled, following Carl Sandburg, "The People, Yes." He cites the pluralities for rearmament, higher taxes for defense, the draft, price control, wage control, rationing, an antistrike law —all approved by the people ahead of Congress. In March, 1940, six months after Hitler's armored divisions marched into Poland, the Army asked Congress for money to build 1,200 fighting planes. Congress appropriated funds to build exactly 59. Yet samples of the American people were showing majorities of nine to one in favor of more air power!

The people are not always right judged by subsequent events; but as Mr. Lydgate shows, they often sense reality better than those whom they elect to represent them. The rank and file are soon lost when questions become technical, but when broad policies are put before them, the polls vigorously support the famous warning: "Never overestimate the people's knowledge, nor underestimate their intelligence."

18

Steps in Opinion Research

To run a poll today is a major operation, in which an amateur would do about as well as he would trying to produce sulfathiazole in the kitchen sink. If the "universe" is all the adults in the United States, as many as 400 skilled interviewers may be needed, stationed at strategic points throughout the country. Perhaps the best way to understand the operation is to follow the process of polling for a public policy question from beginning to end, and note the steps involved. There are eight of them, and we will consider each in turn.[1] Why not save the cost of personal interviews and send questions by mail? Because, as the sad case of the *Literary Digest* made painfully clear, mail returns often introduce a systematic bias.

Step 1: Selecting the Question to Be Polled

Suppose that you are the director of a polling agency; what do you want to ask people about? Granted that it would be interesting to have an answer, is there any reason to believe that enough plain citizens know anything about the topic to make the answer significant? Do not try "free enterprise," for instance, for only three Americans out of ten have a clear idea what "free enterprise" means. Many think it is something given away, like premiums for soap wrappers. Citizens need *background* before they can answer a policy question—unless you are polling specifically to determine the *lack* of background. In 1955 there was a good deal of agitation about a private power combine, called Dixon-Yates, supplying current to the

---

[1] Following Maccoby and Holt, in *Journal of Social Issues*, May, 1946.

TVA. Most Americans had no idea of the facts, which were complicated. So any poll you might have taken would be not on the issue but on symbols—"Private Power vs. Public Power," or "Republican vs. Democrat." This would tell you how people feel about symbols, but not about Dixon-Yates.

Again, even if people know about the subject, do they care? This brings up the *intensity* of public feeling; questions which carry low intensities may not be worth the cost of polling. Again, how *permanent* is the reaction likely to be? Questions subject to large and sudden changes in popular attitudes are less meaningful than those which have more stability, unless you are specifically studying changes, as in "panel" polling to be described later, where the same group is interviewed at different periods.

STEP 2: SELECTING THE UNIVERSE

Will the universe be the whole adult population of the country, Negro sharecroppers in Mississippi, Ph.D.'s in sociology, consumers of Post Toasties, unskilled workers in the Ford Motor Company; or what?

Though opinion can be studied not only in the United States but in other Western nations, polls behind the so-called Iron Curtain are unthinkable—and would probably be worthless even if taken because of fear-induced bias. To compare reactions between nations is always interesting and can be important. An international poll asked the question: "Do you think most people can be trusted?" Only 6 percent of Germans said yes, compared with 66 percent of Americans—a penetrating sidelight on feelings of security in the two countries ten years after World War II.

STEP 3: SELECTING THE SAMPLE

Individuals, as we have seen, must be selected from the universe in such a way as to represent the universe. Here the amateur goes completely out of his depth. As director you choose among various alternative methods: "random sampling," "quota surveys," and so on. You choose the one which seems best to fit the universe—remembering too your client's pocketbook.

Random sampling means using some automatic method of choosing which gives each individual in the universe an equal chance of being included in the sample. If one is sampling marbles, random sampling is quite satisfactory. It can be done by picking up a handful anywhere, though it would be a good idea to shake the whole collection first. If, however, one is sampling people, random sampling is more complicated. Suppose we want to know how many members in a given service club go regularly to church. Here is the card file, with tens of thousands of club members' names. Now pick up a book, any book, and open it at random. If the page is 64, take 4, the last digit. Good, we will start with the *fourth* card in the membership file, and take every hundredth card thereafter. If we want to work to a larger sample and thus a smaller margin of error, take every twentieth card. Prior experiments have proved that when some *person*, however wise, tries to pick the random sample, bias gets in.

A *quota sample* tries to arrange the units in the sample in the same proportions as in the universe. If the universe is total adult population, then divide the sample into corresponding proportions of rich, poor, white, Negro, farmer, city man, old, young, skilled worker, unskilled worker, etc. Elmo Roper claims that by asking 5,000 Americans selected on a quota basis whether they expect, say, to take a vacation in the next six months, he can get, within a few percentage points, the same answer that 100 million adult Americans in a complete census would give. If he is correct, and there is strong reason to suppose that he is, the saving in cost is in the order of 20,000 to 1. Incidentally, here is the reason why *you* may not have been polled. (I was polled for the first time a few days before writing this paragraph. It was about United States oil companies abroad.)

The quota theory is sound; trouble comes in making clusters which truly agree with the clusters in the universe. The studies of Dr. Kinsey in sex behavior have been criticized for having too many respondents with college education. This may be true, but the results are still useful. Though the Kinsey samples may not be perfect, they have told us more than was ever known before about the subject, and may quite possibly have laid the foundation for more intelligent sex education in the future.

STEP 4: PHRASING THE QUESTION

How best to word the question is as delicate as approaching the boss for a raise. Here the survey director must use taste, sympathy, intuition, and semantics. There is no such body of knowledge to help him as in the theory of sampling. He is confronted, among other things, with a problem in the meaning of words. What he must strive for above all else—with an exception to be noted later—is to get a completely dead-pan question, to remove all emotion-stirring words[2] so the respondent can answer spontaneously from his own inner feeling.

When Franklin Roosevelt was President it was found that attaching his name to a policy which was being polled increased its popularity—although not necessarily in the Union League Club. Out where votes are counted this produced a bias in favor of the proposal. "Do you think the United States should send food to starving people in Asia?" gets more votes than the same question with "starving" deleted.

Mr. Roper once ran an interesting semantic test. He matched two groups of people so they were practically identical samples, as proved by asking them various questions and getting close percentage results. He then asked each group a series of questions, identical except that for one group a new and ugly word was introduced, the word "propaganda." The general topic was the usefulness of foreign broadcasts by the State Department.

Interviewers asked Group A: "Some people say it is better to explain our point of view as well as give the news: do you agree?" The answer came back "yes," 42.8 percent. Group B got the following wording, *and observe it is substantially the*

---
[2] Sometimes called "purr" words, or "slur" words.

same question: "Some people say it is better to include some propaganda as well as give the news." The "yes" reaction was cut almost in half, to 24.7 percent.

In Step 4, the director has to decide whether to use "closed" questions, "open" questions, or a combination of both. Closed questions are those to which the respondent answers "yes," "no," "don't know," or selects one reply from a number of alternatives. For instance: "If the election were held today would you vote for Eisenhower . . . Stevenson . . . Don't know . . . ." The "don't knows" or D. K.'s, used to go down the drain in some of the polls, but now their importance is emphasized. Public ignorance of certain questions can be measured by the percentage of "don't knows." Percentages based only on those who indicate a preference, adding up to 100 percent with the D. K. vote excluded, can give a strongly biased conclusion.

An open question, on the other hand, is not so clean-cut as the closed variety. It gets in shades of opinion and also may show intensity. The interviewer starts with a big general question and works down to cases, encouraging the respondent to express his views in his own words and think all around the topic. For instance:

"What do you believe will happen to prices in the next year or so? . . . Why do you think so? . . . What are you doing about it in your own buying? . . ."

Open questions are often a better measure of public opinion, but the interviewer must be better trained and work harder, with a much tougher job of coding and note-taking. Instead of ticking off a "no," "yes," "don't know," he must take down nearly all the respondent says—and most of us like to talk.

Another rule in phrasing questions is to ask only one thing at a time. "Do you think it wise these days to put money into real estate and securities?" is bad wording. George Adams may favor real estate and be afraid of securities, while his banker holds the opposite view. Split it into two questions.

The one time when it seems permissible to load a question is in polling for the extent of prejudice. The usual impersonal questions about race and religious prejudices will not be answered honestly. Many Americans are ashamed of their feelings about Jews or Catholics or Negroes. They will give stereotyped replies based on the Declaration of Independence. But when the interviewer says: "Well, we're through with that. Now tell me what you *really* think about those so-and-so's?" prejudice emerges from its dark den. Marie Jahoda has reported that this technique may cause a 25 percent shift.

Miss Jahoda also says that when parents are polled about corporal punishment, 80 percent give the textbook response: they are against it. But when followed up by a probe of actual behavior 70 percent of the same people are found not to be sparing the rod.

STEP 5: THE TEST RUN

After we have the question worded to our satisfaction, the next step is to put it into the wind tunnel and measure reactions. This gives us the "feel" of what to expect in the larger project. In a study which I followed closely, 22 questions were tried out on a preliminary group of 100 people. The ultimate sample was to be 5,000, for a universe including all United States adults. In this sample of a sample, the interviewer took down replies in full and asked respondents to explain what they meant by all their answers. Thus cloudy wordings were identified and corrected before the final survey.

STEP 6: THE INTERVIEW

Poorly trained interviewers can ruin everything we have arranged so far—the universe, the sample, the wording, the test run. It is easier to train an interviewer for closed questions than for open, but good judgment is always required. He needs it, to get people talking. (As a matter of current practice, most interviewers are not he's but she's—intelligent matrons working part time.)

An interviewer on an unemployment survey must never say:

STEPS IN OPINION RESEARCH

"You're not working now, are you?" but always: "Are you looking for a job now, or are you waiting for a while?" Thus the respondent is permitted to keep his pride. Also an interviewer must never put answers in the respondent's mouth. "Do you say that because of the high cost of living?" will cause many a respondent to follow the leader with, "Sure, that's why." Then bias is in.

Four main causes can make trouble in the communication line between interviewer and respondent: (1) deliberate misstatements, (2) pretense; the respondent assumes a special role for the interviewer's benefit, (3) psychological blockages in the respondent, (4) honest mistakes.

Some respondents try to influence poll results. This is especially true of community leaders who want to make a good showing for the town's schools, or crime record, or whatever the question is. Unless the ground is well prepared, a troop of interviewers invading a small community will start a blizzard of rumors. To cite a case: After all the families in "Springdale" had been briefly contacted by a team, two contradictory rumors spread through the town: the interviewers were FBI agents; no, they were communist spies!

The Fund for the Republic retained two big polling agencies to find out what was worrying Americans in the middle 1950's.[3] It appeared that we were not nearly so much upset about Communists in the State Department, or even in Russia, as we were about our jobs, our health, and our families. Each agency, of course, had its own squad of interviewers, but they asked the same questions of different respondents. Both groups of respondents represented samples of all adult Americans. Here was a rigorous test of the technique of interviewing, but it was brilliantly met. The results, when tabulated, were almost identical.

STEP 7: TABULATING RESULTS

Interviewers have made the rounds, and sent their notes to the central office. The modern method is to make punch cards, one

[3] Samuel A. Stouffer, *Communism, Conformity and Civil Liberties.*

per respondent, and let a computing machine tabulate them. In practically no time at all it will sort and count the cards in as many ways as the director desires.

Attaching equal numerical weights to all responses and adding them, performing least squares and other fancy mathematical operations upon them, could result in a fearful hash. The data should be kept relatively simple. For depth interviews—where the respondent gives the interviewer the whole background of his answers—statistics must be used with great caution. These data are still beyond the mechanical level, a handicraft job for highly skilled interviewers. Depth interviews are also the only way to find out *why* people hold the opinions they do.

STEP 8: REPORTING THE FINAL RESULT

The director of the survey now takes the figures, discusses them with his staff, and sits down to write his report for client or press. An advertising client may be handed a special market survey of how his new TV set is liked, while George Gallup's reports have been widely syndicated in the newspapers.

The report must explain clearly not only what the figures show, but also what they do *not* show. The common habit of generalizing from insufficient data can raise havoc with any poll not carefully guarded. The director must repeatedly caution his readers against generalizing the findings to a different universe from the one being measured. For instance, if the universe is *Iowa farmers*, guard against extending the results to *United States farmers*.

A LOOK AT THE FUTURE

All the eight steps are now under scientific microscopes. The *sample* is increasingly subjected to mathematical analysis and verification. The *questions asked* are being developed from a static to a dynamic phase, registering changes in opinion through time. Louis Harris of the Roper organization described the progress of polling to me.

We began years ago, he said, with a simple yes-or-no. *Do you approve of UNESCO?* Anwer yes or no.

Then we discovered the critical importance of "don't knows." A lot of Americans had never heard of UNESCO.

We went on to "cafeteria questions," where the respondent is asked to select one:

Do you highly approve of UNESCO? Mildly approve? Mildly disapprove? Highly disapprove? No opinion?

We experimented with such multiple questions, using the *index* method and the *scaling* method. Sometimes we arrange a series of questions all bearing on a single topic. Take, for instance, race prejudice. We put, *"Do you approve of complete segregation?"* at one end of the scale, and *"Do you approve of mixed marriages?"* at the other end. In between are a number of questions registering reaction to such things as desegregation in schools, F.E.P.C., Negro players in big league baseball, joint housing facilities, and so on—all in scale between the two poles. The result gives us a deeper insight into the respondent's feelings.

The "panel" method is used more and more to follow shifts in feelings. We used to ask a sample what they thought about a given topic, say on January 1, and then ask another sample on June 1. Now we ask the *same people*: they are the panel. Ask 1,000 people on January 1 if they approve of admitting Red China to the UN. Ask them again on April 1, and again on August 1. This gives us a picture of change, and it develops interactions. The technique can be used to bring out the various pressures and influences which bear on the respondent and influence his opinion—such as his trade union, his industry, his church, his region.

We are a long way from the old one-two, said Mr. Harris, though we still use it for some questions; but we still have a long way to go. Harris believes that ultimately a great deal will be discovered about human behavior by this method.

Here are some areas where opinion research was especially active in the mid-fifties:

Consumer opinion. Paid for by advertisers, businessmen, government. It includes product research, design research, impact of advertising, behavior of consumers in the market, cost of living, TV and radio ratings.

Worker opinion. Paid for by management and labor unions. How employees feel about the boss, the company, the union, the foreman, their jobs.

Public opinion. Paid for by government, foundations, the mass media, business. Includes popular opinion on United States foreign policy, international problems, internal security, political pressures, studies dealing with the fear of communism, behavior in disasters, education—a long list.

A significant report on political pressures was made by a group of social scientists who conducted panel studies in Elmira, New York, covering the 1948 elections.[4] Results have formed the basis for a startling hypothesis about the workings of political democracy, upsetting many cherished ideas of the past. We will save the story for Chapter 24, which deals with political science more specifically. Enough that it shows how opinion research, as conducted by qualified experts, can fertilize new political, economic, and social theory.

We will let Samuel Stouffer sum up the subject. Polls, he says, can replace myths with facts when people are discussing current political questions in press, radio, TV, or barber shop. "We, as social scientists, have an obligation to make the tools better and better, and we as citizens have the obligation in and out of government to see that these powerful instruments are wisely employed. . . . There is no turning back."[5]

[4] See Berelson, Lazarfeld, and McPhee, *Voting.*
[5] *Scientific Monthly,* December, 1946.

19

Is Economics a Science?

"The Republican congressional leaders are preparing to go ahead with their plan to cut taxes, but economists disagree as to whether a reduction would be inflationary or deflationary. Those fellows have the whole thing down to an inexact science."

As one who has written several books on economics, I confess that my mirth at this crack in the *New Yorker* is somewhat forced. Our "science" is fortified with many learned theories and many impressive curves and graphs, but repeatedly it proves unreliable for prediction, the acid test of science as we have seen. George Soule once wrote a book called *The Useful Art of Economics*, but one may ask—and many do—how useful is a body of doctrine which says that things will go up which then go down, or will go down which presently go up?

Despite the frequent failure of prediction, economics is a popular subject, with flourishing departments and business schools in the universities. It wins great attention in financial sections of the newspapers, and is pursued in magazines, monographs, and books without number. If, for the purposes of discussion, we divide the field into three parts, General Theory, Special Theory, and Practical Economics, a pleasanter and more revealing landscape appears.

The two big General Theories in the world today—Ricardian and Marxian—are dogmatic, contradictory, and not reliable for prediction. What the theory says will happen usually does not happen.

The Special Theories cover a more modest area—like Berle and Means's discussion of the evolution of the modern corporation, Colin Clark on the tertiary trades, Keynes's analysis of business depressions. These are capable of verification, and close to social science₁.

Practical Economics, or the use of economic tools, is often excellent, and a great help to government administrators and businessmen in planning and forecasting their operations. The United States economy in World War II, as we shall see, would probably have jammed without the work of economic administrators and statisticians.

All three departments, however, lose by their failure to draw on the behavior sciences—especially the General Theory department. Economists have worked late, employing some high-powered mathematics, trying to find dependable laws for the behavior of money and prices, without sufficiently realizing that prices often fluctuate with the way people *feel* about the situation—a phenomenon in behavior.

A scientist armed with the operational definition would look in vain for any world of economics functioning according to a system of laws of its own. He can find only the behavior of people—as workers, consumers, managers, borrowers, lenders—concerned with getting a living, achieving security, protecting the family, fortifying their egos. He can record and classify this behavior in a number of ways, such as:

Producer behavior—on the farms, in the crafts, factories, mines, laboratories.

Financial behavior—first in the form of barter, then in the invention and use of money, followed by the scramble for the division of the money income in a given society.

Consumer behavior—the impulse to spend or not to spend, the impact of advertising, the stimulation and satisfaction of wants, and so on.

It all goes back to people's needs, drives, desires, fears, hopes for security—psychological incentives. Recall again the girls in the relay room at Hawthorne. This is the reason why the Big Theories ring so hollow. They either leave out human behavior altogether or assume a psychology which does not exist in flesh and blood. They speak of "other things being equal," when things are not equal, and of "self-evident truths," which cannot be proved.

FIFTEEN FORECASTS

To illustrate the inadequacy of much economic theorizing, suppose we glance at some confident predictions of recent years.

1. Following the prompting of leading bankers and financial experts, Britain returned to the gold standard after World War I. They were confident it would restore her economic position in the world. It did nothing of the kind. After six years of steadily accumulating financial difficulties Britain abandoned gold in 1931.

2. When the U.S.S.R. proposed her first Five Year Plan in 1927, it was ridiculed by economists in London, Paris, and New York. The U.S.S.R. was bankrupt, they said, and where would she raise 60 billion rubles to invest in capital assets? Where would the money come from? At the end of five years the factories, power dams, railroads, transmission towers, schools, housing developments, steel plants were there, ugly, solid and substantial, as planned. Where *did* the money come from?

3. In 1928 there were almost no economists in the United States who saw the looming depression. On the contrary, many were coming to believe that the business cycle had been smoothed out and permanent prosperity reached.

4. After the stock market collapse in 1929, few financial experts would admit that it was more than a little swerve—and a healthy one at that. Prosperity, we were told, was "just around the corner."

5. In 1935 a noted financier and economist announced that unless the federal budget were promptly balanced, a dire inflation would ruin the nation. I remember it well, because I debated the question with him before the Economics Club of New York. He won the debate hands down, but the budget was not balanced and the inflation he predicted for the 1930's never came.

6. When Hitler proposed to rearm Germany, the cry went up from the highest authorities: "Germany is bankrupt, she cannot even pay reparations; Hitler has no gold or foreign exchange; where will the money come from?" So the rest of us breathed easier to think of ragged, bankrupt Hitler.

7. A leading economist cited by Beardsley Ruml said in 1937 that unless federal expenditures were brought into line with revenues, the interest rate would rise to 6 or 8 percent. Deficits continued as before, and the interest rate continued in the deep freeze.

8. In 1940 economists affirmed that with a federal debt of the staggering proportions of $45 billion it would be difficult if not impossible to finance a program for defense and rearmament. It proved, on the contrary, surprisingly easy. In 1940, indeed, there was not an economist in the country—including your author—who would have dared to suggest that the United States could shoulder a debt of $280 billion by 1945.

9. As we entered the war economists sternly bade the nation choose between guns and butter; we could not have both. We got both—the mightiest assortment of guns in human history, and a total volume of consumer goods slightly greater than before the war, though differently divided among the population.

10. In the fall of 1941 a flood of articles and news stories assured us that Japan presented no real danger. The long years of war in China had exhausted her resources; she had no gold and was nothing but a hollow shell economically. The attack on Pearl Harbor came as these pronouncements were at their height. The hollow shell gave us a painful amount of trouble for more than three years.

11. In 1943, the Bureau of Labor Statistics estimated that there would be 7 to 12 million unemployed six months after the war's end. The actual number in March, 1946, proved to be 2,710,000. Unemployment during reconversion never went above three million.

12. Early in the war economists were having nightmares over

what they ominously called the "inflationary gap." The gap never opened—not, at least, in any ominous way. Citizens did not spend their money the way economic theory said they should.

13. Many economists opposed any plan for general price control at the beginning of the war. It was believed to be unworkable and would only make the price situation worse. As J. K. Galbraith said: "Standard pedagogy had emphasized this conclusion quite literally for generations."[1] The Office of Price Administration was set up nevertheless, and worked astonishingly well, holding most prices within narrow limits throughout the war.

14. On July 3, 1946, as Congress was enthusiastically dismantling price controls, the National Association of Manufacturers ran full-page advertisements saying:

If price controls are permanently discontinued, the production of goods will rapidly mount and, through free competition, prices will quickly adjust themselves to levels that consumers are willing to pay. . . . Then as production gets rolling again, supply will catch up with demand. . . . prices will be fair and reasonable to all.

For at least 20 months thereafter, prices for most goods continued to increase. What happened to the leveling power of free competition the NAM economists have never explained.

15. In the spring of 1947 most expert opinion held that the peak of price inflation had been reached, as the merchants of Newburyport made their well-publicized 10 percent price cut across the board. A business survey announced that signs of a business recession were abundant, and that it would strike in the late summer. August came and golden September, and all lines continued their mighty zoom upward.

This melancholy story could be indefinitely continued. Business economists, government economists, labor economists, great bankers and fiscal experts, college professors, financial editors, your author—all have missed the boat by alarming margins.

[1] *American Economic Review*, June, 1947.

What is the trouble? No other branch of the social sciences which we have been examining has such a record. Reviewing it, one can scarcely be surprised that the man on the street thinks himself an economist as competent as the professors.

There must be some good reason why such grave miscalculations keep coming from serious and intelligent scholars. Various explanations have been offered by members of the fraternity as well as by outsiders. The *Economist* of London has put its finger on one source of the trouble. As perhaps the leading economic journal of the world the *Economist* speaks with authority:[2]

Economics is a curious science, if indeed it is a science at all. The investigator who digs down through the textbook generalizations in the physical sciences finds at their root a series of facts, checked by carefully controlled experiments, and as accurately known as human ingenuity can compass. The investigator who does the same for economics, penetrating the smoke screen of curves and mathematical symbols, will find not facts, but a series of elementary psychological assumptions checked, if at all, by crude common sense. And, like most assumptions of this kind, he will find that most of them are wrong. . . . It is this lack of a solid factual basis which has brought it about that, while the Army is alleged to be always winning the last war, economists are almost invariably engaged in defeating the last slump. The characteristic of a genuine science is that its practitioners . . . can tell the practical man what to expect around the next corner. Economists may sometimes do the same; but as often as not they have to wait to formulate their theory until the practical man has himself turned the corner. . . .

There have of course been correct predictions. Roger Babson achieved a prodigious reputation by forecasting the great slump of 1929 in his business letter a few weeks before it struck. But observe, if economics were social science[1], the majority of the profession would have checked his calculations and agreed with him, instead of being practically to a man on the other side of the fence.

[2] July 27, 1946.

As things are now, one faction is delighted at the discomfiture of another school when a forecast fails to materialize. The opponents of John Maynard Keynes were overjoyed when the prediction of the Bureau of Labor Statistics about unemployment after the war proved wide of the mark. But the man on the street took it as one more sign that *all* economists are unreliable. Real scientists take pride in their discipline and are concerned when careful forecasts go wrong. Can one imagine, for instance, a group of astronomers rubbing their hands and saying: "Splendid! Halley's Comet never came around the way he said it would"?

BIG THEORY: RICARDO

For almost a century, economic theory has been dominated by two schools which largely contradict each other. The laissez faire or classical school holds that the government should keep out of practically everything, while the Marxist school holds that it ought to get into practically everything. The former has been preferred by most American economists, the latter by many European. It is now the official philosophy—if not indeed the official religion—of the U.S.S.R. and her satellites.

Classical theory was first formulated in a comprehensive way by Adam Smith with his epoch-making book, *The Wealth of Nations*, published in 1776. His ideas were refined by David Ricardo early in the nineteenth century, and were summed up in the term "laissez faire"—let things alone. Ricardo became the chief theoretician of the classical school—the economics which my generation was taught in college.

The theory says that when each individual seeks his own interest and is given opportunity to do so, a higher harmony is established, which cancels out the apparent selfishness, coincides with "natural law," and makes for the maximum of wealth and happiness. The intervention of the state is fatal to this harmony, and must be kept to the absolute minimum necessary for law and order. Let the free play of the market determine prices, wages, rents, interest rates, and let profit be the judge of those entrepreneurs who are to survive.

The culture in which Adam Smith, Ricardo, John Stuart Mill, and the other giants of the classical school did their writing was barely past the handicraft stage, with mass production all but unknown.[3] The machine age was in its infancy: an economy of little markets, little mills, and little ironmasters. Classical theory may have fitted that scene—though this is in some dispute—but it fails to fit the world of electronics, jet planes, and billion-dollar corporations.

Ricardo was trained in the London brokerage business, with little first-hand experience in industry. His powerful mind elaborated the imposing logical structure which came to be called laissez faire. The philosophy was never verified but for a century and more students in all the universities of the Western world have been drilled in its syllogisms, and even expected to go out and run their businesses in accordance with it.

Elton Mayo, from his post in the Harvard Business School, declared it impossible to square Ricardo with practical problems in business administration, or in labor-management relations. He cited Chester I. Barnard, at the time president of the New Jersey Telephone Company, who complained that he could find no treatise in all economic literature which covered business organization as he had to deal with it day by day. Mr. Barnard finally had to write his own book about it, which he called *The Functions of the Executive*. Worse still, said Mr. Barnard, economists fail to recognize the extreme importance of *organization* as the principal structural aspect of society itself. That is, the businessman is doing something out there in the real world which economists are supposed to interpret, but which they are mostly unaware of.

Society as viewed by the laissez faire school, Mayo continued, consists of a rabble of unorganized individuals striving to serve

[3] Muskets for the War of 1812 in the United States were manufactured on an elementary mass production principle—uniform parts were made and then assembled.

the self-interest of each, and yet, by a curious alchemy called "natural law," achieving harmony in the whole. Anthropologists have not discovered anything corresponding to this state of affairs. Ricardian economics "is a study of human behavior in non-normal situations, or, alternately, a study of non-normal behavior in ordinary situations." The number of people activated entirely by self-interest is small. Observe again the 14 men in the bank wiring room at Hawthorne. In Mayo's extensive clinical work over a 30-year period he found that human beings relapse into exclusive self-interest only when society has failed them. Hermits and recluses are examples. Meanwhile Linton fails to mention "natural law" among his universals, and reports no Economic Man, except as an abnormal type.

The laissez faire postulates, in brief, run counter to the culture concept as we outlined it earlier, where man is found to be not an atomistic unit in a human rabble, but an integrated member of a band, group, society, bound together by immemorial patterns. Smith and Ricardo can be excused, for they wrote long before Morgan's initial study of the Seneca Indians. It is harder to explain why their followers have consistently disregarded cultural anthropology, sociology, and social psychology right down to the present day.

Economists Support Mayo

Mayo was an industrial psychologist, but many professional economists now agree with him. As far back as 1914, the late Wesley Clair Mitchell, an outstanding American economist, anticipated Mayo by emphasizing the lack of attention paid to the other social sciences. Economists, he said, have "tacitly imputed to the men whose behavior they were analyzing, certain traits consistent with common sense and convenient for theorizing, especially the pleasure-pain principle. . . ."[4] Meanwhile, psychology has abandoned hedonism or pleasure-pain as a governing principle of human behavior. The economics of both Ricardo and Jevons rests squarely upon it. Yet when hedonism

[4] *Quarterly Journal of Economics*, 1914.

was dethroned by the psychologists, were the theories of Ricardo modified by the economists? They were not, said Mitchell; it was ruled that psychology is no concern of the economist. "Thus economics is said to rest upon the simple facts of choice, and the psychological explanation is said to be a matter of indifference to our science."

This neat elision leaves classical economic theory so purified and rarefied that human nature has no place in it. Mitchell called for a restoration of human behavior as the basis for economic assumptions. Only then, he said, will economics "cease to be a system of pecuniary logic, a mechanical study of static equilibria under non-existent conditions, and become a science of human behavior." This was a daring position for an economist to take in 1914, but everything which has happened in the intervening years has served to strengthen it.

Thorstein Veblen anticipated Mitchell in his *Theory of the Leisure Class,* published at the turn of the century. It was an ironical amalgam of anthropology and economics. He undertook to show how members of the upper-upper class in America helped to maintain status by what he called "conspicuous consumption"—big town and country houses, steam yachts, retinues of servants, diamond tiaras, fox-hunting, and collections of Old Masters. The study dates a bit today, but it was acute observation before World War I, and before the graduated income tax.

BIG THEORY: MARX

Karl Marx, who published *Das Kapital* in the 1860's, based much of his theory on Ricardo, but with a special twist. Also he relied heavily on the philosophy of Hegel with its "thesis, antithesis and synthesis," which, despite its fine verbal roll is a hard thing to measure.

We have already noted in Chapter 4 how Marx developed his theory in a state of emotional sympathy for the poor, and emerged with the principle of the class struggle. He made it an absolute, but anthropologists like Linton find it operating only under special temporary conditions. Perhaps such a condition prevailed when Marx was haunting the British Museum, but it is anything but universal in the West today. Let the reader run back through the last two chapters dealing with relations between labor and management, and note how many exceptions to the class struggle can be found. There was a vicious struggle between men and management in Jersey Standard for a time, but after 1917 it changed first to accommodation, and then to active coöperation. A truly scientific postulate cannot seesaw like this, it must hold for all conditions, and for long periods, if not indefinitely.

Marx predicted, and Lenin repeated the prediction, that as capitalism developed, the rich would grow richer, and the poor would grow poorer. In America, both groups have become richer, but the graduated income tax shaves more than 80 percent from the income of the very rich. The graduated income tax indeed, both here and in Britain, is a vast machine for the redistribution of income, unthinkable in the Marxian philosophy. The divorce of ownership from management in our great corporations, to be described in the next chapter, is also unthinkable. Capitalism has taken a course utterly different from what either Marx or Ricardo expected, bursting the bonds of both socialistic theory and laissez faire. Ricardo, I suspect, would recast his ideas in line with the facts if he were writing today; Karl Marx was a more obstinate man.

CRITICAL BARRAGE

With the rise of the behavior sciences, both economic schools have been under increasing criticism. Both tend to be static theories, while economic behavior, spurred on by technological change, is dynamic. Both have become "self-sealing doctrines," to use Robert Oppenheimer's phrase, with disciples of each vociferously maintaining that their school is absolutely right, and the other school absolutely wrong.

At a time in the early 1950's when the Moscow radio, in ringing Marxian prose, was calling on the downtrodden peasants of

America to arise and shake off their chains, I was making a survey of the Palouse wheat area in the state of Washington. The State Agricultural College at Pullman reported that the *average* yearly income of farmers in the area was $28,000 a year. After the combines had harvested the wheat crop, the downtrodden peasant and his family got into the new Cadillac and took off for Florida or Southern California.

Is Economics A Science?

We are back at the initial question raised in this chapter, and so far as the two big theories are concerned the answer seems to be "no." When one examines the operations going on inside the National City Bank, for instance, or in the Standard Oil Company of New Jersey, or the Social Security Board, or the Supermarket Institute, or the Hartford Empire Company, or the United Mine Workers Union, or the New York Stock Exchange, or the United States Treasury—the dynamic happenings therein do not correspond to the economic theories about them, either Ricardian or Marxian. The universe of the atom has been described, but not the economic universe—not in such terms that you can make an economic bomb with it. Economic bombs go off, right enough, but nobody knows exactly why.

For 30 years I have been reading economic literature, and as a professional accountant I have had an intimate view of many business enterprises. I have been through all the standard theories—laissez faire, socialism, single tax, social credit, Keynes, the coöperative commonwealth. None of them fits the objective realities which I have seen. Parts fit here and there, but as general systems they do not fit.

I have come to the conclusion that the quest for an economic "system" is a forlorn one, as forlorn as the quest for a complete philosophical system. I have come to believe that prices, wages, costs of production, profits, are expressions of the economic behavior which underlies them—what human beings *do* about them. Such economic behavior, in turn, is only a part of cultural behavior. Economic acts therefore will often be irrational, often elaborated far beyond the necessities pursued by Economic Man, and quite incalculable on any "equilibrium" framework, no matter how powerful the mathematics.

Probably no human being ever lived who possessed the characteristics ascribed in the textbooks to Economic Man. No society ever existed which followed the "economic determinism" formulated as a cardinal principle by Marx and Engels. The perfect "equilibrium" is an economic dream world, beyond space and time. The great words go round and round, but I cannot make them connect except in the most spasmodic and discontinuous way with any reality I know.

Little wonder then that the forecasts often fail to materialize. He who tries to formulate "pure" economic theory is like Alice trying to play croquet with no points fixed. The mallet is a live flamingo, the ball is a perambulating hedgehog, and the wickets are soldiers who like to get up and walk around.

If we economists can break away from the notion that there is one perfect, natural, right economic system to which mankind must adhere no matter what the concrete situation may be, our progress in solving specific economic problems should be more rapid. If we can come to realize that economics is only one aspect of the science of man, closely allied with both the culture concept and social psychology, we will abandon quixotic quests for perfect markets, perfect equilibria, perfect states, and concentrate on techniques to halt *this* depression, curb *that* inflation, eliminate malnutrition here, adjust factory conditions to workers there, prepare for automation, raise living standards as the curve of technology rises.

A good share of this book has been dealing with situations which can in one sense be called economic—the experiments at Hawthorne, the strike at Yankee City, the credos of Middletown, the testimony of the polls, the exponential growth of invention. We cannot tear this living fabric apart. Human society is all of a piece and a genuine science must treat it so.

20

Some Economic Tools

The mass production industries, like aircraft, chemicals, motorcars, are based on the work of scientists, but few of our economic institutions are based on the work of professional economists. Most banks, brokerage houses, public treasuries, supermarkets, chain stores, labor unions, trade associations, the gold standard, Farm Bureaus—either just grew like Topsy or were blocked out by lawyers.

The founding fathers of economics—Adam Smith, Ricardo, Karl Marx—came along, looked over the scene, and retired to their studies to evolve those massive theoretical structures we have been reviewing; and most students coming later were satisfied to choose which structure they preferred. It remained for Wesley Mitchell to call for exhaustive observation of what is actually going on as a necessary condition for the formulation of theory.

Most American economists, until the great depression at least, had, so to speak, been making poems about business. These often fortified the businessman's morale but did not tell him what to do—as Chester Barnard complained. For advice on that the businessman went to a first-class corporation lawyer, or accountant, or public relations man. (Now he is also going to industrial psychologists.)

The depression and then the war put economists to work on practical problems. From this experience came some remarkable new techniques, and the shape of more than one new institution—for example, the Securities and Exchange Commission.

Economists, furthermore, did not work alone but often in teams with lawyers, engineers, statisticians, sociologists.

Here and there, of course, ever since Malthus' famous monograph on population, economists and political scientists have produced sound theoretical analyses of specific institutions. Some of them properly belong in the storehouse of dependable knowledge, having far more than historical interest. I should like to outline briefly three studies published in the 1930's that seem to belong in that class. They are Colin Clark's analysis of shifts in occupation, the work of Berle and Means on the modern corporation, and J. M. Keynes's study of the causes of business depressions.

Conditions of Economic Progress

Colin Clark, British economist, tiring of grandiose economic "systems," produced a solid book of facts and figures entitled *Conditions of Economic Progress*, in which he draws some useful conclusions. With a certain irony he quotes Bacon on the title page: "It cannot be that axioms established by argumentation can suffice for the discovery of new works, for the subtilty of Nature exceedeth many times over the subtilty of argument."

To handle his data he invents at least one new concept and one new measuring device. The concept is a classification of occupations and industries on three levels, while the measuring rod is what he calls an International Unit, defined as the average amount of goods and services which could be purchased for one dollar in the United States over the decade 1925-34.

Armed with these tools, Professor Clark establishes two principal points. First, that the world as a whole is a long way from the age of plenty. Only the United States, Canada, Australia, New Zealand, Argentina, Great Britain, and Switzerland had, when he wrote, a standard of living of 1,000 International Units per head per year or better. These countries account for only about 10 percent of the world's population.

Five hundred International Units, or less, was the lot of 81 percent of mankind. More than half the world, including India and China, subsists on less than 200 International Units. The economy of abundance holds good only in those areas where science and quantity production are energetically applied to both industry and agriculture.

The second point I think is even more important. Colin Clark says:

Studying economic progress in relation to the economic structure of different centers, we find a very firmly established generalization that a high average level of real income per head is always associated with a high proportion of the working population engaged in *tertiary* industries. *Primary* industries are defined as agriculture, forestry and fishing; *secondary* industries as manufacturing, mining, and building; the *tertiary* industries include commerce, transport, services, and all other economic activities.

In the United States, Canada, Great Britain, Australia, and New Zealand, nearly half the working population was engaged in tertiary activities so defined. They include the professions, as well as what are called the "service trades." In other countries of Western Europe, and in the Argentine, from 33 to 44 percent was so engaged just before World War II.

When a country begins to industrialize, Clark's figures for man power show a relative decline in primary industry (agriculture), and an increase in secondary (manufacturing). After a while the secondary industries reach a maximum and in turn begin to level off. This seems to have happened in Great Britain and France after the turn of the century, in the United States around 1920, in Germany in 1925. Thereafter—except in the special circumstances of war production—only the tertiary industries, the service trades, can be expected relatively to expand. Common sense agrees with scientific analysis in this conclusion. As the machine contributes more energy, human beings are bound to contribute less. The number of jobs will increase in intellectual and clerical fields—the professions, education, recreation, government work, and the services generally.

This is a conclusion of great importance to the economic future of the world, and one as yet inadequately appreciated. It amounts to a formula for a mass production society, close to a scientific law. It is close enough for me constantly to advise young people that tertiary occupations offer the widest opportunities for future careers. It is close enough to encourage the government of Puerto Rico to launch an industrialization program, in the hope of getting surplus workers out of the sugar cane fields, where unemployment has been rife, into factories, and ultimately into the service trades.

Modern Corporations

Adolf A. Berle, Jr., and Gardiner C. Means in *The Modern Corporation and Private Property* contributed another conclusion of long-term importance. They took a hard look at big American corporations in the era of President Coolidge: what they owned, what they did, how they priced their products, who owned them, who controlled them. The 200 largest non-banking companies in the country were selected, companies which together accounted for nearly half of all business activity. Means as an economist assembled the corporate statistics; Berle as a lawyer assembled the legal status or analyzed the lack of it.

One effect of the study was to shatter various economic "laws" of both Marx and Ricardo. The great corporations— United States Steel, International Harvester, and the rest—had little in common with laissez faire theory. The legal owners, or "capitalists," were found to be virtually stripped of their power by a new elite of self-perpetuating corporation managers, who controlled the vast properties without owning them—something Marx had never dreamed of. The leviathans thus were left swinging in a kind of property vacuum. As the authors put it: "Ownership of wealth without appreciable control, and control of wealth without appreciable ownership, appear to be the logical outcome of corporate development." A voting proxy is not a means whereby an owner of corporate stock controls his property, but a means whereby control is taken away from him. If he gets his "conventional dividend," however, he does not normally complain.

For the 200 corporations, control was found to lodge as follows:

> In self-perpetuating management   44 percent
> In legal devices, including
> pyramiding, non-voting stock,
> voting trusts   21
> In minority interests   23
> _____
> Total control without majority
> ownership of stock   88 percent

Thus property has come to be a different thing, and ownership a very different function, from most textbook stipulations. In many cases the great companies were found to be beyond and above the free competitive market. Either they were outright monopolies, or they practiced "monopolistic competition" like the great tobacco or motor car companies—a condition called by the awkward name "oligopoly" in another famous study, by E. H. Chamberlin.[1]

Gardiner Means, in a later analysis of prices in the depression, showed conclusively that prices in markets where there was active competition among small units like farmers, tended to fall as demand declined. The "law" of supply and demand worked. On the "administered" markets of great corporations, however, as demand fell, output was curtailed, workers were laid off, but prices were substantially maintained. Supply and demand did not work.

KEYNES AND THE GREAT DEPRESSION

John Maynard Keynes first came to public attention when, as a young man, he wrote *The Economic Consequences of the Peace*. He took a gloomy view of the Peace of Versailles after World War I, and later events, culminating in the rise of

[1] *The Theory of Monopolistic Competition.*

Hitler, turned out to be even gloomier. He wrote with wit and precision, and was widely read through the 1920's; but the publication of *General Theory of Employment, Interest and Money* in 1935 made him world-famous. Hardly a professor could write a paper without discussing him pro or con. For a time it looked as if he were to join the ranks of the Big Theory men, to stand with Ricardo and Marx as a scholar who offered an answer to every economic question.

Now, 20 years later, we are realizing that his contribution was more modest. He analyzed brilliantly what happens in a business depression, and went on to demonstrate how to prevent or halt depressions. He analyzed the up-phase of the cycle too, and showed how to check inflation. His slim volume, *How to Pay for the War*, contained suggestions for curbing inflation which all belligerent governments put to use in some degree in the 1940's, with the result that inflation was better controlled than during any other war in history. (Later it broke loose when the controls he recommended were relaxed.)

Keynes outlined what has been called the "compensatory economy," whereby the business cycle can be leveled out in peace time. The government engineers it, but businessmen and unions coöperate. The basic idea is to promote spending vigorously when the economy starts down, and vigorously restrain further spending and expansion when the economy starts soaring toward the stratosphere. He outlined the various tools to be used, such as public works, interest rates, controls on consumer credit, taxation policy, and so on.

His major thesis was that "the spending of income does not take care of itself automatically in such fashion as to tend constantly toward full employment."[2] He denied the Ricardian assumption that it did. Keynes said, in effect, that when an economy starts up, or starts down, in a major movement of inflation or deflation, political and business leaders had better

[2] I am following Dr. John Maurice Clark's analysis of Keynes, in an article for the *American Economic Review* in 1947.

do something about it, not fold their hands and wait for "natural law" to set things straight.

In a downswing, if consumers have no money to spend, and businessmen are afraid to spend for new investment, then the government had better spend. This policy was as reasonable as it was heretical from the Ricardian standpoint, for it contravened a major postulate of laissez faire: that intervention by the state is an absolute evil. But Keynes was no Marxian either; to the day of his death he was a vigorous defender of free competition whenever and wherever it would work.

He emphasized that men in bread lines, not prices in the market, are the more significant economic data. He split the academic guild wide open, and created a ferment among professional economists which rivaled the ferment Einstein had created among the physicists a generation earlier. He formalized a feeling which many economists were beginning to share, namely, that Ricardian theory did not fit reality closely enough to warrant following its principles in a major depression. Meanwhile not many economists, especially in America, were prepared to embrace Marxism as an alternative; it too was founded on exceedingly shaky assumptions, as we have seen. Keynes came to the rescue with a middle-road, pragmatic program which said in effect: "Don't stand there hoping for a god from the machine; *do* something!" And he made some excellent suggestions about what to do. It may well be that because of his work, no large nation will ever again submit to such a catastrophic depression as that of 1929-39. J. K. Galbraith, speaking of the United States, after the promises of the Republican administration to halt a downswing in 1954, puts it this way:[3]

There is a widespread notion that one of the most primitive of modern ideological choices is whether a government shall be Keynesian or not. In fact, faced with the reality of a depression, this comes to nothing more or less than a choice of whether or not to commit political suicide. . . . No present or future administration really has the non-Keynesian choice, come a serious depression, of

[3] *Economics and the Art of Controversy.*

trying to balance the budget and letting nature, unemployment, farm prices . . . all take their course.

Keynes offers national administrations anywhere a three-point formula to stop depression: (1) lower taxes so that consumers can spend, (2) liberalize credit, (3) promote public works. It is to be presumed that no administration will refuse the gift after the harrowing lessons of the Great Depression.

While Keynes discussed in his writings the "propensity to consume," and the "propensity to save," which look like psychological factors, it is doubtful if he ever really grasped certain fundamentals of economic behavior. He was primarily an economist, not a sociologist. His economic theory did not allow, for instance, for the behavior of housewives after World War II. His school looked for a sharp depression when war spending stopped; estimates ran up to ten million unemployed in America unless the government took vigorous compensatory action. No action was taken, and unemployment never went above three million. Why? Because five long years without durable goods —refrigerators, washing machines, houses, automobiles—had built up a tremendous spending drive in millions of American households. Consumers descended on the market after the war like a tidal wave, bought everything in sight, and clamored for more. It would be hard to find a better illustration of the frailty of economic theory without the study of actual behavior.

NEW DEAL PHILOSOPHERS

"The New Deal" is a label covering a series of congressional and administrative acts over a period of about seven years, 1933-40. The people who originated and refined these acts— the FDIC, SEC, AAA, TVA, and the rest of the "alphabet soup" as critics called it—had no settled economic philosophy at all. They were trying to stop the depression with any means which came to hand. Their efforts undoubtedly helped to stop it, but not until the war boom of 1941 was unemployment finally liquidated.

Two main ideas struggled for mastery in the ranks of the New Dealers. I used to sit in at some of their conferences and listen to the uproar. One group was for accepting Big Business, Big Labor, Big Government, and proceeding from that base with big overall planning. The other group, heavily influenced by Mr. Justice Brandeis, was for curtailing Big Business, enforcing the antitrust law, getting back to the grass roots and small units. Thurman Arnold was one of the leaders of the latter school, with his spirited campaign against monopoly.

There was, accordingly, no ideological unity among the New Dealers, no strong group of embattled followers of either Ricardo or Marx. There were some followers of Keynes, especially in the analysis of savings and investment. There were deliberate attempts, such as the Public Works Administration, to keep dollars moving according to Keynesian ideas.

Political opponents called the New Dealers "agents of Moscow." The actual agents of Moscow, with headquarters in Union Square, New York, called them "lily-livered liberals," "social fascists," and "agents of Wall Street." History, I suspect, will record that the period was marked by intelligent young men, some with degrees in economics, some with degrees from law schools, working 14 hours a day trying to find food and employment for a stricken people, trying to make the economic wheels go round again. In Middletown, we remember, a quarter of the population was on relief.

PRACTICAL ECONOMICS

We have looked at the two Big Theories, Ricardian and Marxian, and retreated in some disorder. At best they are social science$_2$—unverified hypotheses. We have inspected the less lofty formulations of Colin Clark, Berle and Means, Keynes, and found them helpful for a better understanding of what is going on—not *all* that is going on, but some of it.

Now we will sample some of the significant work performed by economists during World War II; work not only useful but soundly scientific and capable of prediction. After the attack on Pearl Harbor, a large number of professional economists and statisticians volunteered for public service. Their activities were divided into these main groups: (1) Price control and rationing, (2) The allocation of materials, (3) Techniques for financing the war, (4) Manpower mobilization, (5) Economic intelligence—such as finding out the economic condition of the enemy, and preclusive buying to keep strategic materials out of his hands.

Galbraith gives us a lively account of economists in action, especially in the price control board.[4] "During the second World War the United States, partly by improvisation, partly by plan, developed a system for mobilizing economic resources that, by commonly accepted standards of performance, proved highly satisfactory." In common with most belligerents, the United States employed the "disequilibrium system," by which Galbraith means that the normal market economy was suspended for the duration. Old motivations were supplanted by new forces for determining economic behavior, among them government control over economic resources and over prices, including rationing.

Ordinary market incentives proved largely useless. Automobile makers, for instance, would not voluntarily convert to tanks and bombers even when guaranteed large profits. Similarly, steel makers declined to enlarge their capacity. Finally, the government through the War Production Board had to lay down the law, telling automobile men and steel men what they must do if the war was to be won.

As prices on many markets had long since been "administered," i.e., kept in line by business management, Galbraith found that in this case "price fixing presents no problem of principle, and the war experience came close to showing that such markets are not the exception . . . The designing of price regulations to fit the structure of such markets and their enforcement was the price administration's ablest piece of craftsman-

[4] "The Disequilibrium System," *American Economic Review*, June, 1947.

ship." Thus the thesis of Berle and Means was amply verified. When war came, the government took over the control of prices from the large corporate or trade association interests which for years had been exercising that supervision, and the transition was relatively smooth.

In those markets where free competition still remained, "price control must be supplemented by rationing. In spite of brilliant initial successes, this was the area of . . . failure in the operation of the disequilibrium system." But the failure was not the fault of the economists. The early rationing programs were ably conceived and ably executed. "A good case could be made that the rationing of meats, canned goods and fuel, were among the outstanding administrative achievements of the war." Meat rationing, in particular, brought order to markets which price control without rationing had reduced to chaos.

Price control, guided by such men as Leon Henderson, Galbraith, Donald Wallace, and John M. Clark, achieved brilliant success in holding prices. It was designed, launched, and administered largely by economists. Yet while it was in full career, Congress suddenly banned professional economists from holding administrative positions! Presumably they had never met a payroll, and did not know what they were doing. This was a savage thrust at social science. Scientists were not only saving the country's morale by holding prices firmly, but also saving billions of dollars for taxpayers. Yet Congress banished them to Siberia.

GNP

The letters GNP stand for Gross National Product, which is an elaborate statistical compilation to estimate the total dollar value of goods and services turned out by a nation in a year. It is a rate of work and so a useful figure for peace as well as war, indicating levels of production, employment, and general economic well-being. A whole complex of studies have clustered around GNP. Isador Lubin believes that war production could not have reached the volume it did without this statistical information. He credits its inception to Wesley Mitchell's work on national income at the National Bureau of Economic Research years before.

Thanks principally to the GNP studies, everybody who is interested in the economic shape of his world now knows that there are three, and only three, agencies which can spend money: (1) the ultimate consumer, (2) the businessman, (3) the government. Gross National Product is the total of their combined efforts. If the total begins to shrink, the first step is to find out which agency is curtailing its outlays, and why. The second step is to offset the shrinkage by stimulating one, or two, or all the agencies. This is the heart of the "compensatory" program for maintaining permanent prosperity.

Keynes, like Einstein, introduced the idea of relativity into his science. An increase in government spending at a time of full employment is an invitation to harmful inflation, but an increase at a time of serious unemployment is a blessing. More money placed in the hands of business when investors are alarmed by fears of depression will not "trickle down" to the consumers, but will remain frozen. When business investors have confidence, the reverse is true. It all depends upon when, and by whom, the spending is done—the judgment is relative, not absolute.

OTHER WAR ACTIVITIES BY ECONOMISTS

Stacy May headed a brilliant statistical group in the War Production Board that not only helped to find raw materials, but calculated the proper allocation between essential and less essential uses. The central control agencies, such as the Requirements Committee and the Controlled Markets Plan, were largely devised and staffed by economists, including E. S. Mason, W. L. Thorp, Clair Wilcox.

Then there was a series of Anglo-American economic control boards, some headed by economists like Thomas Blaisdell. There were economists in the War Shipping Board, in the Office of Defense Transportation, in the Board of Economic Warfare, in the Treasury advising on war loans, in the Bureau of the

Budget and in the Federal Reserve Board. Chairman Marriner Eccles was himself a profound student of economics.

The war called for all the analytical and administrative talents which classroom teachers of economics had ever concealed. It gave them full scope to show what they had in them. They responded magnificently but they worked within a closed system. The *end* was given: to win the war. Only the means were sought. This wartime experience, however, represented an important stage in the relation of economists to society. Thousands of them streamed across the bridge from uncertain theory to practical reality.

SOME FINANCIAL LESSONS OF THE WAR

Perhaps the major economic lesson of the war is the one underlined by the International Labor Office at its 1946 convention in Montreal: "A nation can afford anything it can produce." If this lesson had been learned before the stock market crash of 1929, there never would have needed to be a serious depression. Factories and workers were all there, ready to produce. But in 1929 it was believed that the country could not "afford" to let them go to work. This catastrophic cultural lag has now been pretty well overcome.

Beardsley Ruml continues the theme.[5] New discoveries due to war have not been limited to the natural sciences, he says. Great advances have also been made in the fields of finance and economics. The full impact is not yet understood, but we "know enough to know that some things which many competent people thought were true, are either false or true in a different way than was believed." For instance, during the 1930's most people believed that a budget deficit must have an inflationary effect. Now we know that this is not necessarily so.

"The plain fact is," says Ruml, "that the war was actually financed on a declining rate of interest. What does this mean? It means that a *new relationship* has been created between the private money market and the national state." To meet its ex-

[5] In a speech to the New York Employing Printers' Association in 1946.

penses, a nation can either tax or borrow. Borrowing postpones the tax. In the past this has meant higher interest rates charged by the private money market as the national debt has grown. Thus up to 1940 the private market—in the United States we call it Wall Street—dictated the terms for government loans, and usually dictated the tax structure.

In World War II this system was outgrown. Financing became too great for private lenders to handle. Private bankers no longer have the final word on the fiscal policies of the United States government, and control, says Ruml, must henceforth come from the whole community, not from private lenders. Washington, not Wall Street, is now the financial center of not only the country but the world. "It follows that our federal government has final freedom from the money market in meeting its financial requirements. Accordingly the prime consideration in the imposition of taxes has become the social and economic consequences."

It is interesting to note that while Ruml was describing this great historic change in the relative positions of Wall Street and the Treasury, Communists in Moscow were reviving their ancient slogans to the effect that Wall Street was out to dominate the planet. The Communists suffer more from cultural lag than many American conservatives.

Perhaps there is nothing to be called an "economic system" and therefore no laws foretelling its overall performance. But if somebody wants to operate a Central Bank, or float a bond issue, or finance a war, or halt a depression, or arrange an international loan, there are many useful tools now in the hands of economists to assist the process.

Both the great depression and the great war shook economists out of their classrooms into the market place—the real market, where they had to face the National City Bank, United States Steel, Henry Kaiser, John L. Lewis, Ed O'Neal of the Farm Bureau Federation, and the embattled Cattlemen's Association. Their classroom theories were of little use to them in the "disequilibrium" system, but their habits of analysis and of suspended judgment, their ability to handle statistics, were of the greatest value. They got rid of their academic frustrations[6] by experience in practical policy-making and administration.

[6] ". . . Long-standing frustration on the part of many economists that economic theory gave no answers to questions of economic policy . . ." Paul T. Homan in *American Economic Review*, December, 1946.

21

New Dimensions

We have applied the test of the scientific method to three departments of economics—General Theory, Special Theory, and Practical Applications. The first was found to be shaky, but the other two stood up well. Let us now look at some experiments, hypotheses, and studies in the economic field today which are opening a new dimension in economic thinking.

OPERATION BOOTSTRAP

The island of Puerto Rico is smaller than the State of Connecticut, but has a larger population. It is a beautiful, mountainous island, with sugar fields along the coasts, white beaches, palm trees, old Spanish forts, and the incredible colors of the Caribbean sea all around. Those economists who have been fond of erecting theories with Robinson Crusoe's island as a model—a two-man economy—might turn with more profit to Puerto Rico, where they find a two-million-man economy.

"Operation Bootstrap" is an attempt to shift from a one-crop sugar culture to a diversified industrial society in a few years' time and do it without exploiting workers or surrendering democratic freedoms. It took the United States nearly a century to become a society primarily industrial. Political democracy was maintained, but the condition of workers in factories and mines, especially in the early years, left a good deal to be desired. It has taken the U.S.S.R. forty years to become partially industrialized. Many reports still describe slave labor camps, miserable living standards, and no vestiges of political democracy.

In America our economic slogans have celebrated the individualism of Ricardo, in the U.S.S.R. the collectivism of Marx. But in Puerto Rico we find a more realistic and scientific approach to economic problems. Operation Bootstrap is not "capitalism," or "socialism," or "labor unionism," or any other -ism. Its standard is the well-being of the whole island, using whatever agency—government, private business, coöperative enterprise—best serves that goal.

One would have expected a more ideological approach from the political party of Governor Muñoz Marin, for when it rose to power in 1940, the party was frankly socialistic. Early reforms were along socialist lines, with government corporations set up for both agriculture and industry, and plans for further nationalization on the drawing board. Private owners were to be bought out at a fair price (which is of course not the communist idea of nationalization) and the state was to become the major entrepreneur. The government acquired a cement plant, and built factories for the manufacture of shoes, paper, glass, clay products. It began collectivizing the sugar industry.

Presently the program got into management troubles, labor troubles, credit troubles. The cement plant did fairly well, but the other four state factories showed persistent losses. A serious difficulty was that the labor unions, who thought that a socialistic government was *their* government, expected exorbitant favors.

With the economy beginning to crack, the Governor and his staff abandoned socialism as a policy guide, and inaugurated Operation Bootstrap. They deliberately designed it to encourage the development of private business on the island, and to get the government out of losing enterprises. The five plants were sold to local capitalists who had demonstrated their managerial ability, and the proceeds were promptly used for new construction. Hotels and factories were built, to be leased or sold to businessmen. Proceeds from these were later reinvested in a kind of perpetual revolving fund. Taxes on new enterprises were abated for a series of years, and the labor force required was trained by the government.

Local businessmen and businessmen from the States began to

feel differently about a government which was so mindful of their interests, and good relations grew apace. While I was investigating the program in 1951, I used to hear American businessmen, interested in establishing a branch in San Juan, damn Washington as a nest of interfering bureaucrats, and in the next breath praise the staff of *Fomento* (Operation Bootstrap) as gentlemen and scholars. Their whole ideological mechanism seemed to have gone into reverse.

This was a strange but cheerful shift of gears. It meant that neither the structure of modern business, nor that of government, necessarily prevents friendly coöperation for common goals. The difference is ideological, not structural. Also it means, I am afraid, that Puerto Rico has forged far ahead of the mainland in developing this new dimension.

A major goal of the program is to cut down the birth rate, increase employment opportunities, and so reduce emigration to congested areas in New York and elsewhere. Industrialization, as population experts have demonstrated, always reduces the birth rate. It also reduces the death rate, especially of babies. I do not know whether this goal of balancing births against jobs can be reached, but there seems to be a good fighting chance. What nobody can overlook who studies the island is that Puerto Rico now offers a unique and significant laboratory for experimenting with economic change and economic behavior.

Other Economic Laboratories

There are other laboratories exploring the new dimension, though none so tidy as that of Governor Muñoz. Sweden has long practised the "Middle Way," with wide areas of agreement among businessmen, government men, and the managers of large coöperative associations. The powerful Social Democratic Party however, is committed to a mild type of socialism, as is the British Labour Party. Turkey provides another interesting laboratory in rapid economic and social change.[1]

[1] The U.S.S.R. has the largest economic laboratory of all but publishes no dependable results. The best guess is that it is old-fashioned in labor policy, and very hard on agriculture, but does turn out a surprising volume of munitions.

The Tennessee Valley Authority has developed close coöperation with businessmen in the Valley, but not with businessmen elsewhere, especially executives in the power and light industry. The United States Atomic Energy Commission is now promoting joint projects with private business in developing peacetime uses of atomic fission. In the manufacture of aircraft, partnership is well advanced; some 95 percent of all United States airplanes are built in private plants to government order, with the aid of research in government laboratories.

The fact of partnership in common goals is widespread, but only in Puerto Rico has a cease fire in the ideological battle of "Bureaucrats" vs. "Profiteers" been declared.

COUNTERVAILING POWER

Probably the most arresting economic theory since Keynes is the concept of "countervailing power," advanced by J. K. Galbraith in 1952.[2] Puzzled because the "disequilibrium" system had not foundered, despite the gloomy prophecies of both conservatives and liberals, he sought a theory to explain the relative stability of the American economy in recent years.

Five massive political and economic forces, he finds, have supplied the checks and balances to keep the system on a reasonably even keel. They are: (1) Big Industry; (2) Big Distribution—the great mail-order houses, chains, supermarkets; (3) Big Labor; (4) Big Agriculture—with probably the most powerful lobby in Washington; and (5) Big Government.

When one of these giants attempts to dominate the national scene, the others—one or more of them—make a countermove, thus producing in effect a competitive system on the highest level. If Big Industry gets too tough, Big Distribution will build its own factories to cut the price on washing machines or TV sets. If Big Labor thinks it owns the roost, Big Business, Government, and Agriculture may join to slap it down with a Taft-Hartley law. If Big Government tries to extend its industrial controls, the others may combine to set a limit. The old com-

[2] *American Capitalism.*

petitive system of small units, says Galbraith, has passed into history; but this supercompetition now provides a brake on excessive power in any one place.

It is a stimulating hypothesis, and is being widely discussed. Verification will have to wait for tangible performance over the years. Like the laboratory in Puerto Rico, the theory of countervailing power takes economic thinking into fresh new fields.

THE CONCENTRATES

Adolf Berle in a recent book has pushed ahead with his theory of the development of corporations in America.[3] In his earlier work with Gardiner Means, he demonstrated how control had passed from legal owners to self-perpetuating managers, who might or might not own a share of stock. This demonstration helped to overturn traditional ideas about "capitalism"—as noted in the last chapter.

In the quarter-century since the publication of *The Modern Corporation*, the big firms in America have continued to grow, and owners have become still more detached from their legal property. Competition among giants, sometimes called monopolistic competition, is very different from competition among the little firms of Ricardo's day. "It means quite another thing when four or five large units are grinding against each other." In motorcars, only three giants now grind, and if Chrysler is not careful, there may be only two. The few great companies grinding within a given industry Berle calls a *concentrate*. "Competition within a concentrate is more a struggle for power to balance supply against demand, than to secure customers by price competition."

Concentrates are found in oil, sugar, railroads, electric power, meat products, aluminum, chemicals, rubber, and many other mass production industries. Where are they headed? Nobody knows, but Berle ventures some preliminary speculations. "We are nibbling," he says, "at the edges of a vast, dangerous and fascinating piece of thinking." Americans are not used to think-

[3] *The Twentieth Century Capitalist Revolution.*

ing of Big Industry as the political institution which it has now actually become. We have not created any frame of responsibility, any formal mandate to make the concentrates legitimate.

"There is no recognized body of doctrine by which they themselves must test their choice as they act from day to day . . . no one has ever made a blueprint of the community desired by Jersey Standard, Sears Roebuck, Southern Pacific, Ohio Edison, least of all the corporations themselves."

I would like to pause for a moment here, and quote Mr. Frank Abrams, who as Chairman of the Board of Jersey Standard, once told me something of the future he desired for that vast enterprise. Its mission was to use scientific research to explore new and better ways of providing things that people wanted. It must become a kind of public service, said Mr. Abrams, responsible to at least four publics: to the consumers of its products, to its employees on all levels, to suppliers of its materials, and to government as representing the whole community. Unless Jersey Standard holds steadfastly to this role, Mr. Abrams prophesied, it will not survive—not in the kind of world which lies ahead.

To return to Mr. Berle: he calls in effect for the kind of corporate conscience expressed by the Chairman of the Board of Jersey Standard. Such conscience has not been widely developed. The "concentrates" swing in a legal and political vacuum, turning out half of America's goods, holding enormous interests abroad, "capable of becoming one of the master tools of society —capable also of surprising abuse. . . ." A common abuse today is for a concentrate to pick up and leave a town—say Manchester, New Hampshire—tearing the economic heart out of the community as it goes.

Berle finds that 135 nonbanking corporations control 45 percent of United States industrial assets and account for a quarter of the manufacturing output of the world. Their managers decide: (1) the activities of millions of workers—subject to certain checks and balances by Big Labor and Big Government. (2) whether and how to carry on operations, whether to get out

of a city regardless of its future. (3) what markets to serve—
either to meet a public demand, or create one. (4) the important
function of technological development—for example, deciding
how much automation to introduce, and how rapidly. They try
(5) to influence public opinion through mass media. Finally (6),
managers control the extent and rate of capital expansion, making
that cardinal contribution to gross national product (GNP)
noted in the last chapter.

The above six powers of management, says Berle, add up to an
informal planned economy, leaving the "judgement of the market
place" far behind. Some two thirds of the funds for expansion,
furthermore, do not come from borrowing in the market place,
but from sources within, or available only to, the concentrates—
reinvested profits, depreciation and other reserves. Of $150 billion
of new capital improvements, 1946-53, about $9 billion, or 6 per-
cent, came from stock issues. Only at this point do "we approach
the risk capital so much relied on by classical economic theory.
The capital is there; so is capitalism. The waning factor is the
capitalist."

The concentrates, says Berle, share the goal of most American businessmen: "Fundamentally they all want not a perpetual
struggle but a steady job—the job of producing goods at roughly
predictable cost, under roughly predictable conditions, so
that goods can be sold in the market at a roughly predictable
price." They want, of course, to grow in size and power.

Well, there it is, the economic powerhouse of half America,
and a quarter of the world, the climax of a long process, mark-
edly accelerated since 1930. Mr. Berle wants the managers to
get religion, and feel greater responsibility for their massive institution, now in effect a political institution. Mr. Abrams seems
to feel it, so does Murray Lincoln, the insurance company executive and coöperative leader, and one could name a few more.
Most managers, one suspects, have little comprehension of the
role into which history has thrust them.

Here then is another new dimension, demanding scientific
analysis. It connects with the thesis of countervailing power. We

find in the concentrate the essence of America's secret of production. It is indeed a secret in the sense that nobody knows much about the forces which brought it to pass, or the trend it rides. To declaim about "our glorious free enterprise system" explains nothing. To declaim about "the blessings of competition," is not much better, until the extraordinary character of the competition, the grinding of the concentrates, and the countervailing thrusts of other institutions, are explained.

"If ever corporation managers base their continued tenure on power and not on reason, the end is disaster." Social scientists have plenty of work cut out for them here. Mr. Berle is of course not alone in the field, others are making contributions too—including acute studies of the new corporation structure by David Lilienthal and Peter Drucker.

RESEARCH IN ECONOMIC BEHAVIOR

New institutions obviously cannot be successfully analyzed with the tools of traditional economic research. The behavior sciences, including opinion research, must all be enlisted to help. To begin with, the postulates of the traditional Big Theories need more examination, not necessarily to refute them, but to determine what drives really underlie the behavior we call economic. Will an increase in wage rates, for instance, induce more or less work from the society? The Hawthorne experiments tell us something but not enough. Should a government seeking more output from citizens raise income taxes or lower them; make tax rates more steeply graduated or less? There is plenty of theory both ways, but what are the facts? We need more research on the behavior of unions, the behavior of household consumers—where, for instance, is the do-it-yourself movement taking us?—the behavior of large financial institutions, of government managers, as well as corporation managers.

What does "full employment" mean in human terms? What are the consequences of consumer attitudes on future economic conditions? Is there any saturation point to consumer demands? What is the process by which a new product— TV, for instance —is absorbed? What makes consumers spend or save? The above questions, raised by a member of the economics faculty at Yale, are fundamental to an understanding of the American economy, and for most of them we have only tentative answers.

STUDIES AT MICHIGAN

George Katona of the University of Michigan, writing in the *Scientific American* (October, 1954), supplies some answers based on sampling United States consumers in recent years. After the outbreak of war in Korea, he says, prices rose sharply, with little increase in government spending or money in circulation—the classical reasons for inflation. But in the spring of 1951, when government spending in the form of rearmament outlays really began to roll, United States householders ceased their panic buying and began to save their money—contradicting traditional theory again. "People's economic behavior appeared to be governed more by their expectation of what was going to happen, than by the situation at the moment."

Katona reports that five sets of variables should be considered when research into economic behavior is undertaken: (1) enabling conditions—assets and income of the group being studied; (2) precipitating circumstances—a new house, a new baby; (3) habits as imposed by the culture; (4) contracts already in force —for installment purchase of the new car, for rent, insurance; (5) psychological state of consumers at the time. "As a result of group identification and mass communication, similar changes in attitude often occur among very many people at about the same time," and so a measurable trend can be plotted.

In an economy held to bare subsistence such trends will not appear, as all income goes for stark necessities. As abundance comes in, the definition of a "necessity" expands, and consumers' choices become more complicated. Analysis of economic behavior becomes increasingly essential as living standards rise. Katona offers the following generalizations:

Keynes said that in prosperous times, people whose income declines will draw on savings to maintain standards. Research shows this to be correct, provided they expect the decline to be temporary.

Keynes said that as consumer income rises, savings also increase.

No, says Katona, our studies show that spending often goes up faster than income. In the period 1947-50, people with rising incomes borrowed the most; people with declining incomes came second; people with steady incomes borrowed least.

Classical postulates say that if people expect prices to go up they will buy; if down, they will not buy. Advertised bargain sales contradict this conclusion, and such sales have a substantial effect on consumer behavior today.

If people think prices are "about right" they will buy briskly; this is the condition most favorable to consumer spending. The current business policy of aiming at price stability, tempered with bargain sales, suits householders.

There is no "saturation point" in buying-as-a-whole, says Katona. If people have enough cars, they will send their children to college. "We give up aspirations when we have failed, not when we have succeeded." Following the American success saga, our buying proceeds from one level to another. "Saturation" for most people comes only when they feel economically insecure. (For some of us, however, saturation comes with material comfort. Personally I do not want to be bothered with any more stuff, and buy less than I did 20 years ago. But my status in the culture depends on my work as a writer, not on keeping up with the Joneses, and so I am probably an abnormal case.)

The last generalization of Katona's is encouraging. His surveys show no reason to expect a depression automatically following a period of prosperity, but rather the contrary. Consumers do not behave in a way to give the business cycle any regularity of ups and downs. (Perhaps we ought to drop that word "cycle" as a semantic misfit.)

We have learned enough from these surveys, Katona says, to know that "economic psychology very usefully supplements the theoretical and statistical approach of traditional economics." Mr. Katona is too modest: his surveys do not so much supplement the traditional approach as make a shambles of it.[4]

[4] Another fruitful lead in this connection is the work of a team composed of Oskar Morgenstern, economist, and John von Neumann, mathematician. Their book, *Theory of Games and Economic Behavior*, brings the laws of probability to bear on decision-making by executives and other economic agents.

Reviewing the art and science of economics today, one finds encouraging signs of a new dimension. Fortified with studies in behavior, in probability mathematics, and aided by electronic computers—as in Leontief's "Input-Output" calculations[5]— some fresh and important economic theory may be close at hand. Galbraith and Berle are obviously on the edge of it, and a whole school may blossom quite suddenly. It will not be grandiose, full-whiskered theory covering the entire economy, but limited, verified theory, which policy-makers in government and in business—and in households too—can put to useful work.

[5] In which the raw material used by every industry is balanced against the finished product of every industry, an impossible statistical achievement before electronics. See his book, *The Structure of the American Economy.*

22

Reforming the Reformers

To one who has been advocating reforms of one kind and another ever since he read Henry George on the single tax many years ago, social science in its more rigorous aspects comes with something of a shock. Your author looks back at his enthusiasms and begins to realize that some of his aims were unachievable, and most of his means were unworkable. Clearly he will have to start again from the beginning, and he is not as young as he was.

We are speaking of reformer$_1$, who genuinely wants to see conditions remedied, without too personal a motive. Reformer$_2$, on the other hand, as the psychologists describe him, is a frustrated individual with something wrong in his home or job or emotional life. He takes to communism, currency reform, or technocracy, as an escape from personal difficulties. Reformer$_2$, furthermore, tends to select a cause where he can do a lot of hating—communism, for instance, is ideal for this, with its hierarchy of demons: "Capitalists," "Wall Street," "Imperialist Warmongers," "Trotskyites." The best service which science could render reformer$_2$ would be to clear up his emotional insecurity.

What can social science do for reformer$_1$? A number of helpful suggestions are on file and more are being accumulated all the time. We have met a few of them earlier in this book and will now try to get them in some sort of order. This chapter is addressed to those who seriously want to change an institution or a custom in the culture, especially in the field of economics.

PERPETUAL MOTION MACHINES

Perhaps the first task for the genuine reformer is to take a look at the history of perpetual motion machines. For centuries, at least as far back as the Greeks, ingenious persons have devoted themselves to a search for the principle of perpetual motion. Some wanted to make their fortunes, others a great name; most, perhaps, were just curious.

Whatever their motives, the inventors spent years constructing frictionless wheels, ball-bearing spheres, dissolving chemicals, and mechanical constructs that would amaze cartoonist Rube Goldberg. The wheel which the Marquis of Worcester devised in 1660 was 14 feet in diameter and elaborately rigged with 40 sliding weights of 50 pounds apiece. Even Leonardo gave his attention to a wheel to turn itself forever by quicksilver. The screw of Archimedes, the "hydrostatical paradox," capillary attraction, were all employed by the savants. Crackpots to this very day are working on electronics, magnetism, natural heat, and liquid air, hoping to give their construct a shove which will keep it going forever.

As early as 1775 the Paris Academy of Science refused to receive any more schemes for perpetuum mobile, though the theoretical refutation was still incomplete. When the first and second laws of thermodynamics were laid down a little later, perpetual motion machines were thrown finally into the scientific ash can. Nobody in his right mind would ever again waste time on them—except to sell a gold brick to the scientifically illiterate.

How many social and economic mechanisms for reform— agitated and supported by leagues, societies, institutes, celebrities, mass subscriptions, and high-priced publicity agencies—are perpetual motion machines? Every week as I open my mail and the appeals and summonses to action drop out, I finger them and ponder how much of a perpetuum mobile is this, and had the Marquis of Worcester anything to beat that?

The social scientists have not yet produced generalizations as elegant and definitive as the first and second laws of thermo-dynamics, but they have produced enough to raise a large question mark over my mail. They are certainly as far along as the Paris Academy when it banged the door on callers with a box of sliding weights. Already they have chilled my crusading zeal, built up my bank account, and caused me to get a larger waste-basket.

Here is a sample from an aspiring inventor. During the great depression I received literally hundreds of such plans, representing incalculable devotion by their authors.

Dear Mr. Chase:

The fateful years prior to and during the late war with their terrible aftermath have impressed all thoughtful people with the pressing need for some basic change in our social system.

In my manuscript, *The Perfect Answer*, I have outlined a plan to eliminate the boom-and-bust economic cycle, as well as the peace and war political cycle. I have also devised a transition period which would ultimately give us the perfect world of tomorrow through a form of evolution allowing complete fairness to all concerned.

Feeling that you would be interested, I am mailing you a copy of my plan. Please send me your comments as soon as possible and suggest what publisher would be most interested in it.

Yours very truly,
Ernest Mead

Mr. Mead—I am shielding his real name—is obviously on the side of the angels. But I am afraid that he was beaten by the laws of the culture concept before he started.

Linton explains in one sentence what is wrong with most Utopias and with such omnibus schemes as Mr. Mead's. "The greatest difficulty which confronts a leader who seeks to develop a new society is that he has to start with persons who have already been trained to live in some other society." The Utopia builder can compose admirable constitutions and codes; but the wayfaring citizen is unable to accept them outright no matter how much he may desire to. "People live mainly by habit, acting as they have been taught to act without stopping to think first."

If we were suddenly transported to Utopia we should have to stop and think before nearly every act we performed, and would go stark mad long before we acquired a whole new set of automatic habits. We should be like the centipede who was asked which leg came after which, only to fall exhausted in the ditch, considering how to run.

Training to live in one's culture, as we have seen, begins at birth. By the time George Adams is even half-grown he has accumulated a mass of unconscious habits closely fitted to his Middleburg society. If George's little son were sent to live in a Burmese village, the boy could probably shift over within a few years. But if a large group of Americans go to live in Burma, they will take most of their culture with them and not even learn the language. The typical Utopian reform is like trying to move a whole American town to Burma and make it a Burmese community overnight. It is a perpetuum mobile. So is the converse, sometimes attempted by missionaries and economic advisers—making a native community behave like Americans.

When Reform Has a Chance

A second fundamental principle for practical reformers is that a successful movement requires enough tension and frustrations in the society to offer political leverage. When the majority of citizens are going contentedly about their business, the reformer had better teach canasta or give a course on the Great Books. A good illustration is the postwar period in the United States. With practically full employment all large plans for housing, health, minimum wages, inflation control, were received with yawns. There was not enough frustration to give such reforms a chance, however useful they might have proved.

A major problem of the reformer is to determine when the lag between popular credos and real need is great enough to promise some success. Franklin Roosevelt, who was far from being a typical reformer, happened to arrive when the lag was long, and a change overdue. Three years of economic paralysis had made the need for jobs, food, security, abnormally great.

The credos of the American culture, with their insistence on self-help, had come to sound unrealistic, if not positively cruel. Action was accordingly possible over a wide front, and Roosevelt and his New Dealers moved briskly in with a whole alphabet of reforms. The tensions and the frustrations were there; and though the old credos began to be heard again on Main Street after 1935, the needs of the mass of the people were strong enough to reëlect Roosevelt repeatedly, a political phenomenon without precedent.

Had Roosevelt been aware of these cultural laws he might have laid his communication lines more wisely and achieved wider agreement. Unfortunately he saw the situation as a fight, good people against bad, when it was not that kind of two-valued situation. He called the "bad people" a number of hard names—"moneychangers," "economic royalists," and the like. Naturally this infuriated the well-to-do; and they heaped on Roosevelt all their depression-born frustrations and fears. If the President had consistently spoken for *all* the people whom the depression had hurt or bewildered, including the upper brackets, and summoned all brackets to move toward recovery and freedom from fear, he might have averted much of the Roosevelt-hating. The point is that the great depression provided one of the few periods in history when a large majority of the people were ready for change.

CLASS STRUGGLES AGAIN

Many reform movements, as we noted earlier, assume an inevitable conflict between the classes and the masses. Two types of conflict are always latent, though they do not often follow the Marxian pattern. They arise between the individual and society, and between groups inside the society. The individual is kept in line by formal or informal penalties, ranging from ridicule, through ostracism and imprisonment, to death at the hands of the law. The important thing to remember, observes Linton, is that these penalties are rarely used. Most individuals are successfully conditioned to the patterns they are expected to conform to, and carry them out unconsciously. The thief and the murderer get the headlines, but they are exceptions.

In handicraft societies even stealing is rare. Among the Sakalava of Madagascar, for instance, when a person steals for the first time the circumstances are carefully investigated. If the thief was actually hungry, he is given land and a chance to reform. If he steals again, he is speared—not in a spirit of revenge but because he has shown himself a public liability.

Struggles between groups, or class struggles, are not frequent in societies where all members have a fixed place in the culture, as noted earlier. They arise when status is being undermined—as the factory system undermined it in Europe in the nineteenth century. Factory workers were under continual tension because they had no accepted place—until labor unions were invented to give them one. In the United States status has never been rigid, except perhaps for Negroes. Classes here are mobile, as the proverb "shirtsleeves to shirtsleeves in three generations" indicates. Few Americans care for the role of "proletarian," while the managers of industry, as Berle and Means pointed out, have superseded the "owner" and split the solid front among the "capitalists."

I would venture a guess—a wild one to be sure—that more than half the reform energy in this country over the past 50 years has been directed to a perpetuum mobile. The reformers' research, such as it was, had never included a controlled study of human behavior. Old-line socialists, dimly recognizing this, used to complain about the "dumb" workers who could not be brought to recognize their class interest. How could they recognize what they did not have?

In Chapter 12 we observed a few perpetual motion machines in efforts to improve race relations. We concluded that where a caste system exists, as in the deep South, reforms based on logic, justice, reason, are unavailing, while strong-arm measures are likely to boomerang. People in the deep South hold their belief systems as sincerely as people in the North. To them, logic, reason, and justice are on the side of caste. They will fight any one who tries to destroy caste abruptly or violently. Reformers who neglect these scientific findings are squandering their energy, to say nothing of the funds of their well-meaning subscribers.

Factors of Social Change

W. F. Ogburn, whom we met as a student of social change, advises reformers[1] to figure out the social forces which will aid the change, and those which will oppose it. The next step is to study carefully three factors which are bound to affect any but the smallest change, namely: (1) the natural environment; (2) the biological factor of heredity; (3) the culture, including customs and beliefs.

Natural environment changes only over long periods, but man can control it to a degree by using oil-heated houses, igloos, woolen clothing, umbrellas, air conditioning, snowplows, headlights, deep freezes, TVA systems, irrigation, contour tillage, rain-making.

Human heredity has apparently not changed much since Cro-Magnon man. Eugenic programs to modify homo sapiens deliberately are mostly talk, though we see what might be done in the effects of deliberate breeding on plants, fowls, and race horses. Fortunately, in the present state of knowledge we cannot tamper with our genes, which are singularly well encased against reformers. Even sterilization does not get far; Hitler provided some revolting examples in this department. The genes possessed by different family lines, says Ogburn, are not well known. The best thing we can do now is to reform our diets, especially by the better feeding of babies, and so improve each generation. Already we can measure the effects of orange juice, green vegetables, and plenty of milk on the present generation of American college girls and boys. As a group they are taller, heavier, and larger-footed than their parents.

Moving on to the third factor, culture, Ogburn says that progress can be made if the reformer carefully fits his program into

[1] Letter to *The New York Times*, September 29, 1946.

the folkways and allows for cultural lag—a precaution which Franklin Roosevelt did not take. One New Deal reform, however—the Food Stamp Plan—did exactly that. So skillfully did Milo Perkins, its inventor, map his campaign that when the plan was finally launched on a nation-wide basis it was everywhere applauded, without a single vested interest in opposition.

Head-hunting, a strong cultural trait in various primitive societies, may lead to rapid depopulation, and colonial administrators are always trying to check it. In Sarawak, British reformers have abolished the active practice but have wisely kept the tribal credos unimpaired. Officials accumulate old skulls as trophies and issue them when needed for a given ceremony. Among the Papuans, meanwhile, bridegrooms have been persuaded to offer a boar's skull to their brides. It is pointed out that a boar is harder to bring down than a human, especially a woman or a child, and is therefore a better proof of manhood.

These, like the Food Stamp Plan, are examples of really effective reforms. Belief systems are maintained while the harmful practice is eliminated and a better one substituted.

Laboratory for Testing Plans

Such prevision and calculating take time, while the typical reformer is in a hurry. "Unbridled social idealism," says George Lundberg in *Can Science Save Us?* "unbalanced by scientific criteria as to possibilities and cost, is a social liability and in effect a type of fraud on the body politic." The American prohibition law of 1920 was probably of that type. It was promoted, at least in part, by fanatics who lacked the remotest idea of the culture concept and the probable psychological effects of their reform. Alcoholism is a social calamity, but it must be controlled by a different strategy.

Social scientists have been at a disadvantage in competition with eager reformers who promise panaceas. But now scientists are getting into a position to tell us not only what won't work, but what might. I, for one, would like to see a series of competent scientific reports on such current proposals as:

Plans for the control of atomic energy (like the Lilienthal-Acheson
  proposal).
Restoring international free trade.
Federal World Government.
Calendar revision.
The Social Credit proposals.
A wide extension of Rochedale coöperatives.
Protecting witnesses in congressional investigations.
Installation of the metric system by all nations.
Adoption of a universal language.

Proposals such as these cry for analysis, and every day there is
a new one, judging by my mail. Perhaps a permanent laboratory
should be set up by scientists to dissect economic and social reforms. It might even be made self-supporting. When an inventor
is seized with a plan to save the world, he might take his blueprint to the laboratory, and for say $100, get a report on any
stray elements of perpetual motion it might contain.

Inventors of nonpuncturable tires and plastic TV selectors
can choose among a number of testing laboratories, to say nothing of patent attorneys, and Consumers' Research and Consumers' Union. Social inventions are much harder to analyze,
but a scientific appraisal would be welcomed by those whose
goal is benevolence, not hatred, and who really want to get a mess
cleaned up.

THE MUCKRAKERS

Lincoln Steffens made a significant contribution to political
science during the great muckraking era after the turn of the
century. He cut through the stereotype of the big, wicked political boss, and gave us the real story.[2] Low-income people
in the great cities of the power age have deep-seated needs,
both material and emotional. Their economic security is low,
their status indeterminable, and their relations with city neighbors uncertain and often unsatisfactory. Into this situation steps
the city boss. He finds out what people want and, in exchange

[2] In his autobiography.

for votes, tries to satisfy these desires. He sends groceries to a hungry family, finds a job for an unemployed bricklayer, delivers coal when the thermometer drops to zero. Above all, through the "organization," he re-creates the face-to-face group. It may be a sorry substitute for the immemorial village community but it is something.

Thus the boss not only wins votes for the party and power for himself, but reduces frustration, bitterness, and even violence. If the Japanese-Americans at Poston had had a "boss" to discover their needs and satisfy them, tension might not have mounted so high. A case could be made, though I do not remember that Steffens ever made it, that the political boss is the institution which keeps Megalopolis from disintegration, especially during its melting-pot period.

In contrast with this shrewd analysis, most reformers, muckrakers, "do-gooders," Steffens pointed out, conducted their strategy on the hypothesis that bosses were "bad," politics "dirty," poor people weak and gullible—and not very clean either[3]—and that "good government" with a spry businessman in the mayor's swivel chair was the answer.

After many spirited reform campaigns, businessmen swiveled in dozens of chairs but they did not prove to be the answer. The voters, it turned out, missed the boss. If Uncle Timothy dies, the boss calls to express his sympathy and helps out with the funeral expenses. The boss can tear up a parking ticket or help out a juvenile offender for a grieving mother. "All of these rewards," observe Miller and Dollard, "are immediate and therefore more effective than the delayed consequences of good government." The real task of a municipal reformer is thus very different from the assumed task; *it is to beat the boss in finding out what people need and meeting those needs.* Indeed it is similar to the task of the foreign aid administrator in the international field—to get ahead of the communist infiltrators in satisfying local wants.

[3] Bathtubs, if any, were used for storing coal, according to the stereotype.

NATIONAL ECONOMIC PLANNING

Reformers who advocate planning can find some excellent advice in the files of the London *Economist*. Suppose, said the *Economist*,[4] that after the war Britain had called her best social scientists together to plan for demobilization and reconstruction. *First*, the planners would use polls to find prevailing attitudes. What do people want most—what will they stand for? *Second*, they would appraise Britain's foreign balance of payments, exports, imports, United States loans and lend-lease contracts, with a cold eye. *Third*, they would similarly appraise Britain's production possibilities. *Fourth*, they would study the attitudes of the government of the U.S.S.R., the Indian leaders, for areas of possible international conflict and danger.

On the basis of these hard looks, the scientists would block out a flexible program, and use all the modern arts of communication to put it before the British people and also the people of the United States.

But what actually happened? asked the *Economist*. The Labour Government then in power did not use polls; it had no clear idea of the needs of the people at all. It made too many campaign promises. When the government tried to keep some of them, like permanent housing, it found the program completely out of place in the postwar emergency. It forgot other promises, and hushed up bad news; yet psychologists know that in many emergencies people stand things better if they are frankly told the worst. In an earlier crisis, Winston Churchill had promised nothing but blood, sweat, and tears.

Finally and most serious of all, said the *Economist*, the Labour Government wasted valuable time trying to nationalize industries on the Marxian formula. The coal industry was breaking down because of ever deepening shafts and *had* to be nationalized, but other nationalization proposals—like steel—were dubious even in normal times.

[4] December 14, 1946.

In a democratic state, the planning must be done by political parties. Yet no economic policy is right at all times, and the skilled economic planner must know when to reverse his engines. But political parties are not equipped with reversing gear. In 1931 the Tories showed how stubbornly they could defy the facts and follow a policy of contraction in the middle of deflation. Their performance has been equaled by the Labour Party since 1945, with its devotion to the trade union doctrine that it is always right for the pay envelope to grow. Clearly, if it is unsafe to let the Tories out of jail in a slump, the Labour Party ought to be locked up in times of inflation. . . . However, in spite of the doubts, mankind is not now going to abandon the resolve to be master of its economic circumstances.

If the *Economist* is right in believing that nations will increasingly try to plan their economic destinies, the social scientist becomes a consultant of the first importance. Working in a team of specialists, everlastingly digging for the facts—he can advise a government whether its plans have a chance to succeed, or are just so many perpetual motion machines.

23

The Behavior of Groups

The scientific analysis of face-to-face groups was launched in the 1930's by a social psychologist who came to America from Germany, the late Kurt Lewin. His experiments with children making masks have become a classic in the field of group dynamics, like Elton Mayo's classic experiments in the labor-management field.

We have crossed the trail of small groups repeatedly throughout this book. Not only did the relay room and the bank wiring room at Hawthorne illustrate group behavior, but so did the informal teams in aircraft factories, the solidarity of combat fliers in World War II, and many more.

HANDICRAFT CLASSES

Shortly before World War II, Lewin, with Ronald Lippitt and R. K. White, made an intensive study of ten- to twelve-year children in handicraft classes at the Iowa State Welfare Station. The scientists were allowed to rearrange the classes, and they set up three structures: autocratic, democratic, and anarchistic.

In the first an adult leader told the youngsters exactly what to do; in the second he kept his hand on the group, but let the children make most of the decisions; in the third he left them to make *all* the decisions, without any real leader. Children were shifted from group to group to make sure that structure, not personality, was chiefly responsible for results.

Conclusions from the experiment proved heartening to believers in democracy and the techniques of participation. The autocratic group caused a good deal of internal friction, forcing some youngsters to leave, and began to disintegrate after the adult leader withdrew. The anarchistic type fell apart almost immediately. But the democratic group, starting slowly, built up so much internal stability that when the adult leader left, it went right on functioning.

The experiment demonstrated that participation and so-called "permissive" leadership make a stronger, more productive group than either autocratic leadership or a policy of everyone for himself. The results agree with other experimental findings, as well as with much practical experience. They still need more detailed laboratory checking, especially in other kinds of situations, and more theory to explain them.

Expanding Laboratories

The movement Lewin started is now literally sweeping the country. Face-to-face groups, of course, had been studied before,[1] but Lewin added precision, and deliberately undertook to make it social science,. His books are concerned with experimental techniques in group behavior; how controlled experiments may be set up and verified, how research may be applied to change.

The famous National Training Laboratory, now operating each summer at Bethel, Maine, was founded by Lewin, and "little Bethels" are spreading across the nation to the Pacific Coast. I have visited the Maine laboratory three times, and find it a fascinating enterprise. "Delegates" who work professionally with groups at home—teachers, adult educators, business executives, union leaders, Y.M.C.A. secretaries, government administrators, Army and Navy officers—are formed into experimental groups of various sizes, with various tasks, under various kinds of leadership. Their performance is analyzed by a competent research staff, using observers, tape recordings, a special ques-

[1] As in the work of E. C. Lindemann, Charles H. Cooley, Mary P. Follett, Alfred Sheffield, and others.

tionnaire called "PMR" (post meeting reaction), and other techniques.

Sometimes a giant role-playing project is set up. In 1954, members of the laboratory impersonated various citizens of a community faced with a crisis in its school building program. I played the part of a member of the planning commission, and became increasingly involved as the crisis developed. Role-playing, much used in group analysis, has the strange effect of involving one's emotions in the role he is playing, and making him share the other fellow's feelings. Our school crisis at Bethel took two days to work through. It is safe to say that everyone who participated will approach a real crisis in his own town with greater awareness of the forces involved.

The goal of the Bethel Laboratory is to learn to predict how people will react in face-to-face groups, and to improve performance, both individual and collective. The field for practical application is virtually unlimited—school committees, P.T.A. meetings, directors' meetings, classroom teaching, Army training, faculty meetings, fraternity meetings, union meetings, business conferences, international conferences, UN meetings —an endless array now full of headaches and frustrations. Perhaps Americans hold too many meetings. Bethel can help us find out.

One of the staff at Bethel, Herbert A. Thelen of the Education Department of the University of Chicago, has dramatically demonstrated how the techniques may be put to work.[2] He used them to set up a series of block organizations in the Hyde Park district of Chicago, a large section with many fine houses, which was threatening to become a "blighted area," if not a slum. Homes had been thrown on the market for sale, white residents were beginning to leave, real estate values were dropping, rumors were rife and violence in the air.

Today, five years later, more than 400 blocks have been organized by white and Negro families together, in a coöperative

---

[2] See Dr. Thelen's account of the experiment in his book, *Dynamics of Groups at Work.*

effort to improve the section and make it a better place to bring up children. The city and the University have started a huge redevelopment project for the seedier blocks, and it looks as though Hyde Park will be saved. A vigorous application of group dynamics has helped to save it.

The adult education movement is vitally interested in group analysis, both to improve performance in classes and as a subject for study. Its magazine, *Adult Leadership*, keeps up with the latest research findings.

Lewin said that if a person is to change his habits, he must change *as a whole*. This can often be done best through a group. Alcoholics Anonymous is a good illustration, in which members, trying to break the drinking habit, support one another's resolution. It has proved far more effective than lectures, logical arguments, or taking the pledge.

Alexander Bavelas was one of Lewin's associates at the Massachusetts Institute of Technology. He continues there as an experimenter and industrial consultant, arranging ingenious structures to test face-to-face groups. He gives the example of introducing a new machine in a factory, a machine which requires a rearrangement of jobs. If it appears suddenly on Monday morning, already connected, the morale of the whole department is likely to be shattered. If, however, the machine is placed on the floor unconnected, and its functions are carefully explained—"Look, this is how it works"—disorganization will be less. But the best method, says Bavelas, is to consult with the men *before* bringing in the machine. If the workers themselves can be involved in its adoption, the new machine will be introduced without a tremor. Such a course can transform an impending change "from a misfortune to be resisted or endured, to a positive step to be willingly taken."[3]

Group dynamics has already developed a body of principles, of which these six impress me as particularly helpful:

[3] Confirmed by Edmund Brunner, when studying the introduction of a cane cutter and harvester in Hawaiian sugar fields in 1937.

1. Identify oneself with other members in the group, rather than play a lone hand.
2. Encourage maximum participation in activities and discussions.
3. Practice democratic or "permissive" leadership.
4. Protect the emotional security of others. Never let a member feel ridiculous.
5. Keep communication lines open.
6. Encourage better listening.

IN CONFERENCE

In Stouffer's laboratory at Harvard is Robert F. Bales, specializing in group analysis.[4] Let us stop for a moment and gaze through his "one-way window." He has important suggestions for us to employ at the next meeting we attend, supplementing the principles listed above.

Here is a room about the size of a small classroom, with blackboard, round table, chairs, and what seems to be a large mirror on one wall. Out in the hall we enter a closet behind that mirror, and find to our surprise that we can look through it and see everything going on in the classroom. One-way glass divides the two groups; a microphone catches all the talk in the classroom, and a tape recorder can preserve it.

In addition, the staff has developed a machine like a typewriter to record changes in group behavior. Twelve standard types of interaction can be clicked off on this machine: three kinds of questions; three kinds of answers; three kinds of negative behavior—disagreement, tension, antagonism; three kinds of positive behavior—agreement, release of tension, friendly solidarity. It takes long training to record these changes rapidly and reliably. All the techniques have been improved since Bales first set up his window in 1947, and thousands of group meetings have now been studied.

What kind of meetings? Many kinds—family discussions, business conferences, labor-management negotiations, classroom

---

[4] See his book, also accounts in *Harvard Business Review*, March, 1954, and *Scientific American*, March, 1955.

seminars, problem-solving meetings. Will people talk freely when they know they are being watched? They are always told, and experience shows that the group usually takes about five minutes, like a motor on a cold morning, to warm up. It then forgets the unseen observers and turns over normally.

PROBLEM-SOLVING

A long study, involving hundreds of meetings, has been made by Bales of groups trying to solve a specific problem—say a business staff discussing a pension system for employees. What happens in such a situation? What is the best group size? What leaders arise? What antagonisms develop? What can be learned to help problem-solving groups elsewhere?

About half the time in a problem-solving conference, the experiment shows, is spent in answering questions. Such a 50-50 balance may be one characteristic of good communication, allowing plenty of give-and-take, so that members do not leave the conference with unresolved doubts. A group decision is not successful unless members feel actually bound by it, as proved in their subsequent behavior. Members feel bound, furthermore, only when they have participated in making the decision. This need not mean an equal amount of talk; some may not even talk at all. It means a *mental* involvement. But a voiced reaction does help for there is "no adequate substitute for some actual verbal participation of each member."

When a real row develops, the observer behind the window is in danger of becoming involved himself. He may have heard the same case discussed many times before, but he is "caught in the illusion of reality" as the temperature in the classroom rises. Here is an example of what follows:

Suddenly the credulity of the observer is strained beyond some critical point. The illusion that the group is dealing with some external problem breaks. It becomes perfectly transparent . . . that emotions have taken over, and that what one member is saying does not refer at all to some external situation but to himself and the other members present. "Facts" are unwittingly invented or are falsified. Other facts drop out of sight entirely. When one member insists that "people in this office should be treated like human beings," it is clear that he refers to himself and how he feels he should be treated. When his opponent insists that "troublemakers should be fired," it is equally clear that he refers to the man who just spoke to him.

If this particular business group reaches a decision—which is unlikely—it will have all the characteristics of a bad dream.

On the other hand there can be too much sweetness and light in problem-solving. A group determined to agree on everything rarely arrives at durable decisions. There must be some give-and-take, some pungent criticism, usually some compromise, to arrive at consensus on tough problems.

The laboratory has determined the best order for discussing a problem, and it happens to be the "exact opposite of that which is characteristic of formal parliamentary procedure." Successful groups go through three steps, always in this order:

First, they assemble the largest possible pool of facts.

Second, they make inferences and evaluations based on these facts, and try to form common opinions on a level *above* the actual problem in hand.

Third, then, and only then, do members begin offering specific suggestions for the actual problem—suggestions fertilized by a rich background of fact and common opinion.

Not all groups do this by any means; many begin with suggestions. Many members "are hardly conscious of any difference between a fact and an opinion." Then trouble lies ahead. A good suggestion given too early either dies for lack of support or "is trampled to death in the general melee."

TWIN LEADERS

Bales and his staff have reached a striking conclusion about group leadership. It is usually assumed that members in a face-to-face group compete for leadership—provided a leader is not designated in advance. They do compete but this is only part of the story. A problem-solving group normally develops *not one but two leaders: a task leader and a social leader.* The function of the first is to keep the boys on the problem. The function of the second is to keep the boys in good temper.

The task leader emerges as a rule in the first session, and often he will be voted "best liked" in the PMR as well. In the second session, however, his popularity wanes as he holds noses to the grindstone. Somebody else wins the "best-liked" role, somebody who can crack jokes, relieve tensions, make members feel good. By the end of the fourth session, on the average, the chance of the task leader also being the social leader has sunk to *one in seven!*

Not many persons can fill both roles because the functions are so different. But it is important for each leader to recognize the other's role, and form a working coalition. "There are indications that such small and durable groups as the family . . . are constructed this way, and apparently the coalition also takes place in many administrative staffs, sometimes consciously but more often accidentally." In the family, presumably, father is the task leader, and mother the social leader. Says Bales:

Millions are spent each year by business, government, and the armed forces in developing means for recognizing leaders—yet it appears that whatever superior qualities the individual may possess he may be unable, just because of the way groups work, to maintain a stable leadership position without a co-leader of complementary qualities.

Quite a window, this of Mr. Bales. Here are some further conclusions, drawn after years of analyzing face-to-face groups:

Seven members are about the limit for problem-solving. Two or three are not enough; they get into power difficulties—one against one, or two against one.

Be wary of too many "high participators," i.e., bright boys who know the answers and are oververbalized. For best results, the group should be salted with a few quiet characters.

If a row is brewing, *back-track to the facts with all possible speed*—before facts become weapons and unrecognizable. Also try to find similar experiences—referents—for the words being used. Unless experiences overlap, the same words often mean different things to different people.

Keep your eyes on the group rather than on a particular member. "Nothing tones up general harmony like a good strong undercurrent of direct eye contact."

Keep your ear, meanwhile, to the ground. Do not become so absorbed in the problem that you forget the play of group tension and interaction. Try to hold yourself and your fellow members "in good operating condition."

I do not know about the reader, but I have a meeting of the zoning board at four o'clock tomorrow afternoon, and I shall take this whole tool kit right along with me.

24

Notes on Political Behavior

Albert Einstein was once asked, at a meeting in Princeton: "Dr. Einstein, why is it that when the mind of man has stretched so far as to discover the structure of the atom we have been unable to devise the political means to keep the atom from destroying us?"[1]

To which the great scientist replied: "That is simple, my friend. It is because politics is more difficult than physics."

Political science, like economics, has many brilliant names on its roster—Aristotle, Marcus Aurelius, Machiavelli. Its large general theories, however, again as in economics, lack adequate verification. The study has been a curious amalgam of philosophy, history, polemics, brilliant prose, common sense, and primitive psychological assumptions. Only lately has there been added a good deal of hard-headed observation, and the beginning of some verifiable theory. Like economics, political science badly needs help from the sciences of behavior. *Who Gets What, When, How?* as Harold Lasswell subtitles his stimulating book on politics, is obviously oriented in this direction.

The political columnist, Gerald Johnson, gives us an example of shrewd psychological observation when he says: "A professional politician may be secondarily a Democrat or a Republican, but he is primarily a professional. His function, as he understands it, is to give the people what they want, and he will supply crass reaction, or creeping socialism, with the complete indif-

---

[1] Reported in a letter by Grenville Clark to *The New York Times*, April 20, 1955.

ference of a haberdasher handing out blue shirts or white, according to the customer's demand."[2]

HIGH TALK ABOUT INEVITABILITY

Some political scientists employ a literary style which carries a special ring of doom. They speak of the "implacability," the "inevitability," and the "remorseless processes," of history, and do not hesitate to chart its predestined course. The career of James Burnham, for instance, shows us how a skillful political writer, equipped with plenty of gloomy foreboding and a forensic vocabulary, may range unchecked over the field. In physics he would hardly get to first base.

In 1941 Burnham published a book called *The Managerial Revolution*, which extrapolated the theory of Berle and Means about the shift in corporate control from owners to managers, and made considerable sense. Its central thesis has been amply vindicated. Along with this solid contribution, however, Burnham has given us a number of predictions, mostly doleful, which have not been vindicated by events. What he announced as "inevitable" at a particular time, later lost its inevitability, to be succeeded by a new inevitable. His score card, according to Lewis Corey, runs like this:[3]

1. In the 1930's Burnham thought the Trotskyite revolution was inevitable. The Stalinites would be overthrown; 100 percent wrong.
2. In 1941 the managerial revolution was inevitable; true up to a certain point.
3. A little later the victory of Germany was inevitable; 100 percent wrong.
4. After the war, said Burnham, three superstates will dominate the world—Germany, Japan, and the United States. Mark him 33 percent.
5. After the war, again, the U.S.S.R. will inevitably break up and be swallowed by Germany on one side, and Japan on the other; 100 percent wrong.

[2] *New Republic*, November 18, 1954.
[3] *Antioch Review*, Summer, 1947.

6. The 1940, or at the very best, the 1944 United States elections will inevitably be the last free elections. Well, we have had 1944, 1948, 1952, and soon 1956, free and flamboyant as usual.
7. By 1947 it became inevitable to Mr. Burnham that Number 5 was wrong, and that war with the U.S.S.R. was inevitable.

He may be right on Number 7, but it is the purest speculation. Political speculation is entirely legitimate provided one posts it as such. Posted as the truth, inevitable as Halley's Comet, it is dangerous stuff. If war with the U.S.S.R. were inevitable, readers of Mr. Burnham might conclude the sooner we began it the better.

THE GREAT SOCIETY

We have encountered many examples of political behavior earlier in this book—in the relocation camp at Poston,[4] the Middletown studies, opinion research, Puerto Rico, in much of the economics section. Economics used to be known as "political economy," a term which recognized that the two disciplines overlap. As part of the concept of culture, we remember the cardinal distinction between formal and informal government. The first carries the written laws, the latter carries the ultimate sanction of what is permissible in the society.

Mass production and the machine are largely responsible for the rapid, often painful growth of formal government. They have increased the division of labor and destroyed the old self-sufficiency of the family and the small community, as in the shoe factories of Newburyport. Acute problems appear—great armies of unemployed, destitute old people, child labor, strikes, breakdowns in transportation, slums and blighted areas, juvenile delinquency, soil erosion, stream pollution—problems which individuals cannot cope with alone. Yet they must be solved if society is to go on. So big government comes in, on federal, state, and city levels, especially the first and the last.

Frederick Jackson Turner produced a famous hypothesis in

[4] Leighton's book is of course an important contribution to political science, as shown in the title: *The Governing of Men.*

1893, called "The Significance of the Frontier in American History." Many of our culture habits, he said, can be explained only by the frontier. In the United States, with its tradition of self-help and rapid expansion, government up to 1900 tended to be loose and flexible. But by the twentieth century, it proved inadequate for its new functions, especially for coping with the great depression. Political scientists have been trying to design improvements to keep pace with the march of the machine, but they still have a long way to go before government structure is adequate to handle the demands put upon it. The old forms come down from handicraft days; George Washington never saw a railroad, let alone a power line.

To study this serious lag, the Social Science Research Council has set up various committees, and some universities have established courses in public administration. These include specialized graduate schools, and whole departments to work on administrative techniques, as in the University of California. In governing a big city, modern methods include the city manager plan, uniform accounting, city planning, public housing and slum clearance, great recreational centers like Jones Beach near New York. Outstanding technicians have come to the fore, such men as Robert Moses, Joseph McGoldrick, Luther Gulick, Louis Brownlow, and the late Clarence Dykstra.

But rapidly as techniques expand, aided by such invaluable organizations as the Public Administration Clearing House, Megalopolis accumulates its problems even faster. The outlook for traffic control was never darker than it is today. Within a year or two, the way traffic jams are now multiplying, Fifth Avenue in New York, and the Loop in Chicago, will be frozen solid.[5] Somebody has said that if you are injured in the Loop, you can get to the nearest hospital faster in a wheelbarrow than in an ambulance.

Fresh ideas on the federal level have come from such men as Thomas Finletter, Paul Appleby, the late Senator Robert M. LaFollette, Jr.—who have seen government from the inside, and

[5] Admittedly an extrapolation.

then generalized from first-hand experience. The President's Committee on Administrative Management, headed by Charles E. Merriam, produced some original thinking on the vast change in the office of the American presidency in recent years. Because of the pressure groups which flatten so many congressmen, only the President can now represent the whole people.

The TVA should be mentioned again as an important new development in political science. Its regional position between federal and local governments gives it many advantages, for it starts comparatively free of red tape and political vested interests. Its boundaries correspond with geographic realities better than do most of the States. Experts come from all over the world to study this new agency, to admire the towering dams, the gleaming instrument panels which control navigation, flood waters, power, as on a great organ. The TVA may be working out a new adjustment to the machine age. It may show us how businessmen, labor men, government men, professional men, can coöperate for their mutual welfare; how decentralization can be carried to the limit consistent with technology. The TVA is still treated, however, as an ideological football.

Eight states have entered into a compact to eliminate pollution in the Ohio River. Two states coöperate in the tremendous tasks of the New York Port Authority; three states try to compose their differences as to who gets what from the Colorado River—with Mexico as a fourth claimant. All such compacts require new political and administrative thinking. If the United Nations takes a further step, and begins to exercise mandates over territory now disputed, a new dimension in international politics will open.

Administrative consultants and government technicians can be aided by electronic computers, says H. M. Davis in the *Scientific American*.[6] The new machines can help us keep up with the machine age by flashing out statistics almost simultaneously with the event. The "curse of bigness" has been due, in part at least, to people's ignorance of what is going on over vast

[6] April, 1949.

territories. One trouble with planning, says Davis, is that the planners cannot learn the facts rapidly enough to keep abreast of their plans. Computers can remedy this lag, and redefine "bigness" upward. "They may even offer a technical means of contributing to world peace by helping to make world government possible."

When the science of polling is refined a bit further, computers can transmit to government leaders what citizens think, and how their ideas are changing about many important political questions—such as foreign policy, disarmament, taxation, the price of wheat, proposals for an annual wage, public housing, health and vaccination programs, school buildings, traffic jams, desegregation. Elmo Roper favors this idea, but says a research agency to carry it should have a status equivalent to the United States Supreme Court—beyond political pressure. Political scientists are here presented with the nice task of designing such an agency.

Political science may be on the verge of great developments. Certainly many of the old patterns, classifications, and theories stand in urgent need of revision. John M. Gaus[7] has outlined a research program along this line, emphasizing the following questions:

What is a realistic foreign policy for the United States in the atomic age?

What are workable relationships between federal, regional, state, and local governments?

What are the proper relationships between executive, legislative, and judicial power today? (Some recent congressional investigations have stretched and distorted these relationships.)

What are the proper line, staff, and auxiliary relationships in government?

What is happening to the presidency? Is it moving toward some quite new status?

What does the average citizen think of his government today?

[7] Memorandum to Social Science Research Council.

What does he want from it? (A kind of perpetual inventory of public opinion.)

LABORATORY IN ELMIRA

In Chapter 18 we noted how social scientists have been analyzing the voters of Elmira, New York,[8] using the panel method of opinion research. Some arresting new theory has come out of the charts and figures. We will describe it briefly, not as the last word on political democracy, but as an example of social science, in action, and a dramatic contrast with the polemics of Mr. Burnham.

CLASSICAL THEORY

The Elmira researchers quote a British writer, A. D. Lindsay: "There is always a terrible gulf between the fine and elevating theories about democracy which we read in books on political theory, and the actual facts of politics." Locke, Burke, Hobbes, Bentham, Mill, and the other great classicists wrote about politics because they wanted to change methods then in practice. Out of their observations and arguments came injunctions about how you and I, as citizens in a democracy, should behave. We have, according to the classicists, four political duties: (1) our interest in politics should be strong, (2) our knowledge of issues should be competent, (3) our political principles should be cherished and acted upon, and (4) our political behavior should be guided by reason and logic. All citizens may not be in such firm possession of these virtues as thee and me, but a majority must possess them, says classical theory, or democracy cannot survive.

How do the citizens of Elmira meet these standards? A panel of 1,000 voters, studied over a period of many months before the 1948 elections, were found to lack all four essential virtues. Their political behavior did not follow the classical theories. As a group they had little sustained interest in politics, their

[8] See Berelson, Lazarsfeld, and McPhee, *Voting.*

knowledge of issues was rudimentary, their political principles were hard to find, beyond voting the way their fathers voted; and often they seemed to exercise their reason in reverse. In brief, the figures showed this sample of United States voters failing on all four counts. So democracy should be deader than the dodo.

Yet democracy in Elmira, and in America, is very much alive. How is the paradox to be explained? The scientists seek to explain it with this hypothesis: Classical theory concentrated on the *individual citizen* and neglected the social system in which the individual operated. Once the requirements of the system are brought into the analysis, it is unnecessary if not positively dangerous for the average voter to exercise all the standard virtues. Why? Because political apathy on the part of a substantial bloc of voters in America has cushioned the shock of disagreement and change. If one does not take his politics too seriously, social change is easier. The United States, we recall, has been a regular roller coaster of change, geographical, technological, cultural.

Again, if too many voters cling devotedly to fixed party principles, change will be impeded, and bitter fights more frequent. A reductio ad absurdum of fixed principles is found in the behavior of that tiny group of Puerto Rican "nationalists," who are convinced it is their high patriotic duty to go around taking pot shots at their own governor, the United States president, and congressmen.

The Elmira research shows that most voters do have some principles, some information, some political interest, and some rationality, but not in the degree called for by the classicists. Happily for the system, voters distribute themselves along a continuum, running from *sociable man* (including many women voters)—who is bored by politics, to *political man*—who takes an intelligent interest, to *ideological man*—who is a party stalwart with rigid principles and a low boiling point. At the outer edge of the last group are characters like the Puerto Rican nationalists. If we were all ideological men, democracy would dissolve in a cosmic Donnybrook Fair. If we were all sociable men, it would expire from lack of motivation.

In the United States we have these types in the proper proportions apparently to make the political system work. (It reminds us a little of Galbraith's theory of "countervailing power" which accounts for the working of the economic system.) "This distribution itself, with its internal checks and balances, can perform the functions, and incorporate the same values ascribed by some theorists to each individual in the system, as well as to the constitutive political institutions."

The die-hards, the apathetic, and the quick changers (mostly youngsters on the make), provide "enough consensus to hold the system together, and enough cleavage to make it move." Too much consensus would be deadening—as in Bales's problem-solving groups at the Harvard Laboratory. Too much cleavage would be destructive—as in the case of various Latin-American republics. Total politics, of course, as Lenin well knew and advocated, leads to one-party government and the monolithic state; the opposition is banished or shot. Total apathy could lead to authoritarianism too, as the man on horseback rides in to fill the political vacuum.

The Elmira studies indicate that American voters have found a happy medium, a kind of mulch in which political democracy can grow. If the hypothesis of these scientists stands up, it may well revolutionize our ideas about democracy, and be one of the few substantial additions to democratic theory since the close of the eighteenth century.

25

Learning Things

Granted that most of our habits come from the culture, how did we learn them? The anthropologists toss this fundamental question to the psychologists, and some of them have accepted the challenge. Practically all agree that it is in the first few years of life that we acquire the basic habits which distinguish one culture from another; which enable us to live with our families and neighbors, communicate with them, and thus go on learning. A child becomes "socialized," or "acculturated," as his nervous system is trained in innumerable unconscious routines. How are we to explain even the simplest of these habits?

The Institute of Human Relations at Yale, backed by many experiments over a long period of years, ventures an explanation. John Dollard and Neal Miller, working with others, including the late C. L. Hull, have formulated and tested a hypothesis which they call "learning theory." They have written two books about it, the first, now a classic, called *Social Learning and Imitation*, the second, which restates the theory and applies it widely, called *Personality and Psychotherapy*.

MONKEYS AND RATS

I visited the authors at New Haven to see some of their experiments. The first exhibit was a small, brown-eyed monkey. He crouched in the back of a cage about three feet square, while the man with the notebook turned the page to trial number 873. The man touched a switch and a bell rang sharply. In one sweeping movement the monkey leaped to the front of the cage, thrust a hand through the bars, and pulled the lever of a small box with a light in it. As he did so the bell stopped ringing and the light went out. He looked up at us with his sad eyes, relieved that the noise had ceased but still worried. He stretched a long finger through the bars again as though to say: "I hope the damn thing is really off." Then he turned around, leaped to the back of his cage, and crouched there again to wait for trial number 874.

The bottom of the cage was made of metal strips capable of giving a mild electric shock. After repeated exposure the monkey had learned to pull the lever to stop the current. Then the shock had been associated by the experimenters, first with the light in the box, next with the bell, on the best Pavlov principles of conditioned reflex. Now without getting an electric shock at all, only an emotional one, the sad monkey pulled the lever to stop the bell.

Next I saw a documentary movie about two white rats and how they learned things—a film that compared favorably with a Walt Disney production. One rat was very hungry, the other not. They were placed in identical cages side by side. The camera would focus first on one cage, then on the other. An ingenious mechanism attached to the cage deposited a pellet of food in a dish whenever a metal bar was depressed.

The hungry rat with quick, eager movements explores his cage for possible food. About the fifth time around, he hits the bar by accident, and down comes a pellet. He gobbles it but makes no connection between cause and effect. Round and round the cage he goes, with now and again another accidental reward. Then light begins to dawn—the bar! At first he presses it deliberately but awkwardly; gradually performs more swiftly and surely, until in the end he does it as nonchalantly as Groucho Marx lights a cigar.

Meanwhile, the well-fed rat continues to digest ruminatively in a corner of the other cage, taking no interest whatever in his slot machine. Unfortunately for him, however, his cage is equipped with a shockable bottom like the mournful monkey's.

A shock is applied and the rat, for all his satiation, leaps to the top of his cage. Then ensues a sort of super-Disney ballet, in the course of which he accidentally hits the bar and shuts off the power.

More shocks are given, resulting in more wild dances and more accidental collisions. Presently rat Number Two learns to associate depressing the lever with a reward—not food, but relief from annoying sensations in the soles of his feet. Furthermore—and this is important—he learns more rapidly than rat Number One learned about food. The pain drive is more powerful than the hunger drive—at least for those white rats under those conditions.

Learning Theory

What lesson have we here? According to Dollard and Miller, the process of learning in the case of the higher mammals, including man, normally proceeds in four steps:

1. A drive—such as hunger or pain, which makes the individual ready for action.
2. A cue—such as the metal bar.
3. A response—such as pulling the bar.
4. A reward or reinforcement—such as food, or relief from electric shock.

After a stiff shot of theory on the learning process in New Haven, I drive home and try it on our cat. Did you ever teach a cat to sit up and beg? The four steps are conspicuous in this act of learning. The drive is hunger. The cue is a piece of meat held well above the cat's head. The first response is an eager reaching, but the reward must not be given until the animal sits erect on its haunches, paws hanging down. I taught Boots in twenty minutes flat—though I admit that he is a smarter cat than most—and he now sits up politely for anything he wants —dinner, a drink of water, to go out of doors, to have somebody play with him.

"After learning has been completed, response and cue are

bound together in such a way that the appearance of the cue evokes the response. . . . The conditions under which human learning takes place . . . are primarily social and cultural. . . ." If the reward is not forthcoming, the response gradually suffers extinction. The reward, as we have seen, can be either positive or negative—pleasure, or relief from pain.

The theory is derived from Pavlov, Thorndike, Watson, and Hull. On human levels the theory has been verified by many experiments with children, students, soldiers. Here is one of Dollard and Miller's simple experiments which you can repeat with a six-year-old.

Candy Experiment

Hide a piece of candy under a book on a bookshelf. Bring the youngster into the room—making sure he is hungry—and tell him to look under the books and find the candy. Then count the books he picks up and keep track of the time. He may take three or four minutes to find the candy, after moving thirty or forty books.

Now send him out of the room again, hide another piece of candy under the same book, call him back as before. He is likely to find this piece within two minutes. Try again and he will get it in less than a minute and, after some ten trials, he will go at once to the right book and find the candy in about two seconds.

You can chart the curve of this learning, either by time or the count of books, and you will find that it starts on a high level at the upper left and descends steeply toward the lower right of the chart. Analyzing it for the four elements, it is clear that the drive was the child's desire for candy; the cue, instructing him where to look for it; the response, searching the bookshelf; the reward, eating the candy.

In more mature learning, of course, the drives become more subtle and remote, the cues more complex. The reward, often deferred, may be a word of approval, the hope of a promotion, even a private feeling of satisfaction. When human reasoning and foresight are interpreted in these four steps, the theory can be widened to include most forms of human behavior. A whole chain of responses may take place inside one's mind, each one becoming the cue to start the next.

The public cue-producing responses, like words and sentences, that are used in social communication receive an enormous amount of social training. The accumulated cultural heritage of generations of trial and error is represented in the categories, common-sense rules of logic, standards of reasonableness, and sequences of orderly narration of language. This greatly increases the usefulness of verbal responses and their derivatives, such as mathematics, in the solution of social, emotional, and instrumental problems.[1]

Behavior in controlled situations can be predicted, even quantitatively predicted—for instance, the number of trials needed to teach a subject a simple lesson, like a set of nonsense syllables. At higher levels, in situations which are really complicated, the scientists cite many cases on which the theory throws light. Meanwhile they realize that much research remains to be done. Miller and Dollard, like good scientists, are willing to take the hard, gruelling path to knowledge, the path of measurement and counting and endless repetition of experiment —the same path the physicists took for so many decades before the clouds suddenly opened.

Meanwhile, parts of the theory can be usefully applied in innumerable ways: for instance, to simplify and improve teaching in school; to help interpret and explain the habits of an individual or even a culture; to win friends and influence people for business, advertising, social, or political reasons; to help people analyze and overcome their neurotic problems.

Like all scientific findings, learning theory has been challenged. Some critics complain that the parallels between animal and human learning have been pressed too far; again, that not all four steps are present in every case—that is, some learning may take place in the absence of either drive or reinforcement; and again, that in the perennial argument of nature versus nurture,

[1] Dollard and Miller, *Personality and Psychotherapy.*

this theory, like others of the behaviorist psychologists, tends to overemphasize nurture.

HEREDITY PLUS ENVIRONMENT

Well, how about nature versus nurture? Probably no scientist today would admit a bias in favor of either heredity or environment, since the importance of both has been so clearly demonstrated. Yet the argument continues in a different form. Perhaps as clear a statement as any of how the two forces interact appears in a study by Norman Cameron of the University of Wisconsin, *The Psychology of Behavior Disorders: A Biosocial Interpretation.* Dr. Cameron is a specialist in both psychology and psychiatry who believes that personality is developed by the interweaving of physiology with training. Every culture, he says, is built to an unrealized extent around the biological needs for food, shelter, mating, and parenthood, all of which are satisfied—or denied—in a *social situation.* The baby cannot eat without help, or keep himself warm or clean; so his comfort or discomfort is connected at every stage with an older person on whom he depends. Thus physical and emotional habits grow together, as one "grows from a biological newborn to a biosocial adult in an environment of other individuals and cultural products. . . . It is always this interplay of biology and society." Thus Cameron explains the connection among individual structure, drive, and learning, in developing the total personality. Nature and nurture are woven tightly together.

CODE FOR PSYCHOLOGISTS

Psychology is easily the most discussed of all the social sciences, far outdistancing economics, its nearest rival. The word "psychology" is bandied about by most of us quite irresponsibly, along with tags and phrases from popular psychology. Big-time baseball players, prize fighters, taxi drivers, salesmen, tycoons, labor leaders, as well as college graduates, claim a working knowledge of its principles: "I used psychology on

him, and he signed up" . . . "She's got an inferiority complex"
. . . "Bad case of Oedipus." And "Too much unsound speculative psychology in the stock market" came over my radio from
a financial expert this morning.

The growing interest in psychology has of course increased
the number of "psychologists," including a considerable group
of gentlemen—and some ladies—who harbor no objections to
turning a fast buck. Anybody with a penetrating gaze and a
command of the lingo could hang out his shingle and line up
the customers. But as our visit to New Haven makes clear,
psychology in the hands of honest investigators is a rigorous
and demanding science. By the time the student has won his
Ph.D., he may have spent as many years as a medical man in
rigorous training. Also he is painfully aware of how many
questions of human behavior are still unanswered.

The American Psychological Association has boldly attacked
this problem. It has set up a code of ethics to stiffen the profession, and to protect the person in need of psychological
counsel from half-trained "doctors" and outright quacks. Thus
it follows the lead of the Bar Association, the medical societies,
and the Certified Public Accountants, in putting an official
stamp on accredited professionals.

The making of the code was a kind of polling operation.
Instead of sitting down and thinking about ethical behavior,
the Association asked its 12,000 members to describe ethical
problems arising from their personal experience. More than 2,000
replies were received, and cases were classified six ways: ethical
behavior (1) toward the public, (2) toward clients, (3) toward
other psychologists, (4) toward students, (5) in research work,
(6) in writing. A code covering all these matters was officially
adopted in 1953. Prospective clients might do well to find out
if the counselor they select is a member of the Association and
bound by the code.

Here is one of the problems sent in: A famous feature writer
visits a clinic to get a story on juvenile delinquency. A psychologist on the staff uses a hypothetical case to illustrate the

clinic's work. The writer seizes on the case, and writes it up as true, with a sensational twist, as the lead for his story. The psychologist objects, and the journalist hits the ceiling. On appeal, the trustees of the clinic think the psychologist ought to play along. "It's good publicity," they say.

What should the psychologist do? The Code indicates clearly that he should refuse to coöperate with the journalist, however fine the publicity. "The psychologist may be expected to offer every assistance to reputable reporters, but he may refuse to give materials to a reporter who does not adhere to the ethical standards of the profession."

Another case: A psychologist is retained to make a market survey for a soap company, using a questionnaire prepared by the publicity department. He complains that it contains a built-in bias for the company's soap against competitive brands. "Take it or leave it," says the management. *What should the psychologist do?* The Code gives him no choice but to leave it.

Thousands of such cases are in the Association's files. They constitute a unique method of establishing professional ethics, one that can be recommended to other professions with ethical problems. Ask the members to participate in digging out the facts, classify the types of problems, and build the code on that objective base. (Notice the connection between science and ethics).

F. H. Sanford, Secretary of the Association, tells us that more than half the members are now outside the universities, acting as consultants and researchers for industry, government, schools, private clients. Industrial psychology is booming. Research is progressing in aptitude testing (such as Flanagan's work in the Army, described earlier), in group therapy, in counseling methods. Many colleges provide counseling service for students worried about their grades or their personal problems. (Nowhere is social pressure more visible and acute than in the case of a student who does not make the team, or the fraternity, or the glee club—the niche in the subcultural structure which gives status and security.) By and large, psychologists give advice to normal people, or people only normally upset; they send severe cases to psychiatrists.

The therapist or counselor, says Sanford, should establish a brotherly relationship with his client, rather than the fatherly role of most doctors and lawyers. The client states his problem, and the doctor or lawyer fixes it for him (or tries to), speaking a special language, keeping his distance. Not so the good psychologist. His task is to listen, talk out, advise, set forth alternatives, *but not to take command and fix*. Human behavior problems "by their nature must be solved by the human beings who have them." The wise psychologist helps people solve their own problems.

Industrial psychologists, Sanford observes, should not make the administrator's decision for him. "That's his job, not yours." (Remember how Leighton waited at Poston, while the administrator, looking out at the desert in the fading light, decided not to call in the Army.) A psychologist often makes a good administrator, but in this role he becomes an ex-psychologist.

A psychologist addressing a meeting, he continues, should also avoid the fatherly approach. Do not talk *down* to the Parent-Teacher Association, talk *with* them. Do not imply that "technical knowledge is only for experts, and that parents, if they had it, would only use it to clobber up the already miserable job they are doing with their children." Give parents new hypotheses, new facts, new ways of testing old ideas, alternative courses. The children are theirs, not yours.

Mr. Sanford adds this somber warning, during a time of many attacks on academic freedom and traditional American liberties:[2]

Societies that become sick . . . restrict first the psychological and social sciences. Individuals who have a violent neurotic need for security are noted for their hostility to knowledge about the inner workings either of personality or of institutions. . . . Only those societies characterized by considerable maturity will tolerate at all those individuals who have new and boat-rocking ideas about

[2] Address at Houston University, April, 1954.

human behavior. . . . Psychologists must do all they can to see that knowledge is available for the solution of human problems. But if psychologists are ever perceived as using their knowledge to impose any sort of control over society . . . they will be the targets of great and deserved hostility.

Perhaps the most important item in the Code of Ethics lies right here.

Social psychology, like economics, appears in many places throughout this book. Chapter 6 is almost nothing else. The present chapter has not attempted to summarize modern social psychology, but to pick up some interesting theoretic material, experiments, and cases, to add to what has gone before.

26

The Communication Sciences

"Much vain disquiet maketh mankind," said the Psalmist —long before singing commercials, broadcasting from airplanes, and mass communications generally, had made the disquiet a good deal vainer.

Every case we have discussed, and every generalization drawn, is also an exercise in communication. Those students who first observed the case received a communication and recorded it. They used language, perhaps the language of mathematics, sometimes maps or photographs as well. Next I, the author, had to study what the observer reported (or what I myself had seen), and then communicate what I found to you, the reader of this book. The line could be broken or distorted between event and observer, between observer and me, between me and you. Communication is almost as pervading as the air we breathe, and often as unnoticed.

Animals, of course, communicate in many ways, mostly by making sounds. Parrots can even imitate the sound of words. But only man has true language. Evolving through the culture, first as talk, and only lately—in the last 5,000 years or so— as writing, language is the most human of all our characteristics, and many scientists think it the most important. Science, literature, abstract thought, logic and reason would be impossible without words.

Yet, at the same time, words can compound misunderstanding and generate needless conflict. Organized warfare would be impossible without language, and so would the savage disagreements about race, religion, and ideologies. We have been given this power, and have proceeded to foul it up. A major goal of the communication sciences is to find out how language works and if possible abate some of its misuse.

The power of words comes home to me as I compare what you and I know, with what Boots my cat knows. His universe consists of the house and the land around it—perhaps three square miles of lawn, garden, orchard, swamp, pasture, and woodland, mostly belonging to the neighbors. He knows the detail of this area better than I do, especially the habits of field mice; he could survive in it during a blizzard as I, without human shelter, might not. He knows the environment which he sees, hears, smells, feels—*and that is all he knows*. He has no means of relating this experience to wider environments in the same town, to environments beyond that in the State and nation, and beyond that to the spinning planet on which we live, and beyond that to the solar system and the galaxies whose light may take a score of light-years to reach us.

Looking inward again, he has no knowledge of the processes in his own body, or the cells which compose it, or the molecules within the cells, or the atoms which nobody will ever see, or the electrons and the packed nuclei which compose them. Out to the almost inconceivably great, and down to the almost inconceivably small, lies knowledge which we humans may master, chiefly because of our command of words.

Language has been taken too much for granted, but we can now report important progress toward understanding this gift so useful and so dangerous. Many, if not most, of the political and social problems which plague us today are at bottom communication failures. Take for instance the big words in the headlines—"aggression," "appeasement," "coexistence," "socialized medicine," "free enterprise," "liberty," "security," "bureaucracy," "welfare state." It is not difficult to prove, using the discipline of semantics, that such high abstractions mean different things to different people, and unless great caution is taken in using them, they become not only meaningless as coin for common understanding, but actively productive of misunderstanding.

Among current problems which are in good part communication failure are the true menace of communism, international relations, labor-management conflicts, advertising misrepresentation. Much of the trouble between man and wife, parent and child, teacher and student, is due to communication breakdown. "Talking it out" might have repaired the line before a small grievance developed into a monstrous injustice. "Reasonable men," said Beardsley Ruml, "always agree if they understand what they are talking about."

Elton Mayo, in *Social Problems of an Industrial Civilization*, observes:

I believe that social study should begin with careful observation of what may be described as communication; that is, the capacity of an individual to communicate his feelings and ideas to another, the capacity of groups to communicate effectively and intimately to each other. This problem is beyond all reasonable doubt the outstanding defect that civilization is facing today. . . . Our international troubles are unquestionably due to the fact that effective communication between different national groups was not accomplished. . . . On the contrary, an effort was often made to "find a formula," a logical statement which should conceal the fact that neither side had any insight into the actual situation of the other. . . .

As Mayo develops it, communication is like the circulation of the blood—the free flow of ideas through structured channels *within* groups of all sizes, and *between* groups, up to nations, to the great alliances, to the United Nations. Communication depends at the lowest cycle on the articulateness of individuals; next on the functioning of small groups where individuals express their needs and desires, and where the expressions are passed upward to the next cycle, and so on. Such flexible communication, helped by the mass media, could respond sensitively to an appeal from the grass roots, from the little people who want peace and reasonable security. It could—but so far it does not.

Education, science, human progress depend on expressing an idea clearly and being understood by one's fellows. As Edward Sapir puts it:

> While we often speak of society as if it were a static structure ... it is a highly intricate network of partial or complete understandings between the members of organizational units of every degree of size and complexity, ranging from a pair of lovers to a league of nations, or that ever-increasing portion of humanity which can be reached by the press. ...[1]

"A network of partial or complete understandings." This is as good a definition of communication as we are likely to find, as well as a dynamic definition of society itself. It suggests that *relations* between people, in patterns that are active and changing, are the important thing. Sapir goes on to point out the three main techniques of human communication: (1) languages; (2) symbols in special technical situations—such as wigwagging at sea, bugle calls, smoke signals, and other wordless devices; and (3) inventions favorable to communication, such as the telegraph, telephone, radio, airplane.

Through these techniques a given culture is spread. It is due to the third, mechanical invention, that the culture called Western civilization has overrun a large part of the globe. But its very speed has produced serious difficulties at every stage. In an individual, blocked communication may be a major cause of mental breakdown. In a group it may cause conflicts of any degree of violence up to atomic warfare.

This new urgency is one reason for the present vogue of communication about communication, and another reason is the expansion of the mass media. We are all being constantly attacked by messages in ever-growing volume, and we need screening and translating devices, as well as sufficient skill to hold our own in the babel. So in various universities we find departments for the study of communication, which include everything from public speaking to electronics engineering. We

[1] In *Encyclopedia of the Social Sciences*.

find great national societies, and new scholarly magazines. Valuable research is being done, not only in universities but by consulting firms. Without attempting to do justice to all this useful work I will try to classify briefly the most active sections of the field.[2]

Twelve Disciplines

It would not be too much to say that every serious study known to man is wrestling with communication, but 12 of them are now particularly concerned with it; four of them full time, eight part time. The 12 cut across that shadowy boundary between natural and social science, for three—physics, cybernetics, and neurology—are classed with the natural sciences. We cannot do much more than list them here with a few comments, reserving for semantics a somewhat closer preview. Semantics is a study with which I, as a writer, have long been concerned. A short, useful definition is that semantics is "the systematic study of meaning."

1. *The Communication Engineers and Cybernetics*

The Bell Laboratories in New York are doing fundamental research into the theory of communication today. It is strictly within the field of natural science, being more concerned with the fidelity of the transmission of messages than with their meaning. But the sciences concerned with meaning also depend in part for their future development on a brilliant analysis by Claude Shannon and his staff. The Telephone Company puts the findings to work in expanding the dial system.

Every message, they say, whether by sounds, words, flashes, flags, gestures, wires, wireless, begins with an *information source*. From this a *signal* in the form of light waves, sound waves, radio waves, is sent out over some kind of transmitter, to be picked up by the *receiving mechanism*. There the message is *decoded* and passed on to its destination. At any point, *"noise,"* as the

---

[2] In the *Tyranny of Words* and *Power of Words*, I have reported at greater length.

engineers call it, may get in to distort the signal. "Noise is universal and insidious"—such things as static, fading, "snow" in television. The engineers' goal is to get the message through with a minimum of "noise." They do not yet care what the message is; it can be dots, dashes, music, pictures, letters, nonsense phrases.

Now let us move to another level. The word "cybernetics" was coined by Norbert Wiener, of the Massachusetts Institute of Technology, from a Greek root meaning *pilot* or *governor*; and he defines it as "a study of messages which control action." Cybernetics has to do with the theory and design of electronic computing machines, those uncanny robots like the famous "Univac," "Eniac," and their kin. I once compared my rate of multiplying four-digit numbers with that of "Number 701," an electronic computer designed by International Business Machines. It did not take long to determine that he was 100,000 times a better man than I!

Computers send messages which control action like the human brain. Like the brain, a computer has a memory system—Number 701 indeed has *three* memory systems. As they build computers for more complicated tasks—say operating an oil refinery, or guiding a Nike, or figuring out the weather a month in advance—the engineers increase our knowledge of how the human brain and nervous system work to encode and decode messages.

2. *The Neurologists and the Physiologists*

These scientists study the impact of signals on the retina or the eardrum, follow their course to the brain, then the corresponding signals sent out by the brain to the muscles for action. Take such a simple case as the light waves coming to you from a car that is veering over to your side of the road, the decoding of the signal in your mind, and the action of your hands on the wheel and your foot on the brake. If you do not interpret the message correctly and rapidly there will be a crash.

The whole process inside us is deeply buried and very complicated, but it is obviously cardinal for understanding communication.

3. Perception Theory

Now we go over the line to the social sciences. A school of psychologists, headed by Hadley Cantril of Princeton, is investigating how we perceive things: how we know that a rose is a rose, or a chair is a chair. They use elaborate apparatus, invented by the late Adelbert Ames of Hanover, and since extended and improved. One comes away from a morning in their laboratories slightly seasick, because of what his eyes, his nerve channels, and brain have experienced.

Unless we have had experience we cannot know. We never see *all* of an event out there—say an object like a chair—only enough to deal with it. We "bet," in the light of past experience, that it is a chair. An Eskimo who has never seen or used a chair would have nothing to bet on. One reason for becoming seasick is that a perfectly good chair, as seen from one angle in the laboratory, turns out from another angle to be nothing but a flimsy arrangement of sticks and wires. The relativity of perception is thus impressively demonstrated to the somewhat disorganized observer, and new light is thrown on the connection between words and things.

4. Animal Psychology

These studies include communication among animals, and also from animals to human beings. Dogs are more eloquent than cats in sending messages to people, while insects apparently don't give a damn. Bees have a mysterious and complicated message system of their own, in the form of an oriented dance. A scout returns and tells the hive where to find a good haul of nectar. He can pinpoint it, says von Frisch, up to two miles from the hive. Studies of higher animals, especially chimpanzees, throw side lights on human communication, and along with startling parallels, emphasize the gulf which separates man from his fellow creatures.

5. Child Psychology

A baby arrives with a cry but it is wordless. He has a fear response, but no true perceptions, for lack of experience on which to base them. Naturally he has no stock of words. He sets about collecting experience immediately, and by about eighteen months he has enough memories stashed away to begin verbalizing. Then for several years his tongue, mouth, larynx, and thorax develop at a furious rate; the drive to talk is on him. He talks with his whole body. Some five-year-olds have been clocked at 35,000 running words a day—not of course all different, but all running.

At an early age, the experts say, normal children in all cultures have mastered the structure of their language. Here is an illustration. Take three words in English: Man, Bear, Kill. These three words can be arranged—or structured—in six different ways, two of them meaningless, and two which mean something dramatically different from the remaining two. Thus:

KILL MAN BEAR means nothing as written.[3]

KILL BEAR MAN means nothing as written.

MAN KILL BEAR and

MAN BEAR KILL means the same satisfactory act.

BEAR KILL MAN and

BEAR MAN KILL mean the same disastrous act.

Junior at three has probably mastered such structural distinctions—a remarkable accomplishment when one stops to think about it—and at six he talks in fairly complex sentences.

6. The Culture Concept

Junior learns his language from the culture, and social scientists say that language is the most important part of any culture. Any two cultures, furthermore, will have cardinal problems of mutual understanding. A joke in one culture, for instance, may be a deadly insult in another.

[3] Spoken and accented you might make something out of it. See C. C. Fries, *The Structure of English*. Harcourt, Brace, 1952.

7. Linguistics

These scientists are very useful on any field expedition. They collect the sounds of a native language and arrange them into patterns. Presently they can describe and predict the basic phonetic structure. They are less interested in writing than in speaking, while grammar as traditionally taught fills them with alarm. It is not improbable that the linguists are on the way to revolutionizing the study of grammar—an idea which most high school students will be able to take in their stride.

Linguists are concerned not with how things *ought* to be said, but how they are in fact said. They are also concerned with nonverbal communication in the form of gestures and facial expressions—a subscience called *Kinesics*. They tell us that while certain tribes may be living under conditions which we call primitive, there are no primitive languages. The tongue of the Australian aborigines—who are about as "primitive" as they come—is more complicated than English. Eskimo has more than 20 words for *snow*—something any skier can appreciate.

8. Metalinguistics

According to Benjamin Lee Whorf, the language we learn tends to control our thinking. In Chapter 10 we illustrated the idea by comparing cultures in the Southwest: in English the clock *runs*, but in Spanish *he walks*. This results in an important difference between the time sense of Anglos and Mexicans, and serious trouble in the practice of medicine. Indo-European languages tend toward black-or-white thinking, while the Chinese language tends toward multivalued thinking, which considers shades of gray. The Hopi language, says Whorf, makes it easier to understand the idea of relativity, with time as a fourth dimension.

9. Modern Physics

Until physicists cleared up their communication they could not tell each other what they had discovered. Every large new advance, especially the theory of relativity, brought a communication crisis. Percy Bridgman, a Nobel prize winner, has ably documented this story in *The Logic of Modern Physics*. New language has been developed by the physicists in mathematics, multivalued logic, operational definitions, probability theory, statistics of aggregates, theory of types. These languages are international, understood as readily in Tokyo or New Delhi as in Pasadena. The operational definition is especially useful to the student of communication. It gives him a verbal screening machine to eliminate meaningless or unanswerable questions. "Is space bounded?" "Can time have a beginning and an end?" are such questions.

10. Group Dynamics

Scientists here are intimately concerned with the relationships inside face-to-face groups, as described in Chapter 23. Much of that relationship takes the form of communication, both by words and by *Kinesics*—the reinforcement of words through gesture. When a member, for instance, leans back in his chair and carefully folds his arms, the message can usually be decoded as, "I won't budge from my position!"

Some of the group analysts are investigating *listening*, the reception and decoding of messages. They are experimenting with listening clinics, with labor-management groups listening to the reading of a contract, and with college students—who, according to some experiments, hear only about twenty-five percent of what the lecturer says.

11 and 12. Semantics and General Semantics

These two closely connected disciplines may well merge in the years ahead. Semantics has been around since the turn of the century, when a book by Lady Viola Welby, *What Is Meaning?* first brought it to public attention. In 1921, C. K. Ogden and I. A. Richards published their classic study *The Meaning of Meaning*, and gave us the useful advice: "Find the referent"—meaning find the thing in the space-time world to which an abstract term refers.

Take, for instance, such a term as "liberty." Floating up there in the stratosphere, it can mean all things to all men. Ogden and Richards would bring it down to earth by asking, *liberty to do what?* "Your liberty to swing your arms," a great jurist is reputed to have said, "ends where my nose begins." "Liberty," like "freedom," "democracy," and "justice" is only a vague sentiment, amiable or quarrelsome, until a referent is found where the idea can be put to work—liberty to criticize the government, freedom to travel, democracy in elections with secret ballot, the justice of letting an accused person cross-examine his accusers, and so on. Political speeches are normally studded with lofty terms which do not have a referent in a carload. Committees of the United Nations have been trying for two years, without success, to define "aggression." They can try for 200 years with no better luck, unless they start with referents and build cautious generalizations from there.

In 1933, Alfred Korzybski, a Polish-American, published *Science and Sanity*, and inaugurated the school of *General Semantics*. It differed from mere semantics in leaning more heavily on mathematics, relativity, neurology, and psychology. Most of us, said Korzybski, are "unsane," in the sense that we scramble communication, and waste time arguing about little men who are not there. Beyond this normal unsanity, there are cases of real mental breakdown which General Semantics can help repair. The first big test came when Dr. Douglas M. Kelley, psychiatrist, tried using General Semantics in treating some 7,000 cases of battle shock in World War II. His hospital in Belgium returned 96 percent of its patients to their units, cured. It should be pointed out, however, that while semantic treatment undoubtedly helped, it was not the only therapy employed.[4]

Korzybski not only analyzed language from a fresh point of view, but suggested ways to make its use more precise, and

[4] This experiment is described at more length in *Power of Words*.

enable people to think straighter. One useful suggestion is never to forget that *a map is not the territory*. Language, he said, is the map, and the territory is a real event, out there beyond our heads. If the structure of the map agrees with the structure of the territory—if north and south are in the same relative positions—we can use the map to traverse the territory. But if our road map shows Toledo west of Chicago, and we want to drive to Toledo, we are in trouble. Korzybski tried to bring language maps closer to space-time territory.

ROAD BLOCKS

At least a dozen road blocks can break the communication line, among them:

1. Confusing words with things. Believing that the map is really the territory, or controls the territory. Say the right words and your enemy will get the pox, or in the modern version, sell the label and never mind what's in the package.

2. Failing to check abstract terms with concrete events. As in the careless use of "liberty," "aggression," and the like.

3. Confusing facts with inferences, with opinions, or value judgments. Most people do not know the difference; they say, "It's a fact that I think she is not as virtuous as she should be."

4. False identifications. We have been treated to a wholesale demonstration of this road block in accusations of guilt-by-association. Reduced to a syllogism these take the form:

President Eisenhower once had meetings with Russian General Zhukoff.

Zhukoff is a Communist.

Therefore Eisenhower is a Communist.

Ridiculous! you cry, and you are right; of course it is ridiculous. But millions of Americans have not learned to avoid this kind of semantic confusion.

5. Thinking in terms of either-or, black-or-white, those who are not with us are against us. If Prime Minister Nehru of India is a so-called "neutralist," he is not with us, and therefore must be in the enemy camp. Isn't it serious enough to

have real Communists against us from Leningrad to Shanghai, without taking on the whole neutralist world?

Other roadblocks to clear communication include the use of gobbledygook, failure to appraise motives, failure to consider major characteristics before passing judgment, and so on.

Enough has been sketched to show that the communication sciences not only are hard at work, but are beginning to form an interlocking front. With every advance the science of man gains strength and direction.

In lighter vein we might end this chapter with another illustration of communication failure.[5]

"Mrs. Lee, do you think women are better housewives than they used to be?"

"Which women?"

"Which women? Why, any women."

"But I don't know 'any women.' I only know certain women."

"Well, then, the women you know. Are they better housewives than they used to be?"

"In the first place, I don't know what they used to be. In the second place, I don't know what you mean by 'better housewives.' Do you mean, do their draperies match their slip covers? Do you mean, do they compare prices before they buy? Do you mean, do they cook vegetables without destroying the vitamins?"

"Why, yes, we mean all those things."

"But I can't answer all those things at once."

"Well, then, answer one of them. Let's say, do the women you know cook vegetables without destroying the vitamins?"

"I couldn't say. I've never tested their vegetables for vitamins. Wouldn't know how to."

"Well, just give us your opinion, Mrs. Lee."

"What good is my opinion? That isn't a matter of opinion;

[5] An imaginary interview by Mrs. Irving Lee, after she had listened to a radio quiz program sponsored by a food manufacturer of "Fluffy Duff."

it's a matter of fact. The only way I can answer that question is to go and test their vegetables."

"But can't you just make a guess?"

"Oh, well, if you want me simply to guess, I can do that. Yes, my guess would be that most of the women I know destroy some of the vitamin value of vegetables by cooking. But actually, of course, I don't have any way of knowing."

"*So*, Mrs. Lee, you maintain that women are not better house-wives today than they used to be. Well, we're all entitled to our own opinions, aren't we, folks?"

"Look here, I didn't say that. I made one little guess and you puffed it up into a big generalization."

"Thank you very much, Mrs. Lee."

"Why don't you quit asking people these ambiguous questions?"

"Thank you very much, Mrs. Lee."

"And what's more, the first time I hear a sidewalk interviewer who can distinguish between statements of opinion and statements of fact, I'll buy a whole case of your Fluffy Duff."

Mrs. Lee has amused us while making a serious point. Most of us don't know what we are talking about when we climb to the level of high abstractions, and neither does anyone else. The communication sciences are trying to haul us back to the base of common understanding.

27

On the Same Planet

Fitzpatrick, the great cartoonist of the St. Louis *Post Dispatch*, has pictured a huge bomb leaning against a wall, and beside it an equally huge question mark. Two small human figures in the foreground—they might be scientists—are looking up at the vast monoliths. The bomb is labeled, "How to Kill Everybody," and the question mark, "How to Live with Everybody." It was sketched when only the A-bomb was loose, but now with H-bombs in production, and cobalt bombs on the drawing board, the point is even more ominous.

Perhaps the choice is not quite so two-valued; perhaps there will be scattered survivors after the next World War; no one can tell. Atomic weapons, said Sir Winston Churchill in 1955, have passed "outside the scope of human control." The fall out on Eniwetok came as a surprise, and scientists no longer know what can happen: what radiation is doing and may do to forms of life on this planet. Heads of state, who use the methods of diplomacy and war which were standard before Hiroshima, are like boys playing with matches beside an open drum of gasoline.

THERMONUCLEAR TRUCE

Sir Winston emphasized another idea which has been gaining ground, a happier idea. The very frightfulness of atomic weapons, he thinks, will tend to restrain their use. Both the U.S.S.R. and the United States (presently Britain) know that if one side begins the assault, retaliation will be a matter of hours. The size of the stock pile makes little difference so long as there are warheads for that first flight of bombers. Realizing that atomic attack is a form of suicide, heads of state may hesitate to launch it.

The world may now have reached a Thermonuclear Truce which could last some years. It will be an uneasy truce, for if a psychotic like Hitler should come to power, he might consider it his exalted duty to press the button. Or some local "incident" might touch it off, or some trigger-happy junior officer. A daring belligerent during the truce might gamble boldly on getting what he wanted with lesser weapons—a "brush fire" war—and lose his gamble.

But there is a chance for time, and so a chance to end the truce by something other than pillars of mushroom cloud on all the continents. Perhaps we can utilize the uneasy years to block out the forms of a durable peace, and so contrive an answer to Fitzpatrick's question. Perhaps not. But all men of good will must now try.

SOME QUESTIONS

Clearly this is the greatest test of the race since it came down from trees, stood upright, and began to talk like men. Have we stood upright long enough? Are there enough mature men and women in the world to see the shape of the present crisis? Do they see the impasse, the dilemma of power and responsibility which we face? It can sound so easy: "We have an explosive that endangers survival; why not get rid of it?" "Everyone wants peace; why not agree to establish it?" These reasonable-sounding questions have difficult and discouraging answers.

Shall we choose death because we cannot forget our quarrels? I appeal as a human being to human beings: remember your humanity, and forget the rest. If you can do so, the way lies open to a new Paradise; if you cannot, nothing lies before you but universal death.[1]

This appeal by Bertrand Russell, eloquent as it is, neglects four serious difficulties.

1. Most of us, in all cultures, cannot forget our quarrels, or "forget the rest," without some intensive training.

[1] *Saturday Review*, April 2, 1955.

2. Most of us have little concept of our "humanity," as a generalization.

3. We have no clear concept of a new Paradise—or even an old one.

4. We cannot imagine "universal death."

To cause ordinary mortals to act requires a method beyond an appeal to reason, however eloquent. Social scientists are beginning to understand the complicated process by which new ideas get into the central nervous system, how the learning mechanism operates, and change takes place. Appeals such as Russell's may be good for the soul, but if great masses of men are to be moved, we must go deeper.

To neutralize the bomb, a psychologist has written me, social scientists must begin at the same conceptual level as the physicists did when they split the atom, avoid haste, and go to the root of the problem. This calls for scientific courage. Men who are doing fundamental research should continue it, even if they fail to see a clear application.

Certain tasks, however, are obvious, and many useful tools are ready to hand. Let us look briefly at some of them, and summarize findings described earlier. First, however, let us consider what sort of agency might assemble and use the tools. We begin by setting up a rough, preliminary structure on which to hang ideas.

UNITED NATIONS CLEARING HOUSE

The United Nations now has a group working on peaceful uses of atomic energy, following the popular proposal of President Eisenhower in 1953. Let us assume that this group expands to become a clearing house not only for peacetime uses of the atom, but for all serious proposals covering security and peace. It should have qualified social scientists on the staff, able to distinguish between workable plans and perpetual motion machines. Its prime objective should be to find a modus vivendi, a method of accommodation, a technique for negotiation, between the Great Powers.

An early task might be to analyze all international machinery now in use. The World Court, the World Bank, the Postal Union, the international weather service, the Geneva Convention, the Red Cross, epidemic controls, Olympic games, uniform weights and measures, air lines and airports, scientific congresses, religious conferences—the list of agencies which at this moment link the peoples of the world together is as impressive as it is little known. How do these agencies work? Which work best and why?

Here, for instance, is the International Whaling Control.[2] In 1930, representatives from 20 governments concerned with whale fisheries met at Sandefiord in Norway. They came from Britain, the U.S.S.R., Japan, the United States, South Africa, Argentina, as well as Norway. They proceeded to set up the International Whaling Convention which specified rules for the annual hunt, for ocean "sanctuaries," for protecting various species, and a rigorous system of inspection and enforcement. In 1950 the world quota was set at 16,000 Antarctic whales of the large varieties, like the blue whale.

Inspectors of whales have the same difficult problem which inspectors of atomic weapons may some day have: they must develop a double loyalty—to the International Convention, and to their own national fleet. There is some poaching, but to date the system is working well. Everyone agrees that without it the whaling industry would have destroyed itself through national competition. All the valuable kinds of whales would have become extinct. An interesting parallel for study.

Atomic Control

Atomic scientists say that the Lilienthal-Acheson plan for atomic control, which looked so promising in 1946, is obsolete. Perhaps, however, a more modern device for the international regulation and inspection of nuclear weapons can be invented. A great prize of, say, a million dollars might be offered to stimulate inventors.

[2] See R. B. Robertson, *Of Whales and Men*, Knopf, 1954.

In essence, we need a method for allaying fear. The United States is afraid of U.S.S.R. conquering the world, waving the banner of communism. (In 1940 we were afraid of Hitler conquering the world, waving the banner of fascism.) The Russians are afraid of the West overrunning the homeland, remembering what Hitler did on his march to Stalingrad, and what Western armies did on Russian frontiers after World War I. The Germans are afraid of the U.S.S.R., the French are afraid of Germany, the Chinese are afraid of a rearmed Japan. If these fears could be reduced, nations would be more ready to sit down around a table.

World peace must also rest on a modicum of economic security. The vast new potential of atomic energy can be used to increase standards of living. Atomic power, isotopes, irrigation of dry areas with sea water desalted by atomic heat, other engineering miracles, are already on the horizon. Energy in one form or another—from slave power to fuel oil—has always laid the base for a civilization. Now we are developing a wholly new energy base for a planetary civilization. Control agencies must be concerned with building things, not just with stopping things. The enterprise must appeal to the idealism of young people, as well as to the common sense of their elders.

CULTURE CONCEPT AGAIN

Every control agency and negotiating group will of course need the culture concept as a guide. Unless leaders understand the universal characteristics which all men share, permanent peace is inconceivable, and temporary machinery very difficult to install.

As things are now, chiefs of state, foreign ministers, war departments, must predict behavior in other countries, friendly and unfriendly, every day. If officials predict that certain nations will not live up to their agreements, or that their citizens are ripe for revolt, or that all the nation respects is force—and if they proceed to stake the future of all of us on such assumptions, we are in serious jeopardy. What a help it would be if predictions about the other nations' psychology could be based on something more than fear and hunches.

Social scientists should be retained to attack seriously this problem of prediction. Others should give serious attention to the matter of in-group versus out-group—a subject on which sociologists, anthropologists, and psychologists have already pooled their interest, and which is close to the roots of nationalism and patriotism. At the primitive end of the in-group scale are tribes, like the Copper Eskimos, who think it perfectly moral to steal from strangers, though not from members of the tribe. At the sophisticated end are diplomats who insist that their great nation wants only peace, and the rival power is doing all the warmongering.

Anthropologists call the attitude of the Copper Eskimos "a kind of personal vanity enlarged to embrace the group." What shall we call its counterpart, among the citizens of a Great Power? Peace may depend on clearly understanding such motivations. Is some insularity necessary to stabilize a society, and if so how much? Would it help—as some students have half-seriously suggested—to declare war on Mars, and so throw the out-group to another planet?

The cultural lag must be reckoned with, and the vitality of current institutions, both at home and abroad. We can make little progress by resolving that such and such an institution should be abolished, especially if it is still serviceable to a powerful minority. The only known way to get rid of a worn-out culture trait is to replace it with a more practical one—which was William James's idea in his "moral equivalent of war." Peace will be won not so much by ceasing to do things—say disarming—as by actively doing something else—say building atomic power plants.

Seven Wants

A group of social scientists, led by Mark A. May of Yale, has made a study of American foreign information agencies, especially the Voice of America. Their report, published in 1953, contains a short list of seven major wants and needs now shared by all the peoples of the world. The list should be rechecked, but as they stand these seven wants give us some valuable leads. Plans which collide with them are suspect. Plans which run parallel are headed in the right direction. People everywhere, the May committee found:

1. Want to know the facts, the truth about domestic and foreign affairs. *Where, they ask, can we go for news which is not twisted for political purposes?*
2. They want peace. It is a universal desire in all countries. *Who is furthering peace sincerely?*
3. They want better standards of living, more security in food and shelter. *Who is promoting such standards? Per contra, who is exploiting the poor?*
4. They want political independence; no more colonialism, no more foreign masters. *Who are the imperialists?*
5. They want their own religious customs and beliefs. *Who is trying to undermine our religion?*
6. They want to know more about other peoples. They would like to go and see at first hand. *Who is afraid of letting us go, or of letting us in?*
7. Finally, they want to be on the band wagon, the winning side. *Whom shall we join?*

The U.S.S.R. is winning on some of these issues, the democracies on others. The Kremlin is aware of them as forces to be dealt with, while Washington and London have often been more concerned with moral issues than with what people want. Any Western politico at the drop of a hat can tell anyone, anywhere, what he *ought* to want. Among other difficulties, however, the oughts collide.

These mass desires again show the wisdom of the rank and file. The things people want, the questions they ask, are direct and human. The answers they get are often slippery and abstract. The people of the world seem to be unconsciously oriented toward survival, like iron filings to a magnet. Their leaders, by their very responsibilities, to say nothing of the grim process which brought them to the top, are oriented toward power. How can the people be heard?

It is hard for Westerners to realize that in the last few years more than 500 million people, a quarter of the race, have thrown off the yoke of colonialism. It is safe to assume that more will do the same, until colonialism is as dead as the divine right of kings. How would Americans, collectively or individually, enjoy the permanent role of underdog? Have we imagination enough to put ourselves in the place of a poverty-stricken peasant, working till dark to raise food which will be eaten by someone higher up? Can we remind ourselves that he has a body like ours and a family relationship not so different from ours? The collection of photographs assembled by Edward Steichen under the title "The Family of Man" can help us to remember. So can the pictures of small orphaned children in Korea holding up their arms to American soldiers.

ATOMIC CONTROL BOARD

One can visualize a new control agency, a kind of super board of directors, composed of a relatively small number of outstanding Americans, the majority certainly not trained in social science. Before making policy decisions, these directors will see that facts are carefully gathered. Many experts will collect them —some on salary, some on contract, others just to help the project along. They will be scientists from all the disciplines, and lawyers, practical politicians, business executives, publicity experts, union leaders, scholars concerned with the humanities and with trends in philosophy and religion.

To find out how citizens feel about various plans and proposals, they can go to the public opinion researchers, the way the Ford Foundation in 1954 consulted Stouffer to find out how Americans felt about civil liberties. For advice on clearing the communication line with United States citizens, or with citizens of other countries, there might be a panel of mass media experts, linguists, semanticists, communication engineers. If we want to know what is going on behind the Iron Curtain we can consult scientists like Alexander Leighton, Clyde Kluckhohn, John Gardner, who have specialized in "area studies"—that remarkable technique for discovering what is going on in a country without going there. Without Leighton's and Murdock's area studies in the Pacific, our losses in landing on alien beaches would have been catastrophic. Russian Research Centers at Harvard, Columbia, and elsewhere have collected an immense amount of information about the Russian people, their government, their economy, their leaders. Can we hope to negotiate successfully unless we have some understanding of the man on the other side of the table? (The Russians would be well advised to make an area study of the United States. What they read in their papers about us is even more biased than what we read about them.)

For advice on rumor analysis, or race prejudice, the board can turn to scientists like Gordon Allport, or Otto Klineberg. If it wants to improve conference techniques, including its own meetings, there is a wealth of material available from the group dynamics people, and in the records of UNESCO's International Advisory Committee. Here a group of outstanding social scientists explored ways to improve international conferences, which carry not only the normal difficulties found in all group meetings, but additional barriers of language and culture. UNESCO can furnish useful experience about student exchanges, techniques for reducing illiteracy, and many other international activities. Studies have been made, for instance, in comparative stereotypes, nation by nation. When you think of a Frenchman what do you see? What are his main characteristics? When he thinks of you, an American, what does he see? UNESCO's report on these stereotypes describes, among other things, how they change over the years. (Remember how most Americans pictured the Japanese after Pearl Harbor, and compare it with the present picture.)

When we need to send delegates abroad, we can call on the Foreign Service Institute at Washington, where social scientists have been preparing young men for careers with the State Department. They are shown how to live in a different culture and appreciate its differences. They also learn foreign languages by a very effective and rapid method based on speaking rather than writing.

The linguists of the Foreign Service Institute, too, have some practical advice on the possibilities of an international language. Henry Lee Smith, Jr., points out that language is always a function of culture, and as we have no world culture, an international language cannot be much more than a signal system, without the richness and overtones of true language. Whatever the shortcomings as a medium of poetry, a universally accepted communication code would simplify the problem of negotiating a durable peace. It would also simplify the problems of tourists and visiting students, and help to break down the bias against "ignorant foreigners talking gibberish." A Gallup poll, conducted in various nations in 1953, asked the question: "Should school children be taught an international language?" The affirmative came back:

Finland	90	percent
Canada	84	"
Norway	82	"
Holland	82	"
United States	78	"

How shall the economic needs of poverty-stricken people be met? This question will continue long after the end of the Thermonuclear Truce and will require every scrap of dependable theory and practice the economists can muster. For the long swing it is perhaps the toughest question before the planet— the balance of population against food supply. Science is pushing down the death rate, doing little about the birth rate, and not nearly enough about the rate of food production.

What we call "Point Four" programs can be of immediate economic aid. They have been tested for a number of years all over the world. Western technicians have been sent to backward agricultural areas to show farmers how to fertilize, improve seed, irrigate, rotate, grow cover crops, conserve water. The program involves a maximum of participation by the local people as they learn to help themselves—and a minimum of cash subsidies. It can be linked with industrialization programs, as in Puerto Rico. Technical aid, however, has often failed because the staff did not allow for the local culture. We recited earlier the sad story of the paymaster in the Near East who wrecked his project by insisting on paying his help on a Moslem holy day.

Political scientists should go to work immediately analyzing the development of nationalism,[3] and the reasons for successful international agreements in the past. Why did the League of Nations fail? How may the United Nations be strengthened? (If I had anything to say about it, I would get it out of New York into strictly international territory, say a ceded island.) The scientists could use to advantage some of Leighton's principles for administrators, worked out at Poston. They could look again at the Human Rights Code drafted by social scientists for UNESCO.

Communication difficulties, we may be sure, will continually haunt us. Mayo said that our international troubles are largely due to ineffective communication between nations. Diplomats have set up a façade of verbal formulas which have concealed the real nature of differences. "The peoples of the world," somebody once observed, "are islands shouting at each other over seas of misunderstanding." We shall need the help not only of scientists skilled in communication theory, but of experts in journalism and publicity.

Let me emphasize again that this is not the author's plan to save the world, but only a rough scaffold on which to hang ideas. Some planetary action the world must take, and this is one way to begin thinking about it. The United Nations has been functioning since 1945; it does not require a Mark May report to prove that the peoples of the world want peace.

This might all seem pretty vague and speculative were it not

[3] See Boyd C. Shafer, *Nationalism, Myth and Reality.*

for what social scientists actually did from 1941 to the war's end. America was in a desperate emergency and needed help in all sorts of problems—finding fliers, training foremen, organizing recruits, setting up rationing and price controls, landing on Pacific beaches, handling Japanese internment camps. The earlier pages of this book are filled with accomplishments, often brilliantly executed.

Now another mobilization is demanded, but on a planetary scale, with the goal of "how to live with everybody." In one way this should suit the scientific attitude better. Science, as we said before, is as international as the north wind. By preference and by tradition it speaks for all mankind.

28

Toward a Science of Man

What have we learned from our rough-and-ready survey across the front of the social sciences, in this second decade of the Atomic Age? The reader must answer for himself, but for the author the journey has been rewarding. This sample, rough as it is, shows that knowledge is now available on a scale which most of us have been unaware of.

The interest in social science, furthermore, is deep and growing. Government, business management, all our major institutions, increasingly depend on its findings. The questions, indeed, are piling up faster than answers can be found. The scientists are under pressure from two sides—on the one hand to speed application and engineering, on the other to maintain research standards. New responsibilities fall upon the psychologists and economists and political scientists; and now the whole faculty is charged with the greatest responsibility of all—to help us safely through the Thermonuclear Truce.

It is no longer necessary to argue whether social science is "science," or what good it is beyond providing credits for a university degree. The *Scientific American,* for instance, has long since ceased to look down its nose at the social disciplines. A count of articles published in 1953 and 1954 shows 38 out of 194 of them in the social field, with nine on the borderline, or almost one quarter not primarily concerned with traditional natural science. We note such titles as "Conditioning and Emotions," "Linear Programming," "Economic Psychology," "What Is Memory?"

Facing the Paradoxes

A more important question is a philosophical one, and it is often raised. Granted that the scientific method has invaded the field of behavior, where is "science" itself taking us? Scientists have produced a weapon which Churchill says is out of human control—not to mention the robots, the "lonely crowds," the unemployed, the juvenile delinquents, the uprooted people, of the machine age. Might it not have been better if Galileo had never dropped his shot from the Leaning Tower; better if the Second Law of Thermodynamics had not been verified; better if Einstein had never demonstrated that energy equals mass times the speed of light, squared?

There are two answers. In the first place, Galileo *did* inaugurate the era of modern science, which the Royal Society presently formalized; Einstein did discover the explosive equation governing atomic energy, and whether science is a good thing or not, it is locked in the culture. Among other results, it has made life possible for far greater numbers than could survive without it. Deprived of mechanized agriculture, serums, and prime movers, at least half the present population of the West would soon be dead.

In the second place, "science" is only one of a whole battery of paradoxes which the mature mind must face. "Science" can blow us off the planet, yes, but it is abolishing disease around the world, and has all but wiped out helpless poverty in the United States. "Language," as noted in Chapter 26, is both a blessing and a menace—"danger: men talking." "Religion" can be a great comfort, but religious fanatics have promoted holy wars. "Liberty" to move and speak freely is priceless; "license," at the other end of the scale, is destructive. "Democracy" can give the fairest form of government yet devised, and also provide a field day for demagogues. It is difficult to think of any large abstract quality which is not at its extremes both beneficent and malignant.

A little semantic analysis helps resolve these paradoxes. *The lofty terms are meaningless as they stand.* Not until referents are found for them can they become meaningful—"liberty" to do what? Once found, referents can be arranged on a scale, or a frequency distribution curve, with the extremes at either end. Applying this idea to the scientific method we find that its uses are legion, on a scale that varies all the way from "how to live with everybody" to "how to kill everybody." Science, someone has said, does not provide an escalator to carry man automatically to Utopia, but an elevator which can carry him either up or down. Every new invention presents him with the challenge of which button to press. We should stop, look, and listen before jumping to the conclusion that "science," or "democracy," or "liberty," is either all good or all bad—any more than an ax is either good or bad. How are you going to use the ax?

How About Ethics?

The scientific method as such is amoral; but Alexander Leighton notes that ethical considerations can influence a piece of scientific research at three points: (1) When deciding what to investigate—say crime and prisons; (2) when selecting experimental techniques—say, no surgical experiments on human beings, however revealing; (3) when deciding how to apply the results—shall automation be allowed to increase unemployment? Remember, too, the oath of Hippocrates, and the ethical code of the psychologists.

Only the scientific method can resolve problems independently of our wills, desires, and emotions. To fudge an experiment, as we observed earlier, slant a conclusion, report anything but the whole truth as one knows it alone in the night, brings ignominy and oblivion. Integrity must follow curiosity in the development of any genuine scientist. In this regard, science is perhaps the most ethical of all man's disciplines, operating above cultures, above nationalism, above all ideological systems. Thus ethics itself can be a legitimate study in social science. One professor I know teaches it as a branch of anthropology.

The culture concept, indeed, can provide a stabilizing element for one's philosophy in this crisis-ridden world. It shows the student, on good scientific authority, that he belongs to something more enduring than one society or one nation. He feels himself part of a process which has been evolving for perhaps a million years. Many standard dogmas—Marxism and fascism for instance—dissolve on continued contact with the idea of culture, leaving something more substantial in their place.

Again in Chapter 12 we saw how science has demolished fixed notions about racial differences. If it has not established complete "equality," it has established the negative proposition which is almost as strong—there is as yet no proof of inherent inequality. We owe to social scientists the cardinal distinction between *race prejudice*, which is deep in one's nervous system and hard to change, and *discrimination*, which can be removed overnight in many cases. Ultimately its removal helps to melt down prejudice. Ethics and science meet in this analysis.

Two Observations

Throughout this book two major observations recur: the place of relativity in scientific work today, and the need for taking down partitions between the disciplines.

Absolutes in science have all but vanished, to be replaced by ideas of order, structure, relation, probability. Few conclusions are 100 percent so; there is always room for a new experiment to increase the probability. Such an attitude is baffling to minds that like stark yes or no answers, but there seems to be no other way to fruitful discovery. On a very few levels, absolutes may still prevail—perhaps C, the speed of light, is an absolute. But in most scientific work, as in climbing a granite face, it is a rocking, flexible balance which gets one up the cliff.

Waldemar Kaempffert meanwhile believes that scientific teamwork saved Britain:

It was not the generals who won the war for the British, but the professors, and they won it by coöperatively applying the scientific method to every phase of fighting. Strange as it may seem, zoölogists, geneticists, mathematicians, psychologists, anthropologists, physicists and chemists, worked together in teams to solve problems presented by German bombers and submarines. . . .

Before the war, emphasis in the graduate schools here and abroad was on training students to be competent, clever, and critical within the walls of their own discipline. One goal was to see who could most effectively annihilate whom. The war reversed this attitude and demanded coöperation between disciplines and an end to intellectual feuding. Social scientists found it hard at first, but many grew to like it. "Each came out of it," says John W. Gardner, "with a new respect for the special competence of the others." How long will it be before a group of graduate students may be freely permitted to submit a joint thesis? Several advance cases are already on record.

This brings us to some notes about training. A professor of sociology gives us a picture of what to expect in a modern department of social science.[1] One of his colleagues is collecting data to determine "what combination of urban and rural living will conserve the values of each, yet avoid the ill effects of both a mass society and provincialism?" Another colleague inquires: "How does the life one leads influence his development and growth?" A third is just back from islands in the Pacific, where he worked out written languages for natives who used only the spoken word. (The poor chaps will now have to learn to spell.) A fourth associate, flying to the scene of tornadoes, earthquakes, plane crashes, is studying how people behave in crisis, and so how to control panic and speed relief in disasters.

The role of a social scientist is now so central, Wilson says, that training is of great importance. It should include, along with his speciality, courses in biology, language, cross-cultural comparisons, statistics, history, philosophy, and logic. The student should be "taught to challenge the easy generalizations by seeking in his own experience a contradictory case." He should learn to state a problem clearly and precisely before he

---

[1] E. K. Wilson in *Antioch Notes,* November 15, 1954.

attempts an answer, and learn to relate his particular problem to a class of problems. "Whatever he sees, he must learn to analyze; and for this he needs background in the logic and tools of inquiry." His training should enable him to separate sharply what *is* from what *ought* to be.

The day is approaching, furthermore, when an intelligent layman will not feel himself competent to decide complicated questions about crime or sex or the federal budget without some background in social science—perhaps a course or two in college, or in the extension field. He does not now claim competence in genetics or astronomy without study, and why should he here? Newspaper editorials deal with social problems every day, but most editorial writers seem quite unaware that there is anything to learn beyond common sense and a fistful of figures.

What do students specializing in social science look like? We said earlier that they may spend as many years at it as a medical student. The Social Science Research Council has made a study of 153 students majoring in the field in 100 colleges.[2] They were a picked group, averaging B plus or better.

Their spelling—like your author's—was found to be "highly original," while their sentence structure was often a deep mystery. Very few have yet developed a clear prose style—as Oxford and Cambridge students usually do at the same age— and one wonders why. Their parents are a varied lot—professional people, business executives, tradesmen, clerks, and skilled workers. It was usually a high school teacher who first aroused their interest. "The fondness and sense of intellectual debt displayed when writing of these teachers are impressive." Sometimes a parent or a college professor opened a window and let in the light.

These students reflect the flexible class structure of America, with parents encouraging children to a professional standing higher than their own. There has been a good deal of moving about the country, giving the youngsters direct knowledge of

[2] SSRC *Items*, September, 1954.

many places and many people. As a group, the students have been good observers, and despite high marks are far from "greasy grinds." They are active in athletics, fraternities, college organizations. The stereotype of the social misfit who retires into a world of books is "simply not substantiated."

The group is less interested in scholarship than in people, but is glad to use scholarly knowledge in trying to understand people. Along with curiosity about human behavior, a majority have a dash of the reformer in them. This helps to keep them interested while they gradually acquire a more scientific approach. (Perhaps Chapter 22 would do them no harm.) Said one: "I want to work in a field which presents challenges in terms of personal satisfaction, and in terms of a world need." On the whole their attitude reflects the observation of George C. Homans: "There is only one paramount reason for studying anything but the multiplication table . . . you are so interested in a subject that you cannot let it alone. . . ."

The proper study of mankind presents plenty of challenges. It is replete with half-answered, unanswered, and slurred-over questions. Young men and women of spirit and imagination have a none too easy career before them if they embrace social science. They will have, too, the haunting certainty that the world's future depends on finding better answers than any which have yet been demonstrated.

But these human problems are more urgent and more dramatic than the problems in any physics laboratory. Here, as the atomic age deepens, is the intellectual adventure of our time, here the unknown continents to be explored and mapped. What can be a greater life work than extending the boundaries of the science of man?

Selected Bibliography

This partial list gives sources cited in the text, along with some background material not directly quoted. Reports of laboratory or field studies are designated R; works especially recommended for students are starred; P stands for pamphlet. Magazine articles quoted are not listed here, but are covered in the text itself by footnotes.

A complete list of important work in so broad a field would clearly be impossible, and many excellent books remain unlisted. This includes the major classics and Great Books in these subjects, which the student can readily find in libraries or in popular editions. Two good recent summaries of the classic economists will be found, by George Soule and Robert Heilbroner. Linton's *Study of Man* is recommended for background in cultural anthropology, Leonard Doob's *Social Psychology* for that subject, and for sociology, both Davis, Bredemeier, and Levy's *Modern American Society* and MacIver and Page's *Sociology* are useful.

Allport, Gordon W., *The Nature of Prejudice*, Boston, Beacon Press and Cambridge, Addison-Wesley Publishing Company, Inc., 1954.

R Anderson, Sherwood, *Home Town: The Face of America*, New York, Alliance Book Corporation, 1940.

Appleby, Paul, *Big Democracy*, New York, Alfred A. Knopf, Inc., 1946.

Arnold, Thurman, *The Bottlenecks of Business*, New York, Reynal & Hitchcock, 1940.

R Bales, R. F., *Interaction Process Analysis*, Cambridge, Addison-Wesley Publishing Company, Inc., 1950.

Barnard, Chester I., *The Functions of the Executive*, Cambridge, Harvard University Press, 1938.

Barnard, Chester I., *Organization and Management*, Cambridge, Harvard University Press, 1948.

* Benedict, Ruth, *Patterns of Culture*, Boston, Houghton Mifflin Co., 1934.

*P Benedict, Ruth, and Weltfish, Gene, *The Races of Mankind*, New York, Public Affairs Pamphlets, Pamphlet No. 85, 1943.

R Berelson, Bernard R., Lazarsfeld, Paul, and McPhee, William N., *Voting: A Study of Opinion Formation in a Presidential Campaign*, Chicago, University of Chicago Press, 1954.

Berle, Adolf, *The Twentieth Century Capitalist Revolution*, New York, Harcourt, Brace & Co., 1954.

Berle, Adolf, and Means, Gardiner C., *The Modern Corporation and Private Property*, New York, The Macmillan Co., 1933.

R Blumenthal, Albert, *Small Town Stuff*, Chicago, University of Chicago Press, 1932.

Boas, Franz, *Anthropology and Modern Life*, New York, W. W. Norton & Company, Inc., 1928.

Boas, Franz, *The Mind of Primitive Man*, New York, The Macmillan Co., 1911, 1938.

Bridgman, Percy W., *The Logic of Modern Physics*, New York, The Macmillan Co., 1932.

Brunner, Edmund de S., and Hallenbeck, Wilbur C., *American Society: Urban and Rural Patterns*, New York, Harper & Brothers, 1954.

Burnham, James, *The Managerial Revolution: What Is Happening to the World*, New York, The John Day Co., 1941.

Cameron, Norman, *The Psychology of Behavior Disorders: A Biosocial Interpretation*, Boston, Houghton Mifflin Co., 1947.

Cantril, Hadley, *The "Why" of Man's Experience*, New York, The Macmillan Co., 1950.

Carroll, John B., *The Study of Language: A Survey of Linguistics and Related Disciplines in America*, Cambridge, Harvard University Press, 1953.

Chamberlin, E. H., *The Theory of Monopolistic Competition*, Cambridge, Harvard University Press, 1932.

PR Chase, Stuart, *"Operation Bootstrap" in Puerto Rico*, Washington, National Planning Association, Planning Pamphlet No. 75, 1951.

Chase, Stuart, *Mexico, A Study of Two Americas*, New York, The Macmillan Co., 1931.

Chase, Stuart, *Power of Words*, New York, Harcourt, Brace & Co., 1954.

Chase, Stuart, *Roads to Agreement*, New York, Harper & Brothers, 1951.

Chase, Stuart, *The Tyranny of Words*, New York, Harcourt, Brace & Co., 1938.

Childs, Marquis, *This Is Democracy: Collective Bargaining in Scandinavia*, New Haven, Yale University Press, 1938.

Clapp, Gordon R., *The TVA: An Approach to the Development of a Region*, Chicago, University of Chicago Press, 1955.

Clark, Colin, *The Conditions of Economic Progress*, London, The Macmillan Co., 1940.

Clark, John Maurice, *Guideposts in a Time of Change*, New York, Harper & Brothers, 1949.

Clark, John Maurice, *Social Control of Business*, 2d ed., New York, McGraw-Hill Book Co., 1939.

Cohen, Morris R., and Nagel, Ernest, *An Introduction to Logic and Scientific Method*, New York, Harcourt, Brace & Co., 1934.

Cole, Margaret, *Beatrice Webb*, New York, Harcourt, Brace & Co., 1946.

Cooley, Charles H., *Social Organization*, New York, Charles Scribner's Sons, 1922.

R   Dahir, James, *Communities for Better Living: Citizen Achievement in Organization, Design and Development*, New York, Harper & Brothers, 1950.

R   Davis, Allison, *Social Class Influences on Learning*, Cambridge, Harvard University Press, 1948.

R   Davis, Allison, and Gardner, Burleigh and Mary, *Deep South: A Social Anthropological Study of Caste and Class*, Chicago, University of Chicago Press, 1941.

*   Davis, Kingsley, and Bredemeier, H. C., *Modern American Society*, New York, Rinehart & Company, Inc., 1949.

R   Dietz, Walter, and Kirkpatrick, Frances, eds., *The Training Within Industry Report, 1940–1945*, Washington, War Manpower Commission, 1945.

Dimock, Marshall Edward, *Business and Government,* New York, Henry Holt & Co., Inc., 1949.

R Dollard, John, *Caste and Class in a Southern Town,* New York, Harper & Brothers, 1949.

* Dollard, John, and Miller, Neal E., *Personality and Psychotherapy,* New York, McGraw-Hill Book Co., 1950.

Dollard, John, and Miller, Neal E., *Social Learning and Imitation,* New Haven, Yale University Press, 1941.

* Doob, Leonard W., *Social Psychology: An Analysis of Human Behavior,* New York, Henry Holt & Co., Inc., 1952.

Doob, Leonard W., *The Plans of Men,* New Haven, Yale University Press, 1940.

Drucker, Peter, *The Practice of Management,* New York, Harper & Brothers, 1954.

R Dublin, Louis I., *The Facts of Life from Birth to Death,* New York, The Macmillan Co., 1951.

R Dublin, Louis I., and Lotka, A. J., *Length of Life,* 1936, rev. ed. with M. Spiegelman, New York, The Ronald Press Company, 1949.

Durkheim, Emile, *The Division of Labor in Society,* New York, The Macmillan Co., 1933.

Fine, Benjamin, *1,000,000 Delinquents,* Cleveland, The World Publishing Company, 1955.

Finletter, Thomas, *Can Representative Government Do the Job?* New York, Reynal & Hitchcock, 1945.

R Flanagan, John C., ed., *The Aviation Psychology Program in the Army Air Forces,* 19 vols., Washington, Government Printing Office, 1948.

PR Flanagan, John C., *American Institute for Research Reports,* Pittsburgh, 1948-51.

Follett, Mary P., *Creative Experience,* New York, Longmans, Green & Co., Inc., 1924.

Frank, Lawrence K., *Nature and Human Nature: Man's New Image of Himself,* New Brunswick, Rutgers University Press, 1951.

Fraser, James G., *The Golden Bough,* abridged ed., New York, The Macmillan Co., 1922.

R Frisch, Karl von, *Bees, Their Vision, Chemical Senses, and Language,* Ithaca, Cornell University Press, 1950.

* Galbraith, J. Kenneth, *American Capitalism: The Concept of Countervailing Power*, Boston, Houghton Mifflin Co., 1952.

Galbraith, J. Kenneth, *Economics and the Art of Controversy*, New Brunswick, Rutgers University Press, 1955.

Galbraith, J. Kenneth, *The Great Crash, 1929*, Boston, Houghton Mifflin Co., 1955.

Giddings, Franklin H., *Studies in the Theory of Human Society*, New York, The Macmillan Co., 1922.

Gillin, John, *The Ways of Men: An Introduction to Anthropology*, New York, Appleton-Century-Crofts, Inc., 1948.

R Glueck, Sheldon and Eleanor, *Unraveling Juvenile Delinquency*, Cambridge, Harvard University Press, 1950.

R Golden, Clinton S., and Parker, Virginia, eds., *Causes of Industrial Peace under Collective Bargaining*, New York, Harper & Brothers, 1953.

Hansen, Earl Parker, *Transformation: The Story of Modern Puerto Rico*, New York, Simon and Schuster, Inc., 1955.

* Hayakawa, S. I., *Language in Thought and Action*, New York, Harcourt, Brace & Co., 1949.

R Healy, William, and Bronner, Augusta F., *New Light on Delinquency and Its Treatment*, New Haven, Yale University Press, 1936.

Hecht, Selig, *Explaining the Atom*, New York, The Viking Press, Inc., 1947.

* Heilbroner, Robert L., *The Worldly Philosophers: The Lives, Times, and Ideas of the Great Economic Thinkers*, New York, Simon and Schuster, Inc., 1953.

Herskovits, Melville J., *The Anthropometry of the American Negro*, New York, Columbia University Press, 1930.

Hicks, Clarence J., *My Life in Industrial Relations: Fifty Years in the Growth of a Profession*, New York, Harper & Brothers, 1941.

Hicks, Granville, *Small Town*, New York, The Macmillan Co., 1946.

Hogben, Lancelot, *Science for the Citizen*, New York, Alfred A. Knopf, Inc., 1938.

R Hollingshead, August B., *Elmtown's Youth: The Impact of Social Classes on Adolescents*, New York, John Wiley & Sons, Inc., 1949.

Homans, George C., *The Human Group*, New York, Harcourt, Brace & Co., 1950.

* Huxley, Julian, *Man Stands Alone*, New York, Harper & Brothers, 1941.

R Katona, George, *Psychological Analysis of Economic Behavior*, New York, McGraw-Hill Book Co., 1951.

R Katona, George, and Mueller, Eva, *Consumer Attitudes and Demand, 1950–1952*, Ann Arbor, Survey Research Center, 1953.

Keynes, John Maynard, *The General Theory of Employment, Interest and Money*, New York, Harcourt, Brace & Co., 1936.

Keynes, John Maynard, *How to Pay for the War*, New York, Harcourt, Brace & Co., 1940.

Kinsey, Alfred C., Pomeroy, Wardell B., and Martin, Clyde E., *Sexual Behavior in the Human Male*, Philadelphia, W. B. Saunders Co., 1948.

R Klineberg, Otto, ed., *Characteristics of the American Negro*, New York, Harper & Brothers, 1944.

Klineberg, Otto, *Race Differences*, New York, Harper & Brothers, 1935.

* Kluckhohn, Clyde, *Mirror for Man: The Relation of Anthropology to Modern Life*, New York, McGraw-Hill Book Co., 1949.

Korzybski, Alfred, *Science and Sanity: An Introduction to Non-Aristotelian Systems and General Semantics*, International Non-Aristotelian Library Publishing Co., 1933, 1941, 1948. Distributed by Institute of General Semantics, Lakeville, Conn.

Kroeber, A. L., *Anthropology*, New York, Harcourt, Brace & Co., 1923.

Lasswell, Harold, *Politics: Who Gets What, When, How?* Gloucester, Peter Smith, 1950.

Lee, Irving J., *Language Habits in Human Affairs: An Introduction to General Semantics*, New York, Harper & Brothers, 1941.

*R Leighton, Alexander, *The Governing of Men*, Princeton, Princeton University Press, 1945.

Leighton, Alexander, *Human Relations in a Changing World:*

Observations on the Use of the Social Sciences, New York, E. P. Dutton & Co., Inc., 1949.

R Leontief, Wassily, *The Structure of the American Economy*, New York, Oxford University Press, Inc., 2d ed., 1951.

Lewin, Kurt, *Field Theory in Social Science: Selected Theoretical Papers*, New York, Harper & Brothers, 1951.

R Lewin, Kurt, *Resolving Social Conflicts*, New York, Harper & Brothers, 1948.

Lilienthal, David E., *Big Business, A New Era*, New York, Harper & Brothers, 1953.

* Lilienthal, David E., *TVA, Democracy on the March*, New York, Harper & Brothers, 1944.

Lindeman, E. C., *Social Education*, New York, New Republic, 1933.

* Linton, Ralph, *The Study of Man*, New York, Appleton-Century-Crofts, Inc., 1936.

R Lippitt, Ronald, *Training in Community Relations*, New York, Harper & Brothers, 1949.

R Lombard, George F. F., *Behavior in a Selling Group: A Case Study of Interpersonal Relations in a Department Store*, Boston, Harvard Graduate School of Business Administration, 1955.

Lorimer, Frank, and Osborn, Frederick, *Dynamics of Population*, New York, The Macmillan Co., 1934.

Lubell, Samuel, *The Future of American Politics*, New York, Harper & Brothers, 1952.

Lundberg, George A., *Can Science Save Us?* New York, Longmans, Green & Co., Inc., 1947.

*R Lydgate, William A., *What Our People Think*, New York, Thomas Y. Crowell Co., 1944.

Lynd, Robert, *Knowledge for What? The Place of Social Science in American Culture*, Princeton, Princeton University Press, 1939.

R Lynd, Robert and Helen, *Middletown: A Study in Contemporary American Culture*, New York, Harcourt, Brace & Co., 1929.

R Lynd, Robert and Helen, *Middletown in Transition: A Study in Cultural Conflicts*, New York, Harcourt, Brace & Co., 1937.

* MacIver, Robert M., and Page, Charles H., *Sociology*, New York, Rinehart & Company, Inc., 1949.

Malinowski, Bronislaw, *A Scientific Theory of Culture*, Chapel Hill, University of North Carolina Press, 1944.

Malthus, Thomas, *An Essay on the Principle of Population*, London, 1798.

Marrow, Alfred J., *Living Without Hate*, New York, Harper & Brothers, 1951.

R Marshall, Robert, *Arctic Village*, New York, Smith and Haas, 1933.

R May, Mark A., and associates, *Seventh Semi-annual Report of U. S. Advisory Committee on Information*, House Document 94 of 83rd Congress, Washington, Government Printing Office, 1953.

Mayo, Elton, *The Human Problems of an Industrial Civilization*, New York, The Macmillan Co., 1933.

* Mayo, Elton, *The Social Problems of an Industrial Civilization*, Boston, Harvard Graduate School of Business Administration, Division of Research, 1945.

PR Mayo, Elton, and Lombard, George F. F., *Teamwork and Labor Turnover in the Aircraft Industry of Southern California*, Boston, Harvard Graduate School of Business Administration, Business Research Studies, No. 32, 1944.

*R Mead, Margaret, *Sex and Temperament in Three Primitive Societies*, New York, William Morrow & Co., Inc., 1953.

Menninger, William C., *Psychiatry, Its Evolution and Present Status*, Ithaca, Cornell University Press, 1948.

Merriam, Charles E., *The Written Constitution and the Unwritten Attitude*, West Rindge, New Hampshire, R. R. Smith, 1931.

Merriam, Charles E., *What Is Democracy?* Chicago, University of Chicago Press, 1941.

Miller, George A., *Language and Communication*, New York, McGraw-Hill Book Co., 1951.

Mitchell, Wesley C., *The Backward Art of Spending Money, and Other Essays*, New York, McGraw-Hill Book Co., 1937.

R Morgan, Lewis H., *Ancient Society, or Researches in the Lines of Human Progress from Savagery Through Barbarism to Civilization*, New York, Henry Holt & Co., Inc., 1877.

Morgenstern, Oskar, and Neumann, John von, *The Theory of Games and Economic Behavior*, rev. ed., Princeton, Princeton University Press, 1947.

Murdock, George Peter, *Our Primitive Contemporaries*, New York, The Macmillan Co., 1926, 1934.

Murdock, George Peter, *Social Structure*, New York, The Macmillan Co., 1949.

Murray, Elwood, Barnard, Raymond H., and Garland, Jasper V., *Integrative Speech*, New York, The Dryden Press, Inc., 1953.

R Myrdal, Gunnar, *An American Dilemma*, 2 vols., New York, Harper & Brothers, 1944.

* Ogburn, William F., *Social Change*, New York, The Viking Press, Inc., 1950.

Ogburn, William F., *The Social Effects of Aviation*, Boston, Houghton Mifflin Co., 1946.

* Ogburn, William F., and Nimkoff, M. F., *Sociology*, Boston, Houghton Mifflin Co., 1940, 1946, 1950.

Ogburn, William F., Odum, Howard, and Hunt, Edward E., eds., *Recent Social Trends*, 2 vols., New York, McGraw-Hill Book Co., 1933.

Ogden, C. K., and Richards, I. A., *The Meaning of Meaning*, New York, Harcourt, Brace & Co., 1923, 1936.

Park, R. E., and Burgess, Ernest W., *Introduction to the Science of Sociology*, Chicago, University of Chicago Press, 1921.

* Parker, Carleton H., *The Casual Laborer and Other Essays*, New York, Harcourt, Brace & Co., 1920.

R Raper, Arthur F., *Preface to Peasantry*, Chapel Hill, University of North Carolina Press, 1936.

R Redfield, Robert, *Tepoztlan, A Mexican Village*, Chicago, University of Chicago Press, 1930.

Rivers, W. H. R., *Medicine, Magic and Religion*, New York, Harcourt, Brace & Co., 1924.

Rivers, W. H. R., *Social Organization*, W. J. Perry, ed., vol. 1, *History of Civilization*, New York, Alfred A. Knopf, Inc., 1924.

R Roethlisberger, F. J., and Dickson, William J., *Management and the Worker*, Cambridge, Harvard University Press, 1940.

* Rogers, Carl R., *Counseling and Psychotherapy*, Leonard Carmichael, ed., Boston, Houghton Mifflin Co., 1942.

Ruml, Beardsley, *Tomorrow's Business*, New York, Farrar & Rinehart, 1945.

Sapir, Edward, *Language: An Introduction to the Study of Speech*, New York, Harcourt, Brace & Co., 1921.

R Saunders, Lyle, *Cultural Difference and Medical Care*, New York, Russell Sage Foundation, 1954.

* Scheinfeld, Amram, *The New You and Heredity*, Philadelphia, J. B. Lippincott Co., 1950.

R Schultz, Richard S., *Wartime Supervision of Workers: The Human Factors in Production for Executives and Foremen*, New York, Harper & Brothers, 1943.

Selekman, Benjamin M., *Labor Relations and Human Relations*, New York, McGraw-Hill Book Co., 1947.

Seligman, E. R. A., Johnson, Alvin, and Lerner, Max, eds., *Encyclopedia of the Social Sciences*, 8 vols., New York, The Macmillan Co., 1937.

Shafer, Boyd C., *Nationalism, Myth and Reality*, New York, Harcourt, Brace & Co., 1955.

Shannon, Claude, and Weaver, Warren, *The Mathematical Theory of Communication*, Urbana, University of Illinois Press, 1949.

* Soule, George, *Ideas of the Great Economists*, New York, The Viking Press, Inc., 1952.

Soule, George, *The Useful Art of Economics*, New York, The Macmillan Co., 1929.

R Spicer, Edward H., ed., *Human Problems in Technological Change: A Casebook*, New York, Russell Sage Foundation, 1952.

Steffens, Lincoln, *Autobiography*, New York, Harcourt, Brace & Co., 1931.

Stimson, Dorothy, *Scientists and Amateurs: A History of the Royal Society*, New York, Henry Schuman, Inc., 1948.

R Stouffer, Samuel A., *Communism, Conformity and Civil Liberties: A Cross-section of the Nation Speaks Its Mind*, Garden City, Doubleday & Company, Inc., 1955.

PR Stouffer, Samuel A., and associates, *Report for the Five Years,*

1946–1951, Cambridge, Harvard University, Laboratory of Social Relations.

Stouffer, Samuel A., and associates, *The American Soldier*, 2 vols., Princeton, Princeton University Press, 1949.

Sumner, William Graham, *Folkways*, Boston, Ginn & Company, 1906.

Taylor, Frederick W., *Scientific Management*, New York, Harper & Brothers, 1923.

R Terman, Lewis M., and Merrill, M. A., *Measuring Intelligence*, Boston, Houghton Mifflin Co., 1937.

Thelen, Herbert A., *Dynamics of Groups at Work*, Chicago, University of Chicago Press, 1954.

Thomas, W. I., *Primitive Behavior*, New York, McGraw-Hill Book Co., 1937.

Thomas, W. I., *The Unadjusted Girl*, Boston, Little, Brown & Co., 1923.

Turner, Frederick Jackson, *The Frontier in American History*, New York, Henry Holt & Co., Inc., 1920.

Veblen, Thorstein, *The Theory of the Leisure Class*, New York, The Macmillan Co., 1899: Modern Library, Inc., 1934.

R Walker, Charles R., and Guest, Robert H., *The Man on the Assembly Line*, Cambridge, Harvard University Press, 1952.

R Warner, W. Lloyd, and associates, *Democracy in Jonesville: A Study in Quality and Inequality*, New York, Harper & Brothers, 1949.

R Warner, W. Lloyd, and Lunt, Paul S., *The Social Life of a Modern Community*, Vol. 1 of Yankee City Series, New Haven, Yale University Press, 1941.

R Warner, W. Lloyd, and Lunt, Paul S., *The Status System of a Modern Community*, Vol. 2 of Yankee City Series, New Haven, Yale University Press, 1942.

R Warner, W. Lloyd, and Srole, Leo, *The Social Systems of American Ethnic Groups*, Vol. 3 of Yankee City Series, New Haven, Yale University Press, 1945.

R Warner, W. Lloyd, and Low, J. O., *The Social System of the Modern Factory*, Vol. 4 of Yankee City Series, New Haven, Yale University Press, 1947.

R West, James, *Plainville, U. S. A.*, New York, Columbia University Press, 1945.

PR Whetten, Nathan L., *Wilton, A Rural Town near Metropolitan New York*, Connecticut State College, Storrs, Studies of Suburbanization in Connecticut, No. 3, 1939.

P Whorf, Benajmin Lee, *Four Articles on Metalinguistics*, Washington, Foreign Service Institute, 1949.

Wiener, Norbert, *Cybernetics*, Cambridge, Technology Press, 1949.

Williams, James Michel, *Our Rural Heritage and the Expansion of Rural Life*, New York, Alfred A. Knopf, Inc., 1925.

R Williams, Robin M., Jr., and Ryan, Margaret W., *Schools in Transition: Community Experiences in Desegregation*, Chapel Hill, University of North Carolina Press, 1954.

* Wissler, Clark, *An Introduction to Social Anthropology*, New York, Henry Holt & Co., Inc., 1929.

Woodward, C. Vann, *The Strange Career of Jim Crow*, New York, Oxford University Press, Inc., 1955.

R Yerkes, Robert M., *Chimpanzees, A Laboratory Colony*, New Haven, Yale University Press, 1943.

Young, Donald, *American Minority Peoples*, New York, Harper & Brothers, 1932.

Young, Pauline V., *Scientific Social Surveys and Research*, New York, Prentice-Hall, Inc., 1939, 1949, 1955.

Index